"If you don't like change, you're going to like irrelevance even less"

Eric Shinseki

Introduction

The Management Consulting Toolkit contains 50 of the most useful, versatile and value-adding tools used by management consultants the world-over. In general, the tools contained herein focus on business analysis and transformation and cover key consulting disciplines such as:

- Business performance analysis
- Future state design
- Transformation planning
- Transformation execution
- Project management
- Change management
- Team management

These tools have all stood the test of time, and the team at Expert Toolkit believes they will continue to be relevant, powerful and value-adding in the hands of the competent practitioner.

We hope you find the contents of this toolkit useful. Please contact us if you have any questions or feedback, or if we can help you craft a tailored training or delivery program for your organization.

the team @ Expert Toolkit

Contents of the Management Consulting Toolkit

1. Accelerated SWOT Analysis Tool
2. Benchmarking Assessment Template
3. Business Diagnostic Findings Template
4. Business Initiative Project Charter
5. Capability Gap Assessment Template
6. Cost-Benefit Assessment Framework
7. Customer Experience Design Framework
8. Data Collection Plan Template
9. Failure Mode Effects Analysis Template
10. Five Whys Analysis
11. Future State Process Change Framework
12. Hypothesis Capture Template
13. Initiative Prioritization Map

Contents of the Management Consulting Toolkit

14. Jidoka Board

15. Pain Point Analysis Tool

16. PEST Analysis Trend Matrix

17. Process Flow Analysis Framework

18. Process Issues Summary Template

19. Project Status Update Template

20. RACI Matrix Template

21. Root Cause Analysis

22. SIPOC Analysis

23. Solution Assessment & Prioritization

24. Solution Ideation & Ranking Framework

25. Swimlane Process Map Template

Contents of the Management Consulting Toolkit

26. The ABCD Tool
27. Activity Accountability Plan Template
28. Business Metrics Framework
29. Business Stakeholder Map
30. Business Stakeholder Tracking Tool
31. Business Transformation Guiding Principles Template
32. Business Transformation Recommendation Template
33. Business Transformation Framework
34. Business Vision Template
35. Communications Plan Template
36. Operating Model Template
37. Operating Rhythm Template
38. Organization Impact Assessment Template

Contents of the Management Consulting Toolkit

39. Project Evaluation Template
40. Project Issues Register
41. Project Risk Register
42. Project Status Report Template
43. Project Executive Update Template
44. Resource Management Plan Template
45. Strategy Pyramid
46. Team Temperature Check Tool
47. Transformation Conclusion Survey
48. Transformation Map Template
49. Transformation Readiness Checklist
50. Transformation Readiness Survey

Accelerated SWOT Analysis

A simple, but powerful method for thinking through strategic choices taking into account market dynamics and capabilities

Accelerated SWOT Analysis – Overview

What is it

The Accelerated SWOT Method is a simple approach that matches corporate capabilities against market conditions to develop strategic choices. The technique uses a grid to present trends, strengths, weakness and strategic choices on a single panel. The method lends itself to a collaborative approach - taking into account organizational strengths and weaknesses, and market trends. At the end of the exercise you will have a set of strategic imperatives that the leadership team can understand and buy into.

When to use it

The Accelerated SWOT Method is best used when a fresh perspective is needed on trends market and how they line up against corporate capabilities. It is helpful in bringing alignment across a leadership team at the strategic level. It is also a great method for validating strategic programs against and overarching corporate strategy – and when time or resources do not permit the use of the more comprehensive SWOT analysis.

Why use it

The Accelerated SWOT helps to solve a variety of problems: Lack of clarity on key strategic imperatives; Lack of confidence that current strategic imperatives take into account current corporate strengths, weaknesses and market conditions; Lack of strategic alignment across the leadership team; Lack of creative thinking around strategic choices that are available to the organization.

Accelerated SWOT Analysis – Method

How you use it

Step 1. Using existing information and stakeholder interviews, document the organization's corporate objectives. If performing the accelerated SWOT on a subset of the organization, use those objectives.

Step 2. Document the key trends that are relevant to the business unit, product, geography used in step 1. Focus on the most influential trends that create opportunities or threats.

Step 3. Document the assessment of internal capabilities. Focus on the key capabilities that are seen as core strengths or weaknesses within the organization.

Step 4. With an eye on the Strategic Objectives captured in the top left box, brainstorm potential strategic choices for the organization. Take on each section (Offensive, Conversion, Utilization, Defensive) sequentially.

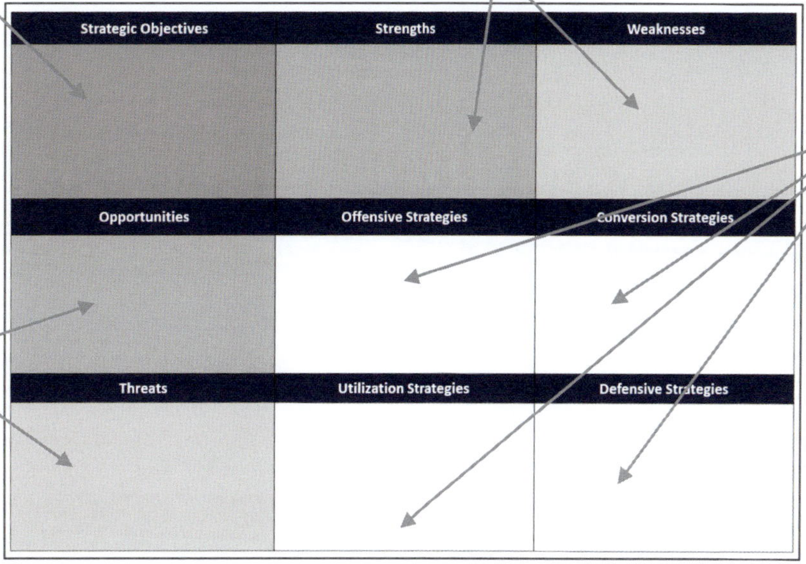

	Strategic Objectives	Strengths	Weaknesses
Opportunities		Offensive Strategies	Conversion Strategies
Threats		Utilization Strategies	Defensive Strategies

A more comprehensive "How to" guide for SWOT Analysis can be found on experttoolkit.com

Accelerated SWOT Analysis – Method

How you use it

Offensive Strategies = Strengths plus Opportunity. Where can a market opportunity be exploited by leveraging a corporate strength.

Conversion Strategies = Weakness plus Opportunity. Where can market opportunities be leveraged to overcome a corporate weakness.

Utilization Strategies = Strength plus Threat. Where can a Strength be leveraged to overcome a market threat.

Defensive Strategies = Weakness plus Threat. What strategy can be employed to neutralize a weakness at the same time as mitigating a threat.

A more comprehensive "How to" guide for SWOT Analysis can be found on experttoolkit.com

Accelerated SWOT Analysis – Template

Strategic Objectives	Strengths	Weaknesses
Opportunities	**Offensive Strategies**	**Conversion Strategies**
Threats	**Utilization Strategies**	**Defensive Strategies**

Accelerated SWOT Analysis – Example

Strategic Objectives	Strengths	Weaknesses
• Drive domestic market share • Improve customer service • Improve operating margins • Expand into Eastern Europe • Lift shareholder value	1. Premium brand 2. Strong balance sheet 3. Offshore distribution centers 4. Retail sales footprint 5. R&D Capability	1. High operating cost base 2. Poor sales processes 3. Complex legacy systems 4. Unionized workforce 5. Limited big deal experience
Opportunities	**Offensive Strategies**	**Conversion Strategies**
1. Eastern Europe Conditions 2. Potential for alliances 3. Technology increasing demand 4. Sustainability agenda	1. (S1+O1+O2) Distribution alliance with XYX in Romania leveraging our brand 2. 3.	1. (W2+O1) Complete a process re-engineering exercise to support efficiency + market expansion 2. 3.
Threats	**Utilization Strategies**	**Defensive Strategies**
1. Increasing competition 2. Pricing pressure 3. Increasing deal complexity 4. Suppliers competing 5. Cyber security risks	1. Leverage balance sheet to purchase #3 competitor (S2+T1) 2. 3.	1. Conduct a cost optimisation program to improve margins and prepare for increasing price pressure (W1+T1+T2) 2. 3.

Benchmarking Assessment Template

A concise layout for comparing the performance and practices of peer organizations as part of a business diagnostic exercise

Benchmarking Assessment – Overview

What is it

The Benchmarking Assessment Template is a clear and simple framework for allowing organizations to be compared across a range of practices, performance measures, metrics or operational attributes in a visually appealing and easy-to-understand format. It can be easily tailored to suit the number of organizations or dimensions being compared, in addition to allowing other qualitative aspects to be highlighted as part of the read-out.

When to use it

The Benchmarking Assessment Template is best utilized as part of an analysis or diagnostics exercise where peer comparisons are being made across multiple organizations with the aim of highlighting areas of significant variation. It is particularly useful when needing to convey comparator variations to a senior executive audience or wide group stakeholders who need to be engaged and involved in action to address apparent performance or practice deficiencies.

Why use it

The Benchmarking Assessment Template is proven to be effective at conveying the critical information emanating from a peer comparison exercise. Its value comes through the ease with which direct comparisons between organizations can be made and, more importantly, communicated to a variety of audiences. Injecting peer comparison insights into a business analysis exercise can be extremely informative at highlighting the need for business transformation.

Benchmarking Assessment – Method (Option 1)

How you use it

Step 1. Capture the key dimensions or drivers that benchmarks, metrics, practices and comparators are being assessed.

Step 2. Capture the metrics, practices, measures in each area that are being assessed.

Step 3. For each metric or practice notate the relative performance and position of your organization compared to peer organizations.

Step 4. Use the correct symbols to notate the appropriate quartile positioning.

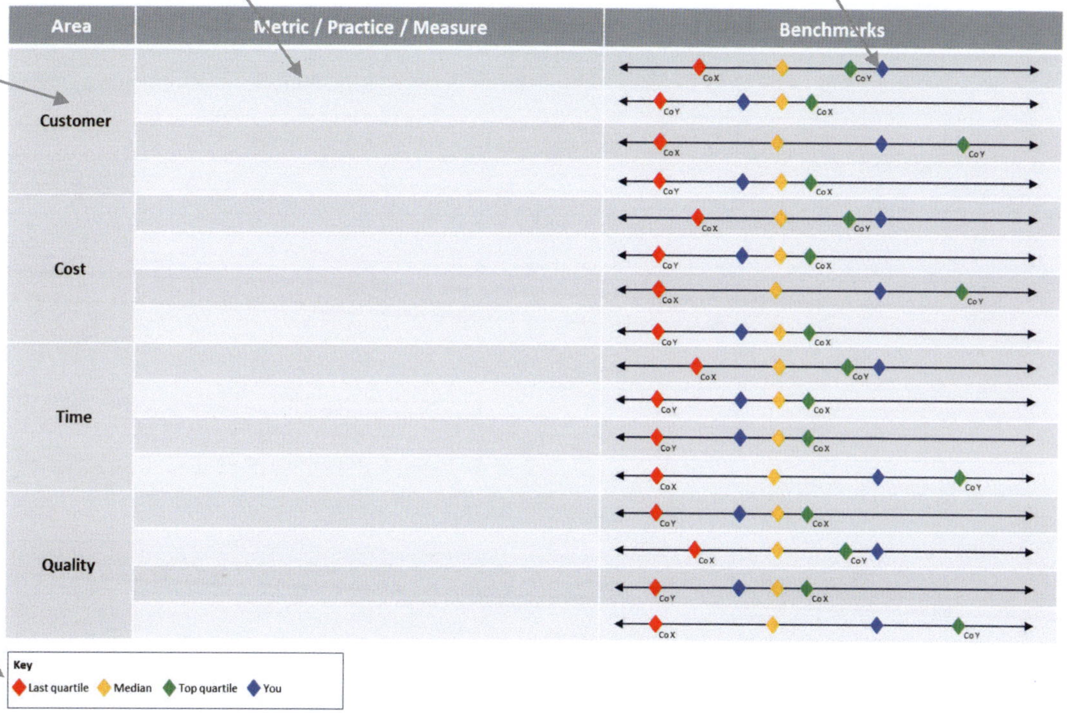

Area	Metric / Practice / Measure	Benchmarks
Customer		
Cost		
Time		
Quality		

Key: ◆ Last quartile ◆ Median ◆ Top quartile ◆ You

Benchmarking Assessment – Template (Option 1)

Area	Metric / Practice / Measure	Benchmarks
Customer		Co X ← → Co Y
		Co Y ← → Co X
		Co X ← → Co Y
		Co Y ← → Co X
Cost		Co X ← → Co Y
		Co Y ← → Co X
		Co X ← → Co Y
		Co Y ← → Co X
Time		Co X ← → Co Y
		Co Y ← → Co X
		Co Y ← → Co X
		Co X ← → Co Y
Quality		Co Y ← → Co X
		Co X ← → Co Y
		Co Y ← → Co X
		Co X ← → Co Y

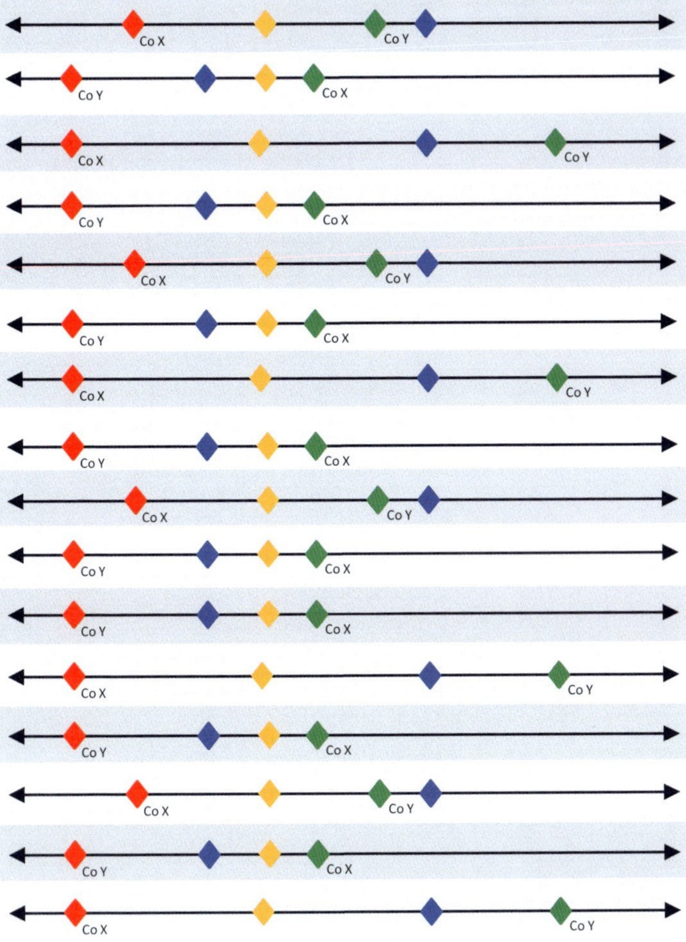

Key
- 🔶 Last quartile
- 🔶 Median
- 🔶 Top quartile
- 🔶 You

Benchmarking Assessment – Method (Option 2)

How you use it

Step 1. Capture the key dimensions or drivers that benchmarks and comparators are being assessed.

Step 2. Capture the metrics, practices, measures in each area that is being assessed.

Step 3. For each metric or practice, notate the relative performance and position of your organization compared to peer organizations.

Step 4. Capture any insights that emerge from the peer comparison and relative position across metrics and practices

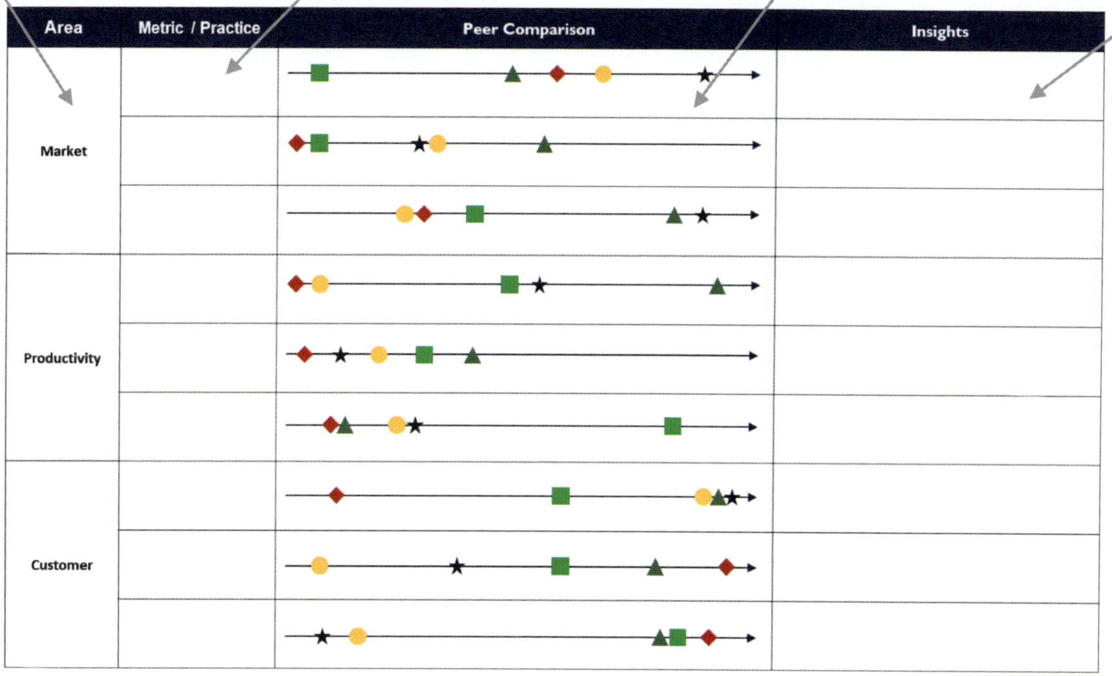

Area	Metric / Practice	Peer Comparison	Insights
Market			
Market			
Market			
Productivity			
Productivity			
Productivity			
Customer			
Customer			
Customer			

Benchmarking Assessment – Template (Option 2)

Area	Metric / Practice	Peer Comparison	Insights
Market			
Market			
Market			
Productivity			
Productivity			
Productivity			
Customer			
Customer			
Customer			

Legend: Comparator A ▲ | Comparator B ■ | Comparator C ● | Comparator D ◆ | Us ★

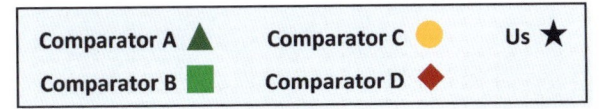

Business Diagnostic Findings Template

A structured approach for presenting findings and observations from a business diagnostic exercise

Business Diagnostic Findings – Overview

What is it

The Business Diagnostic Findings Template is a proven framework for presenting the essential findings and observations from a business diagnostic phase. The format is highly adaptable and is particularly suited to presenting the summary outcomes from an analysis exercise to a group of key stakeholders. Two format options are presented here for selection by the business analyst. The template assumes that underlying analysis exists, providing sufficient evidence of the findings and these can be referenced if required.

When to use it

These templates should be used at the conclusion of a business analysis or diagnostic exercise when the key findings and observations are needing to be socialized with a stakeholder group. The template works for most varieties of analysis exercises – regardless of the focus being process, technology, organization, customer or other. The format for presenting the results works well as the segue into developing solution options or recommendations.

Why use it

The Business Diagnostic Findings Templates presented here are proven to work well with executive audience and are similar to those used by the leading management consultants reporting out findings to senior business executives. The format of the templates provide sufficient detail and are structured in a way to help the reader or audience understand the key facts and insights easily and therefore make informed decisions.

Business Diagnostic Findings – Method (Option 1)

How you use it

Step 1. Describe each focus area of the analysis exercise that has been conducted. This could be product, business unit, service type, systems – or any logical grouping that aligns with the approach and objectives of the exercise.

Step 2. Summarize the findings or observations for each focus area.

Step 3. Describe the likely impact of each finding.

Step 4. Outline potential solutions that could be adopted to counter the negative findings.

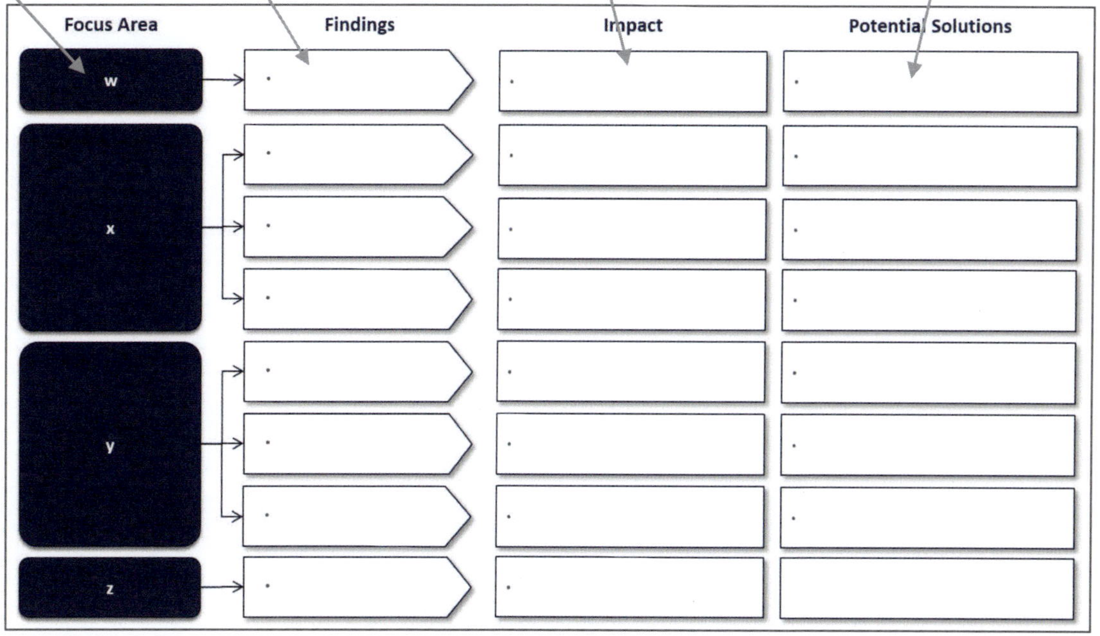

Focus Area	Findings	Impact	Potential Solutions
w	.	.	.
x	.	.	.
x	.	.	.
x	.	.	.
y	.	.	.
y	.	.	.
y	.	.	.
z	.	.	.

Business Diagnostic Findings – Template (Option 1)

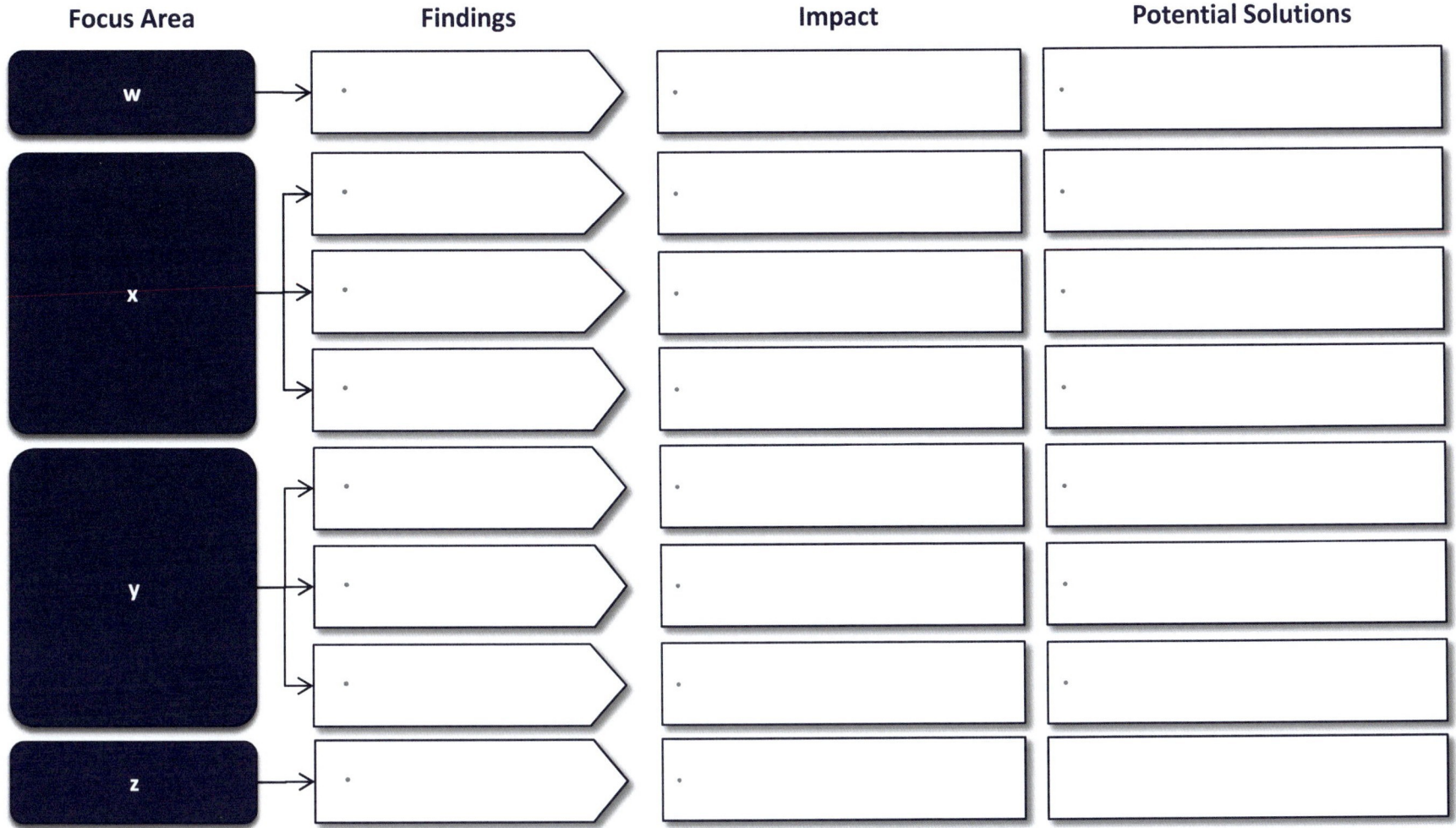

Business Diagnostic Findings – Method (Option 2)

How you use it

Step 1. Describe each observation or finding from the analysis exercise.

Step 2. Provide data, an example or other information as supporting evidence of the finding.

Step 3. Describe the known and potential impacts to the business caused by the finding.

Step 4. Use a key or legend to notate each finding, indicating which organizational dimension is impacted by the finding

Observations	Supporting Evidence	Business Impacts	
•			☺
•			ⓘ
•			$
•			
•			

Impact Areas: ☺ Customer Satisfaction $ Financial Performance   ⓘ Business Efficiency

Business Diagnostic Findings – Template (Option 2)

Observations	Supporting Evidence	Business Impacts	
•			😊 ⬇
•			💲
•			
•			
•			

Impact Areas 😊 Customer Satisfaction   💲 Financial Performance   ⬇ Business Efficiency

Business Initiative Project Charter

A simple, clear, proven and customizable template for the effective definition of a business improvement initiative

Business Initiative Charter – Overview

What is it

The Business Initiative Project Charter Template is a simple, "on a page" view for laying out the key elements of a business analysis or improvement initiative including scope, objectives, activities, deliverables, stakeholders, measures of success and critical success factors. These elements and structures is easily customized to suit the needs of the business environment or project.

When to use it

This Business Initiative Project Charter should be used at the beginning of a project to clearly outline the scope, objectives and work required to be delivered as part of the project. The template can be used with the project team members to ensure alignment and the "job to be done" and can also be used with project sponsorship or other stakeholders to seek buy-in and endorsement.

Why use it

Clarifying and agreeing the scope, mandate and work to be delivered of a business initiative is a critical first step to ensuring success. This template is simple, clear, proven and customizable facilitating the efficient and effective definition of any business improvement initiative.

Business Initiative Charter – Method

How you use it

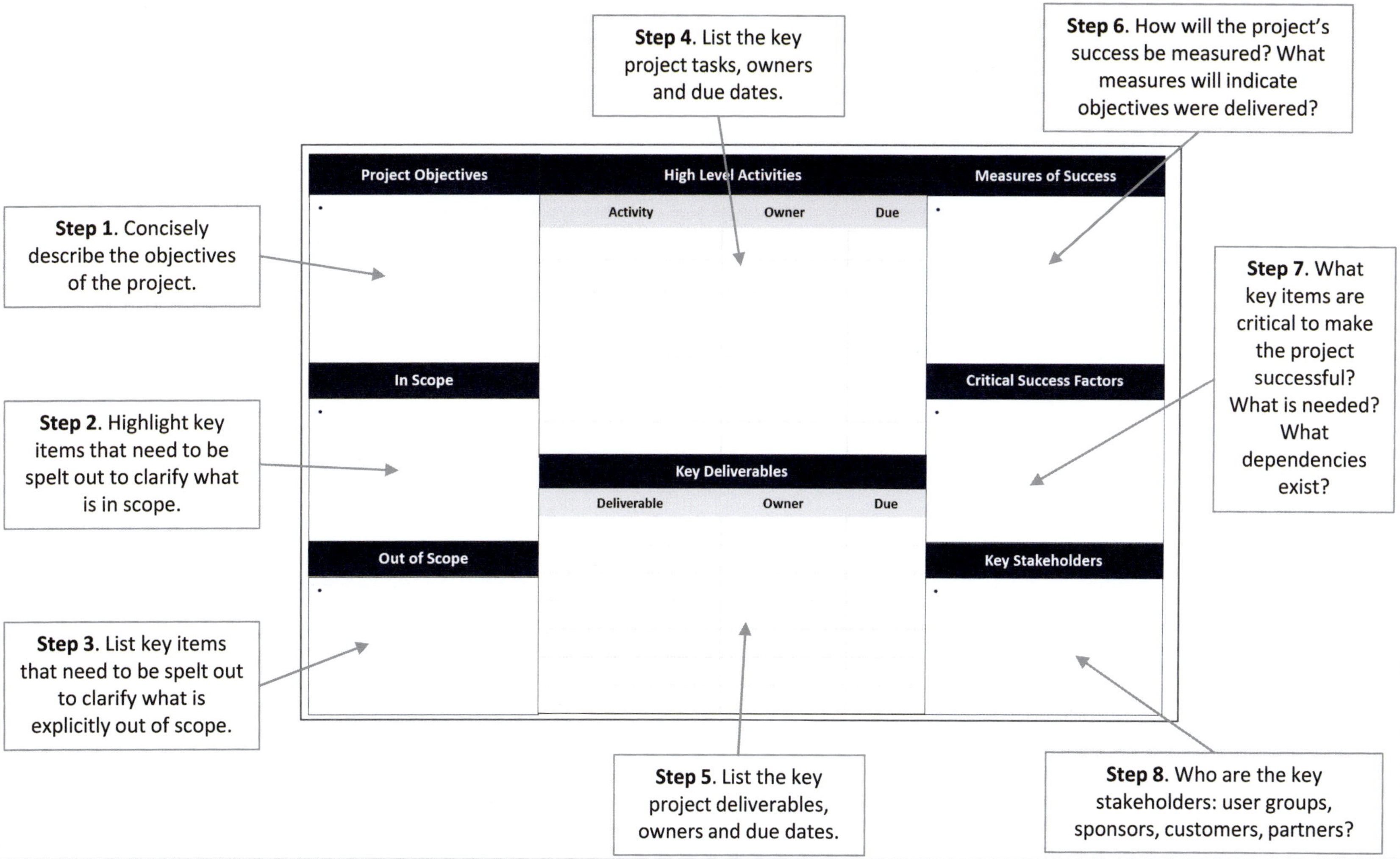

Step 1. Concisely describe the objectives of the project.

Step 2. Highlight key items that need to be spelt out to clarify what is in scope.

Step 3. List key items that need to be spelt out to clarify what is explicitly out of scope.

Step 4. List the key project tasks, owners and due dates.

Step 5. List the key project deliverables, owners and due dates.

Step 6. How will the project's success be measured? What measures will indicate objectives were delivered?

Step 7. What key items are critical to make the project successful? What is needed? What dependencies exist?

Step 8. Who are the key stakeholders: user groups, sponsors, customers, partners?

Project Objectives	High Level Activities			Measures of Success
•	Activity	Owner	Due	•
In Scope				**Critical Success Factors**
•				•
	Key Deliverables			
	Deliverable	Owner	Due	
Out of Scope				**Key Stakeholders**
•				•

Business Initiative Charter – Template

Project Objectives	High Level Activities			Measures of Success
•	Activity	Owner	Due	•
In Scope				**Critical Success Factors**
•				•
	Key Deliverables			
	Deliverable	Owner	Due	
Out of Scope				**Key Stakeholders**
•				•

Capability Gap Assessment

A structured framework for assessing the capabilities that exist within an organization.

Capability Gap Assessment – Overview

What is it

The Capability Gap Assessment is a structured framework for analyzing the capabilities that exist within an organization and presenting this assessment in a clear and simple form. The template allows a business analyst to capture multiple organizational dimensions, assess current capabilities and then outline potential improvement strategies to address apparent capability gaps.

When to use it

The framework is ideally suited to be used at the conclusion of an assessment phase, where findings need to be presented and potential strategies tested with stakeholders. The framework can be applied at a broad organizational level, also at a team or business unit level. Typically, the business analyst will have more detailed analysis and workings in support of the findings presented in the summary framework (such as interview notes, five whys, root cause etc.)

Why use it

This framework is especially useful when conducting a business analysis exercise that requires consideration of the capabilities that exist within the organization. It is highly adaptable and can be applied to tangible and less tangible organizational capabilities and across a range of dimensions including process, technology, people, culture, controls, governance, leadership.

Capability Gap Assessment – Method

How you use it

Step 2. Summarize the capabilities that are required in this organizational dimension for the business to accomplish its objectives.

Step 3. Summarize the current capabilities that exist within the organization in this area.

Step 4. Rate the current organizational capability for each dimension (High, Medium, Low)

Step 5. Identify and capture the potential strategies to lift the organizational capability from the current level to the required level.

Step 1. Capture the dimensions or organizational aspects that are being assessed.

Dimension	Required Capabilities	Existing Capabilities & Rating		Potential Strategies
Brand	• Must have….	• Currently have….	H	• Investigate the option of…
Service			M	
Pricing			L	
Network			H	
Offering			L	
Cost			L	
Invoicing			M	
Suppliers			H	

Capability Gap Assessment – Template

Dimension	Required Capabilities	Existing Capabilities & Rating		Potential Strategies
Brand	• Must have….	• Currently have….	H	• Investigate the option of…
Service			M	
Pricing			L	
Network			H	
Offering			L	
Cost			L	
Invoicing			M	
Suppliers			H	

Cost Benefit Assessment Framework
A proven, simple and flexible model for evaluating the costs and benefits of business improvement initiatives

Cost Benefit Assessment Framework – Overview

What is it

The Cost-Benefit Assessment Framework is a proven and easily customizable model for evaluating the costs and benefits of business improvement initiatives. It allows a business analyst or project owner to summarize the key dimensions that need to be considered when evaluating the worthiness of potential business improvement initiatives. The structure can be tailored to suit the specific requirements of the business, however the layout presented here is considered best practice.

When to use it

The Cost-Benefit Assessment Framework should be used to objectively evaluate business improvement initiatives and socialize them with executive stakeholders for selection and endorsement. The framework is designed to be used at the conclusion of an "analysis and design" exercise where issues are known in-depth and potential improvement projects have been identified, assessed and scoped. It is typical that additional financial worksheets will be created to support the information presented in this framework.

Why use it

The Cost-Benefit Framework is flexible and proven to work across a range of industries, environments and business improvement portfolio types. It provides a concise and structured mechanism for outlining potential improvement initiatives and prioritizing them based on pre-defined objective criteria – such as cost, financial return, strategic alignment, customer advocacy impact and benefit accomplishment risk.

Cost Benefit Assessment Framework – Method

How you use it

Step 1: List the business improvement initiatives being evaluated.

Step 2: For each initiative, provide a qualitative rating of alignment to strategic objectives.

Step 3: For each initiative, identify the pain points that will be remediated.

Step 4: For each initiative, provide a qualitative rating for the extent the initiative will have a positive impact on customers.

Step 5: For each initiative, provide details of Cost (OpEx, CapEx) and benefits (OpEx, Revenue) over 1 and 3 years.

Step 6: For each initiative, indicate the confidence level in the benefits being achieved.

Step 7: Total the results in order to assess the overall improvement portfolio.

Initiative Name	Strategic Alignment	Pain Points Addressed	Positive Customer Impact	Estimated Costs Capex ($m) 1ST YEAR	Estimated Costs Capex ($m) 3 YEARS	Estimated Costs Opex ($m) 1ST YEAR	Estimated Costs Opex ($m) 3 YEARS	Estimated Benefits (3yr totals $m) OPEX	Estimated Benefits (3yr totals $m) REVENUE	Confidence Level of Benefits
Example Initiative Name	High	#1, #2	High	0	0	1.5	2	4	4	Moderate
Example Initiative Name	Medium	#11, #14	Medium	3	5	1	3	10	50	High
Example Initiative Name	Low	#10	Low	1	4	2	6	5	27	Very High
Total										

Cost Benefit Assessment Framework – Template

Initiative Name	Strategic Alignment	Pain Points Addressed	Positive Customer Impact	Estimated Costs				Estimated Benefits (3yr totals $m)		Confidence Level of Benefits
				Capex ($m)		Opex ($m)				
				1ST YEAR	3 YEARS	1ST YEAR	3 YEARS	OPEX	REVENUE	
Example Initiative Name	High	#1, #2	High	0	0	1.5	2	4	4	Moderate
Example Initiative Name	Medium	#11, #14	Medium	3	5	1	3	10	50	High
Example Initiative Name	Low	#10	Low	1	4	2	6	5	27	Very High
			Total							

Customer Experience Design Framework

A proven, simple approach for outlining a customer experience vision and design for an organization

Customer Experience Design – Overview

What is it

The Customer Experience Design Framework is simple-to-use, but very effective framework at structuring analysis and design of customer experience improvement. It uses three components to drive analysis, "visioning" and discussion: 1. The aspirational customer experience; 2. The current customer experience; and 3. The experience delivered by competitors. Using this simple model, aligned to the core steps taken by a customer along their experience journey allows improvement to be targeted for greatest return.

When to use it

The Customer Experience Framework is best suited to a future-state design exercise that is concentrating on the customer experience vision and design of an organization. To be most effective, some level of analysis and insight on the current state and competitor experiences will be available. Using this information, a business analyst can then facilitate a group of stakeholders to design an aspirational customer experience and from there agree on where the maximum improvement effort is required.

Why use it

The power of this Customer Experience Design Framework comes through its simplicity and adaptability. It can be tailored to any customer experience journey, any level of detail and any number of customer journey steps. It is also very effective when used to engage stakeholders during a future state customer experience design or "visioning" exercise in addition to executive socialization discussions aimed at soliciting buy-in and endorsement for process improvement or transformation.

Customer Experience Design – Method

How you use it

Step 1: Identify the process steps that customers move through. The framework can be used at the highest process level or used at lower level process steps (for example the steps to purchase). Add steps along the horizontal as required.

Step 2: For each process step, summarize the experience that is being targeted for delivery to the customer.

Step 4: Draw experience curves that represent your organization's delivered experience and the experienced delivered by your primary competitor.

Step 3: Summarize the key points that represent the experience provided to customers by your primary competitor.

	Customer Lifecycle Step 1 (e.g. Browse)	Customer Lifecycle Step 2 (e.g. Buy)	Customer Lifecycle Step 3 (e.g. Use)	Customer Lifecycle Step 4 (e.g. Pay)	Customer Lifecycle Step 5 (e.g. Renew)
Our Desired Experience					

Experience levels: Wow! / Pleasure / Easy / Procedural / Confusing / Frustrating

Competitor's Provided Experience					

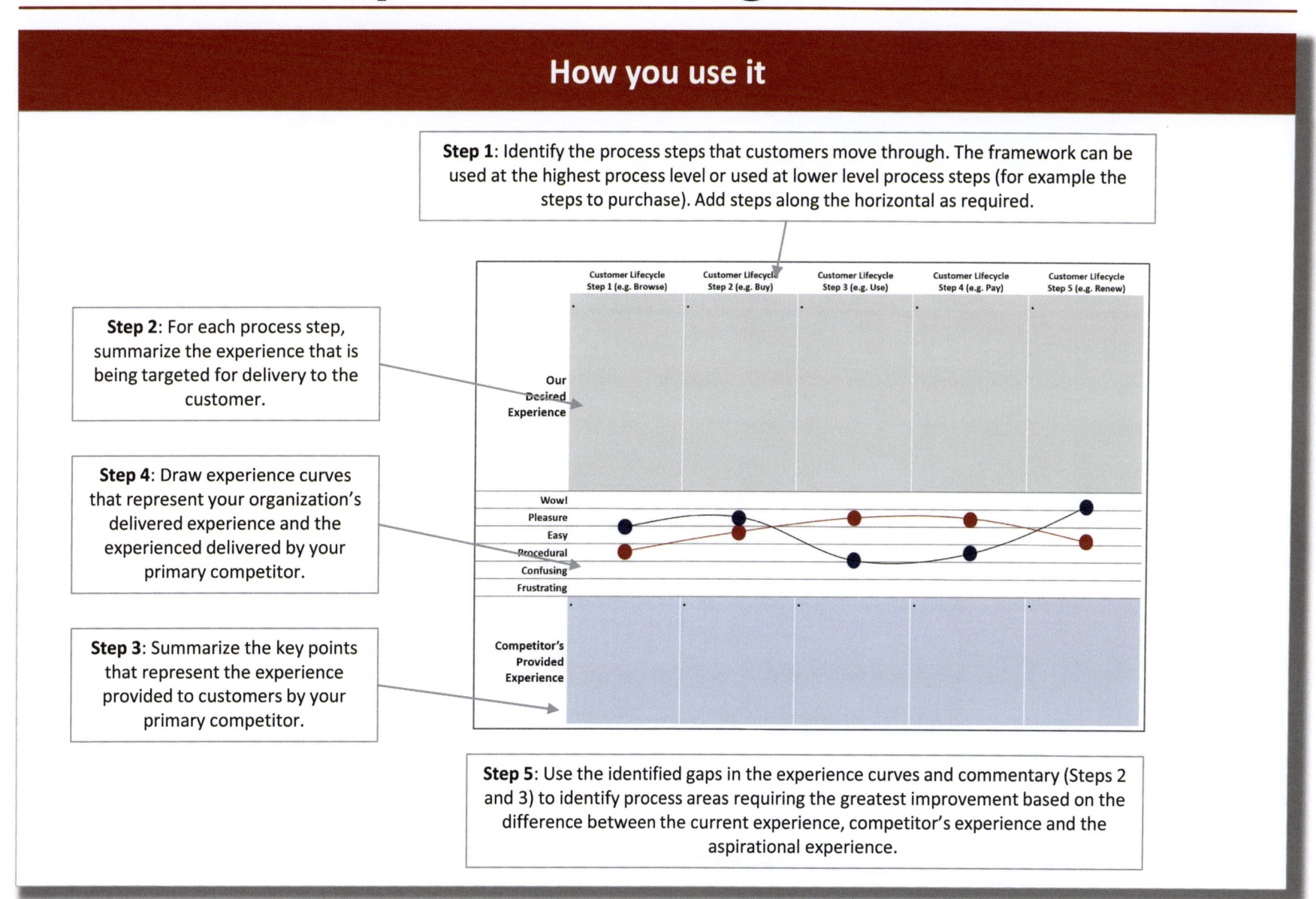

Step 5: Use the identified gaps in the experience curves and commentary (Steps 2 and 3) to identify process areas requiring the greatest improvement based on the difference between the current experience, competitor's experience and the aspirational experience.

Customer Experience Design – Template

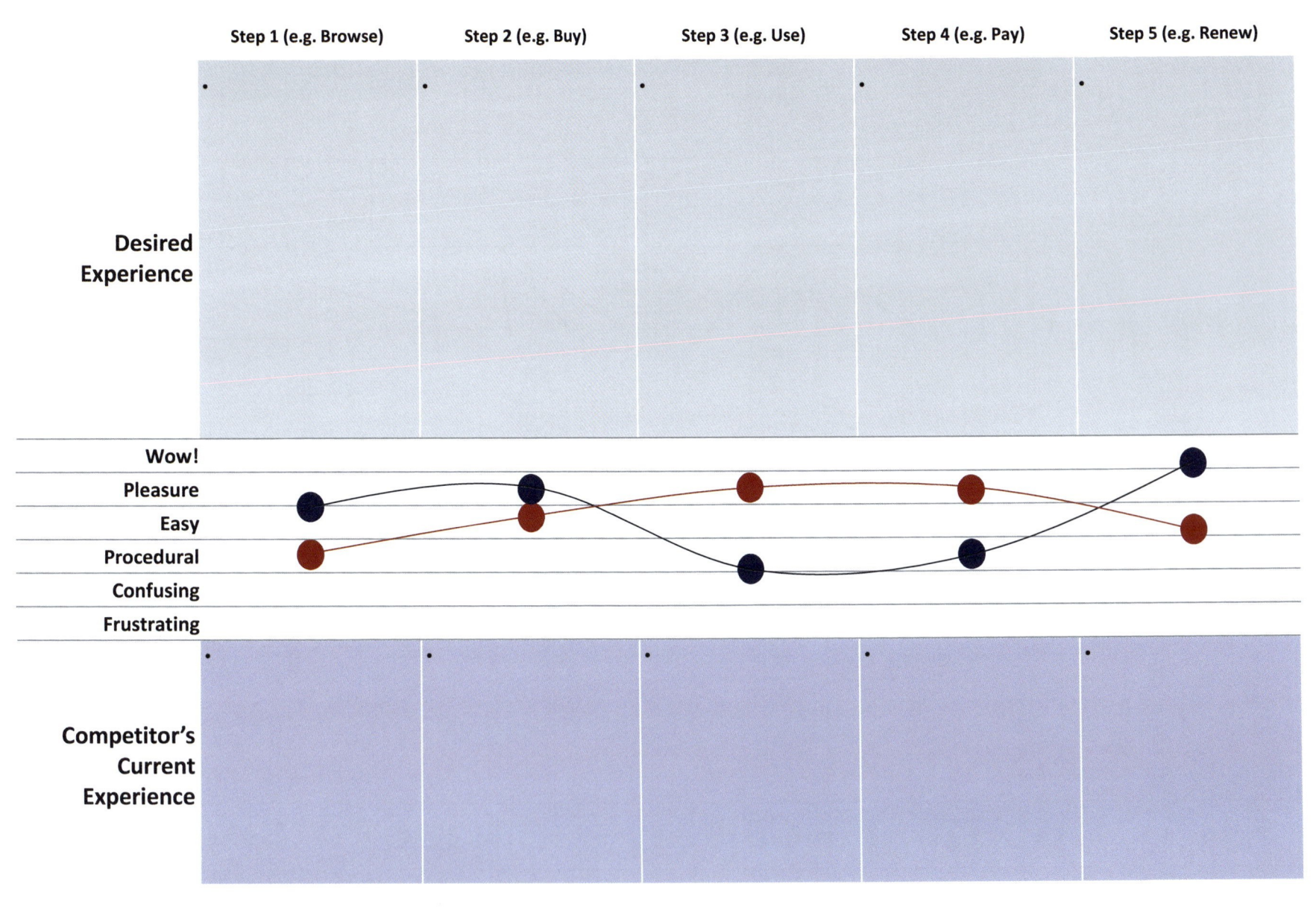

	Step 1 (e.g. Browse)	Step 2 (e.g. Buy)	Step 3 (e.g. Use)	Step 4 (e.g. Pay)	Step 5 (e.g. Renew)
Desired Experience					

- Wow!
- Pleasure
- Easy
- Procedural
- Confusing
- Frustrating

	Step 1	Step 2	Step 3	Step 4	Step 5
Competitor's Current Experience					

Data Collection Plan

A proven template for gathering operational data in support of a business analysis exercise

Data Collection Plan – Overview

What is it

Business analysis initiatives need to begin with a clear understanding of the location, drivers, actors and implications of problems. To obtain this, it is essential the current state is understood intimately and accurately through data. Data is typically available from a range of sources, can be collected in a variety of methods, a variety of formats and can be obtained in different volumes. To gather the right data in the right format, in the right volumes and from the right sources is critical to have a good data collection plan.

When to use it

A Data Collection Plan should be used at the beginning of an analysis exercise that is endeavoring to understand the current state in order to get to heart of business problem drivers and root causes. Once the problem has been defined and initial hypotheses are being established, a data collection plan should be documented to outline and agree the data collection approach, volumes, sources, measurement volumes and time periods.

Why use it

A robust Data Collection Plan is critical to the success of any business analysis exercise. Clarifying the sources of data that will be gathered, analyzed, measured and used in a diagnostic is an important part of scoping, planning and approach definition. The Data Collection Plan template provided here is a proven structured approach for defining this plan.

Data Collection Plan – Method

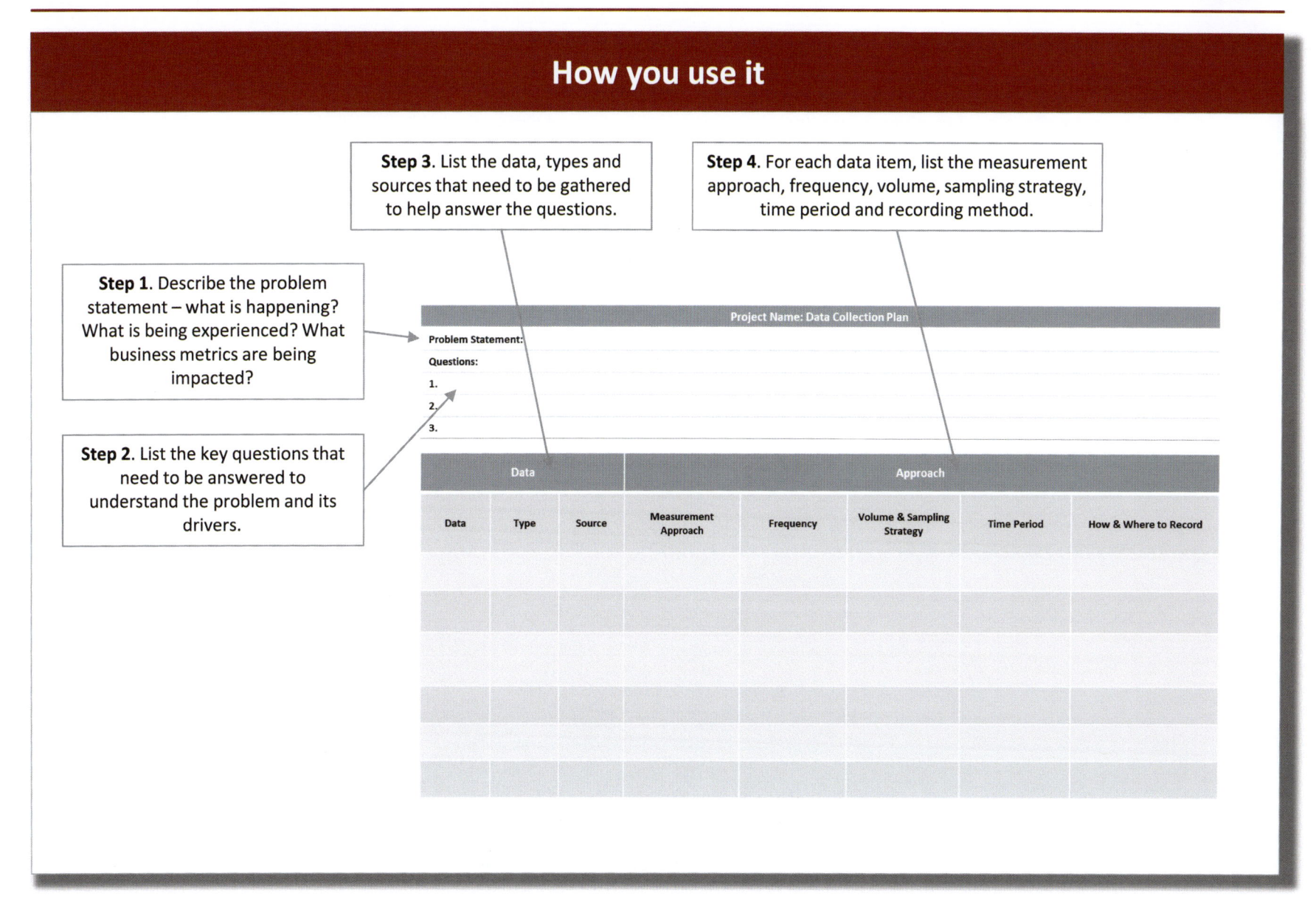

How you use it

Step 1. Describe the problem statement – what is happening? What is being experienced? What business metrics are being impacted?

Step 2. List the key questions that need to be answered to understand the problem and its drivers.

Step 3. List the data, types and sources that need to be gathered to help answer the questions.

Step 4. For each data item, list the measurement approach, frequency, volume, sampling strategy, time period and recording method.

Project Name: Data Collection Plan

Problem Statement:

Questions:
1.
2.
3.

Data			Approach				
Data	Type	Source	Measurement Approach	Frequency	Volume & Sampling Strategy	Time Period	How & Where to Record

Data Collection Plan – Template

Project Name: Data Collection Plan
Problem Statement:
Questions:
1.
2.
3.

Data			Approach				
Data	Type	Source	Measurement Approach	Frequency	Volume & Sampling Strategy	Time Period	How & Where to Record

Data Collection Plan – Example

Project Name: Data Collection Plan
Problem Statement: High volume of customer complaints being received in the contact center by customer using the RixbyPro home integration unit.
Questions:
1. Why are customers calling?
2. Are the complaints related to product, service, pricing?
3. Are their particular types of customers who are calling?

Data			Approach				
Data	Type	Source	Measurement Approach	Frequency	Volume & Sampling Strategy	Time Period	How & Where to Record
Customer Complaints	Call Recordings	Call Quality System	Listening and capturing salient data	Calls to be listened to over a 10 day period	Total of 400 call recordings	3 month period	Hills call center using the call quality playback system
Customer Purchase Experience	Customer Feedback	Live Survey Data	Customer Interviews upon store exit after product purchase	Every customer purchasing	Minimum of 400 store customer interviews	1 month	5 stores across 3 cities
Customer Returns	Forms	Returns Center Customer Forms	Gather customer product return forms and capture salient data	Every customer form	Minimum of 400 return forms	3 month	Springfield Returns Depot

Failure Mode Effects Analysis

A proven analysis method for identifying and preventing business process failures and errors

Failure Mode Effects Analysis – Overview

What is it

Failure Mode Effects Analysis (FMEA) is a method for analyzing potential ways in which a process could fail impacting process performance, output quality, customer satisfaction. FMEA works by using a consistent classification approach in which failures are prioritized based on severity, detectability and likelihood. Failure modes are errors or defects in a process, design, or item, especially those that affect the customer, and can be potential or actual. Effects analysis refers to the evaluation of the consequences of failures.

When to use it

FMEA is a useful method for identifying and analyzing the potential "break points" of a process. It helps ask the questions – "where could this process go wrong, how bad will it be when it goes wrong, how likely will we see it has gone wrong and be able to correct it". Using the objective assessment and scoring approach, FMEA can be used to focus improvement efforts in areas likely to cause greatest impact. FMEA is a valuable technique to utilize in any process analysis exercise where control and output quality is critical.

Why use it

A successful FMEA activity helps a business analysis team identify potential failure scenarios based on past experience, similar products or processes. This then enables improvements to be crafted that design those failures out of the process or system with the minimum of effort and resource expenditure, thereby reducing development time and costs. FMEA is widely used in a variety of industries and is applicable to product and service oriented processes.

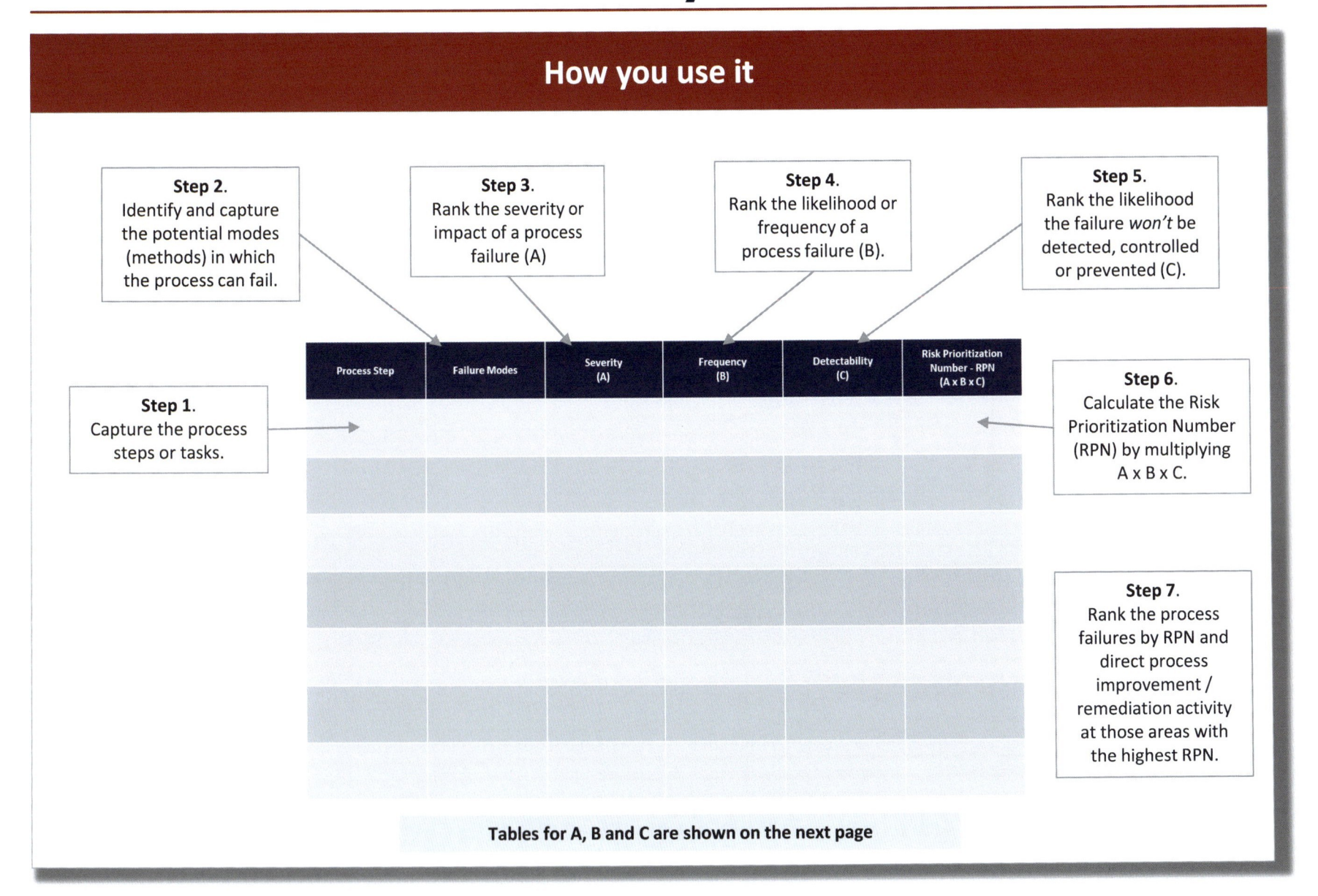

Failure Mode Effects Analysis – Method

How you use it

Step 1. Capture the process steps or tasks.

Step 2. Identify and capture the potential modes (methods) in which the process can fail.

Step 3. Rank the severity or impact of a process failure (A).

Step 4. Rank the likelihood or frequency of a process failure (B).

Step 5. Rank the likelihood the failure *won't* be detected, controlled or prevented (C).

Step 6. Calculate the Risk Prioritization Number (RPN) by multiplying A x B x C.

Step 7. Rank the process failures by RPN and direct process improvement / remediation activity at those areas with the highest RPN.

Process Step	Failure Modes	Severity (A)	Frequency (B)	Detectability (C)	Risk Prioritization Number - RPN (A x B x C)

Tables for A, B and C are shown on the next page

Failure Mode Effects Analysis – Method

How you use it

Step 3. Severity (A)

Rating	Meaning
1	No effect
2	Very minor – only noticed by highly discriminating customers
3	Minor – noticed by the average customer but functionality not affected
4-6	Moderate – most customers are frustrated by the error and will complain
7-8	High – loss of primary function and customers likely to defect, cancel
9-10	Very High and Hazardous – inoperative, could result in critical error, injury or death

Step 4. Frequency (B)

Rating	Meaning
1	No known occurrences on similar processes
2-3	Low – relatively few failures
4-6	Moderate – occasional process failures
7-8	High – repeated failures occur
9-10	Very-High – almost inevitable that failures will occur

Step 5. Detectability (C)

Rating	Meaning
1	Certain – tests will detect fault
2	Almost certain fault will be detected
3	High likelihood fault will be detected and prevented
4-6	Moderate likelihood fault will be detected and prevented
7-8	Low – manual inspection required and high likelihood faults will be missed
9-10	Fault very likely to be passed on to customer

Failure Mode Effects Analysis – Template

Process Step	Failure Modes	Severity (A)	Frequency (B)	Detectability (C)	Risk Prioritization Number - RPN (A x B x C)

Five Whys Template

A structured and disciplined method for identifying drivers of business problems

Five Whys – Overview

What is it

The Five Whys Method is a disciplined, powerful technique for questioning a business performance situation in order to understand "why things are the way they are" to arrive at a true, underlying root cause – not a symptom. The name is derived by the principle of asking "why" at least five times to get to the real cause or driver for a business problem. The actual number of times "why" is asked will vary from situation to situation – but the goal is always to get to and true root cause of the problem experienced.

When to use it

The Five Whys Method has incredible versatility and facilitates a range of perspectives being gathered in a short time period through its inclusive nature. It is therefore very useful in situations where there is a high degree of time pressure associated with solving a business performance issue and there are a range of stakeholders with insights to be provided regarding the issue and its likely causes. It can be used in one-on-one settings (such as focused interviews) or in workshops involving multiple participants.

Why use it

The Five Whys is effective at getting to potential business problem drivers quickly. Although qualitative in nature, the structured questioning and probing combined with the collective knowledge of a range of stakeholders makes it particularly useful in discovering problem drivers quickly and then using the knowledge gathered during problem identification to begin solution ideation.

Five Whys – Method

How you use it

Step 1. Clearly describe the problem statement – what is happening? What is being experienced? What business metrics are being impacted?

Step 2. List the stakeholders that will be interviewed as part of the problem diagnosis.

Step 3. For each interviewee, capture the answers to each why. The first why box captures the answer to "why is this problem happening" (or similar). Each subsequent why box captures the answer of why the previous answer is happening.

Step 4. After each interviewee has been asked enough whys (3-5 recommended) some common themes should emerge for the underlying root cause.

Step 5. Based on the common theme root cause, brainstorm potential solutions or containment measures with the interviewees.

Problem Statement:

Interviewee	1st Why	2nd Why	3rd Why	4th Why	5th Why

Underlying Root Cause:

Potential Solution or Containment Measure:

A more comprehensive "How to" guide for the Five Whys can be found on experttoolkit.com

Five Whys – Template

Problem Statement:

Interviewee	1st Why	2nd Why	3rd Why	4th Why	5th Why

Underlying Root Cause:

Potential Solution or Containment Measure:

Future State Process Change Summary Template

A concise format for outlining the key changes and improvements required to optimize a business process

Future State Process Change Summary – Overview

What is it

The Future State Process Change Summary Template is complementary to the Process Issues Summary Template. It is a clean and structured method for highlighting proposed improvements to a process in addition to the corresponding initiatives that need to be initiated in order to implement the improvements.

When to use it

The Future State Process Change Summary should be used at the conclusion of a process analysis exercise to convey in a summary form the information necessary for stakeholders to understand the recommended improvements. The change summary should be supplemented by more detailed process analysis conducted by the business analysis, which should support the findings and recommendations.

Why use it

The Future State Process Change Summary is a proven, clear and logical format for conveying the changes and initiatives necessary for driving business process improvement. It works very well with a variety of stakeholders and is particularly useful with executive audiences who primarily need to know the summary of the recommendations requiring endorsement.

Future State Process Change Summary – Method

How you use it

Step 1. List the roles that are involved in supporting the future-state process.

Step 2. List the key tasks or process steps that are involved in delivering the future-state process.

Step 3. Describe in detail the changes that are proposed in the current process to implement the future process.

Step 4. Document the initiatives and fixes that need to be implemented in order to deliver the changes required of the future-state process.

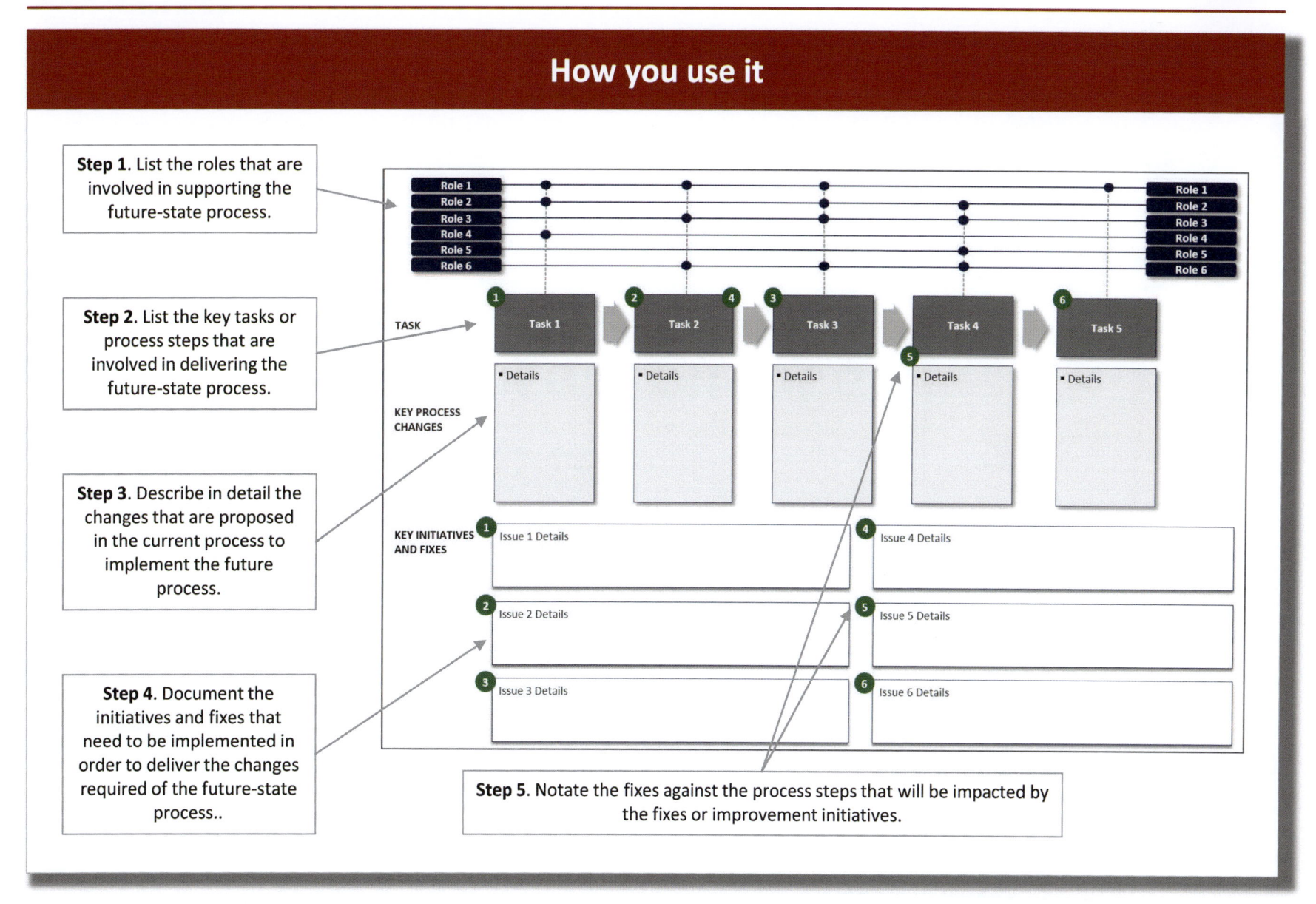

Step 5. Notate the fixes against the process steps that will be impacted by the fixes or improvement initiatives.

Future State Process Change Summary – Template

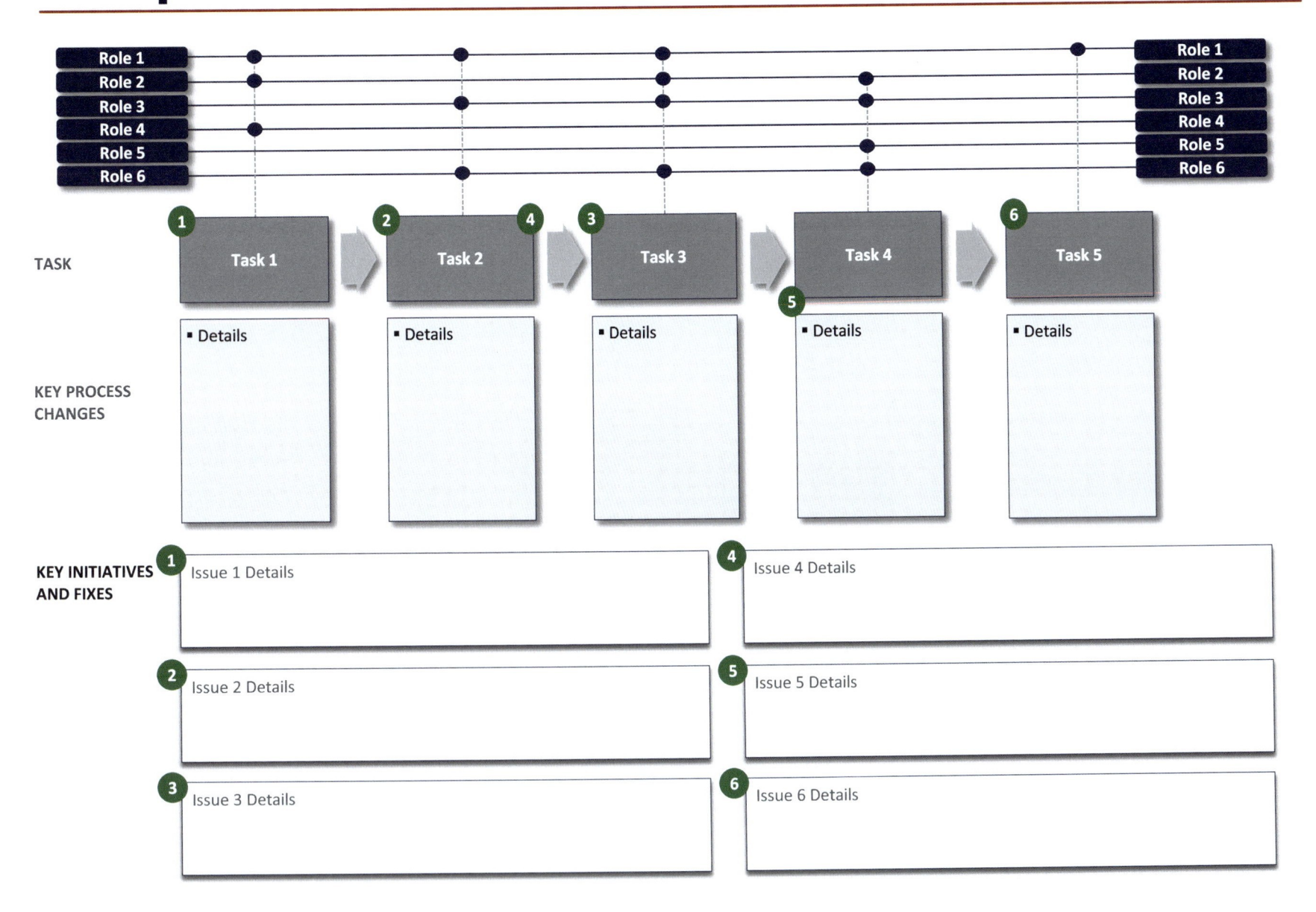

Role 1, Role 2, Role 3, Role 4, Role 5, Role 6

TASK

1. Task 1
2. Task 2
4. (between Task 2 and Task 3)
3. Task 3
5. (between Task 3 and Task 4)
   Task 4
6. Task 5

KEY PROCESS CHANGES

- Details (Task 1)
- Details (Task 2)
- Details (Task 3)
- Details (Task 4)
- Details (Task 5)

KEY INITIATIVES AND FIXES

1. Issue 1 Details
2. Issue 2 Details
3. Issue 3 Details
4. Issue 4 Details
5. Issue 5 Details
6. Issue 6 Details

Hypothesis Capture Template

A structured framework for capturing hypotheses and driving fast-paced inductive business analysis

Hypothesis Capture – Overview

What is it

Hypotheses are developed during an inductive analysis (as compared to deductive analysis) exercise. Hypotheses are educated guesses that are then tested to assess if evidence confirms they are true or if they are false (dis-proven). Hypothesis-based business analysis facilitates fast-paced discovery and development of strategic choices. This Hypothesis-capture template is a proven and structured framework for capturing the necessary information associated with hypotheses as they are explored and tested.

When to use it

Hypotheses-based analysis is best used in circumstances where there is sufficient knowledge of the business environment and context to allow quality hypotheses to be developed and sufficient data and resources are available in order to test the hypotheses. When choosing to take a inductive-reasoning approach to a business analysis exercise, this template is useful in managing the various hypotheses and "lines of inquiry" that are evaluated.

Why use it

Hypotheses-based analysis is beneficial in facilitating an efficient and timely discovery of problems and opportunities by focusing the analysis effort in areas guided by the professional judgement of people closest to the subject matter. The alternative, deductive analysis, can be very time and effort intensive as it seeks to take a "bottom-up" approach of analyzing all available data to discover problems and opportunities for improvement.

Hypothesis Capture – Method

How you use it

Step 1. Clearly describe the problem statement – what is happening? What is being experienced? What business metrics are being impacted?

Step 2. State the assertion which is an underlying belief or possible driver related to the problem. A good assertion leads to the development of a good quality hypotheses.

Step 3. Craft the hypothesis. The hypothesis is the item to be tested through analysis and should be developed based on professional judgement.

Step 4. List the lines of inquiry or data sources that need to be investigated and analyzed to confirm or refute the hypothesis.

Step 5. Following the analysis of the data sources and lines of inquiry, list the key findings or insights that were revealed.

Step 6. Document that conclusions as a result of the analysis. Was the hypothesis true or false? Is there work to be done to implement a measure to address the proven hypothesis or explore an alternate hypothesis?

Problem / Question	Assertions	Hypotheses	Data Sources / Lines of Inquiry	Findings / Insights	Conclusions

A more comprehensive "How to" guide for Hypotheses-based Analysis can be found on experttoolkit.com

Hypothesis Capture – Example

Problem / Question	Assertions	Hypotheses	Data Sources / Lines of Inquiry	Findings / Insights	Conclusions
Are we losing orders through poor quality sales processes? Sales orders and in-store stock are not reconciling.	There might be fraud occurring on the front-line which is causing the appearance of lost sales. This is a common problem in this industry and we have experienced it previously.	Absence of in-store controls are allowing sales orders to be manipulated resulting in stock loss and no corresponding order.	Order Data Stock Data Store Mystery Shopping Store Observations	At stores X, Y, Z stock levels and order levels are inconsistent by 3500 units (13%) for the month of April. We have large number of orders being processed to dummy accounts with no customer attached. These orders are concentrated amongst a finite set of sales reps.	The hypothesis is confirmed. There is an immediate need to implement proactive process and system controls to prevent fraudulent store sales.

Hypothesis Capture – Template

Problem / Question	Assertions	Hypotheses	Data Sources / Lines of Inquiry	Findings / Insights	Conclusions

Initiative Prioritization Map Template

A proven framework for categorizing and prioritizing business improvement initiatives

Initiative Prioritization Map – Overview

What is it

The Initiative Prioritization Map is a structured framework for displaying, evaluating and prioritizing business improvement projects based on a simple two-by-two framework which generally considers a measure of the value of the initiative against a measure of the risk associated with delivering the initiative. Using this framework, initiatives can be categorized into different treatment groups to take forward.

When to use it

The Initiative Prioritization Map is ideally suited for use at the conclusion of an "Analysis & Design" project to evaluate potential improvement ideas, recommendations and initiatives. For effective use of the framework, initiatives should have already been identified and scoped to a sufficient level to know the relative business benefit and risk associated with delivery. The framework is also very useful for conveying a view of a prioritized improvement portfolio to senior executives for awareness and endorsement.

Why use it

The Initiative Prioritization Framework is simple, clear and easy to use – but powerful in its ability to stratify potential improvement initiatives into logical treatment categories to take forward. It is also proven to work well with senior executive business leaders for facilitating decision making on investments and garnering buy-in programs to take forward and those to defer or drop.

Initiative Prioritization Map – Method

How you use it

Step 1. Confirm the dimensions of the matrix. The typical approach uses business value on the vertical and ease of delivery on the horizontal. Other options are cost to deliver, delivery risk, customer impact, pain point resolution.

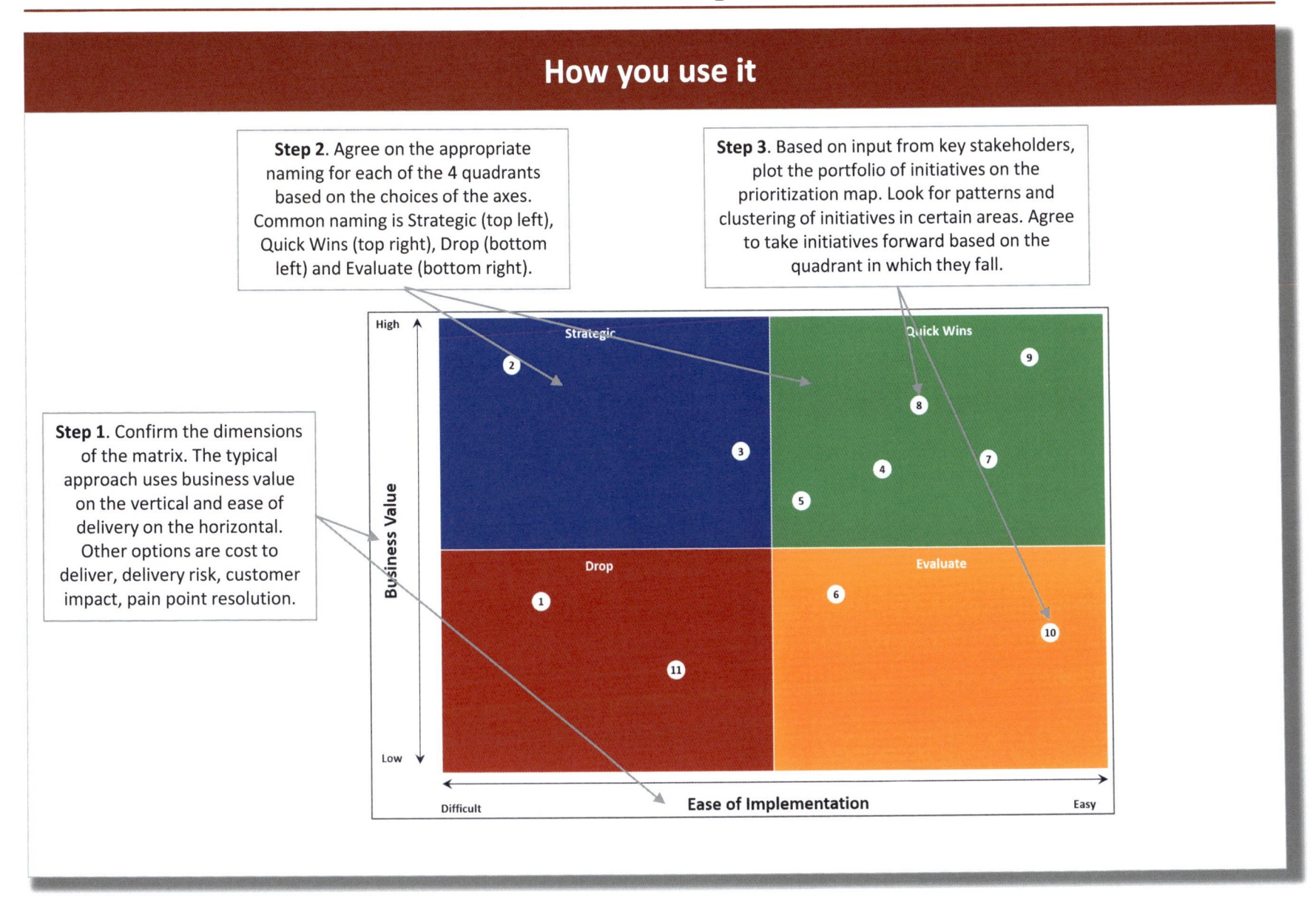

Step 2. Agree on the appropriate naming for each of the 4 quadrants based on the choices of the axes. Common naming is Strategic (top left), Quick Wins (top right), Drop (bottom left) and Evaluate (bottom right).

Step 3. Based on input from key stakeholders, plot the portfolio of initiatives on the prioritization map. Look for patterns and clustering of initiatives in certain areas. Agree to take initiatives forward based on the quadrant in which they fall.

	Strategic	Quick Wins
Business Value (High / Low)	2, 3	4, 5, 7, 8, 9
	Drop	Evaluate
	1, 11	6, 10

Ease of Implementation (Difficult → Easy)

© 2019 Expert Toolkit | ALL RIGHTS RESERVED | USAGE PERMITTED AS PER USER AGREEMENT

Initiative Prioritization Map – Template

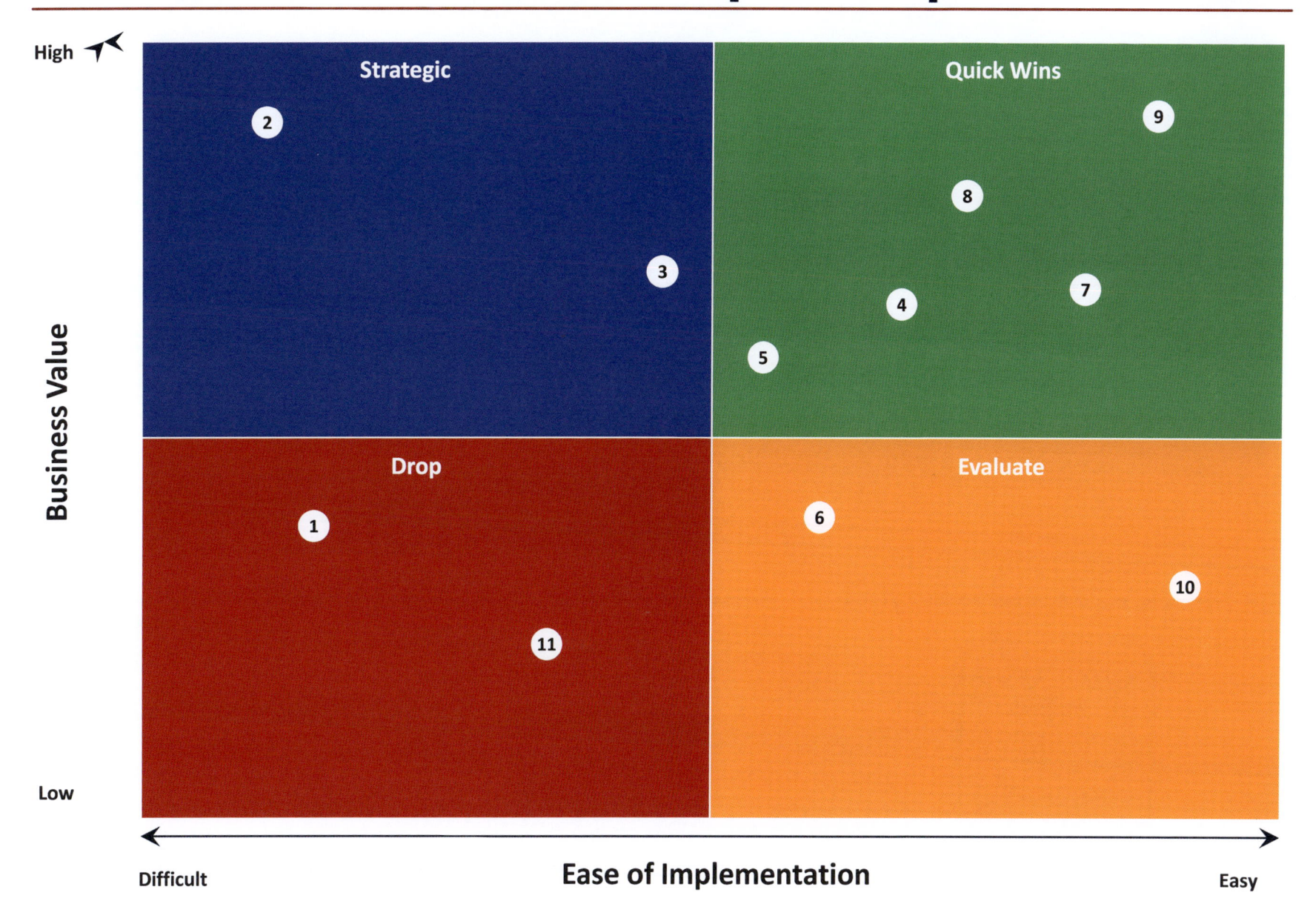

Business Value (Low → High)
Ease of Implementation (Difficult → Easy)

- **Strategic** (High Value, Difficult): 2, 3
- **Quick Wins** (High Value, Easy): 4, 5, 7, 8, 9
- **Drop** (Low Value, Difficult): 1, 11
- **Evaluate** (Low Value, Easy): 6, 10

The Jidoka Board Method

A structured, agile and disciplined method for identifying drivers of business process problems

Jidoka Board – Overview

What is it

Jidoka is a core pillar of lean thinking that requires management to develop processes that stop "production" immediately whenever an error or issue occurs. This stoppage then necessitates immediate error highlighting, resolution and error-proofing. At the heart of the philosophy is the principle that every user of a business process has the permission to stop a poorly operating process or raise issues that require remediation to improve performance. This makes Jidoka a powerful business analysis method.

When to use it

Jidoka has incredible versatility and facilitates a range of perspectives being gathered in a short time period through its inclusive nature. It is therefore very useful in situations where there is a high degree of time pressure associated with solving a business performance issue and there are a range of stakeholders with insights regarding issues and likely causes. It can be used in one-on-one settings or in workshops. It is also particularly powerful in an operational setting – facilitating continuous process improvement.

Why use it

The Jidoka Method is effective at getting to potential business problem drivers quickly. Although qualitative in nature, the structured questioning and probing combined with the collective knowledge of a range of stakeholders makes it particularly useful in discovering problem drivers quickly and then using the knowledge gathered during problem identification to begin solution ideation, development and implementation.

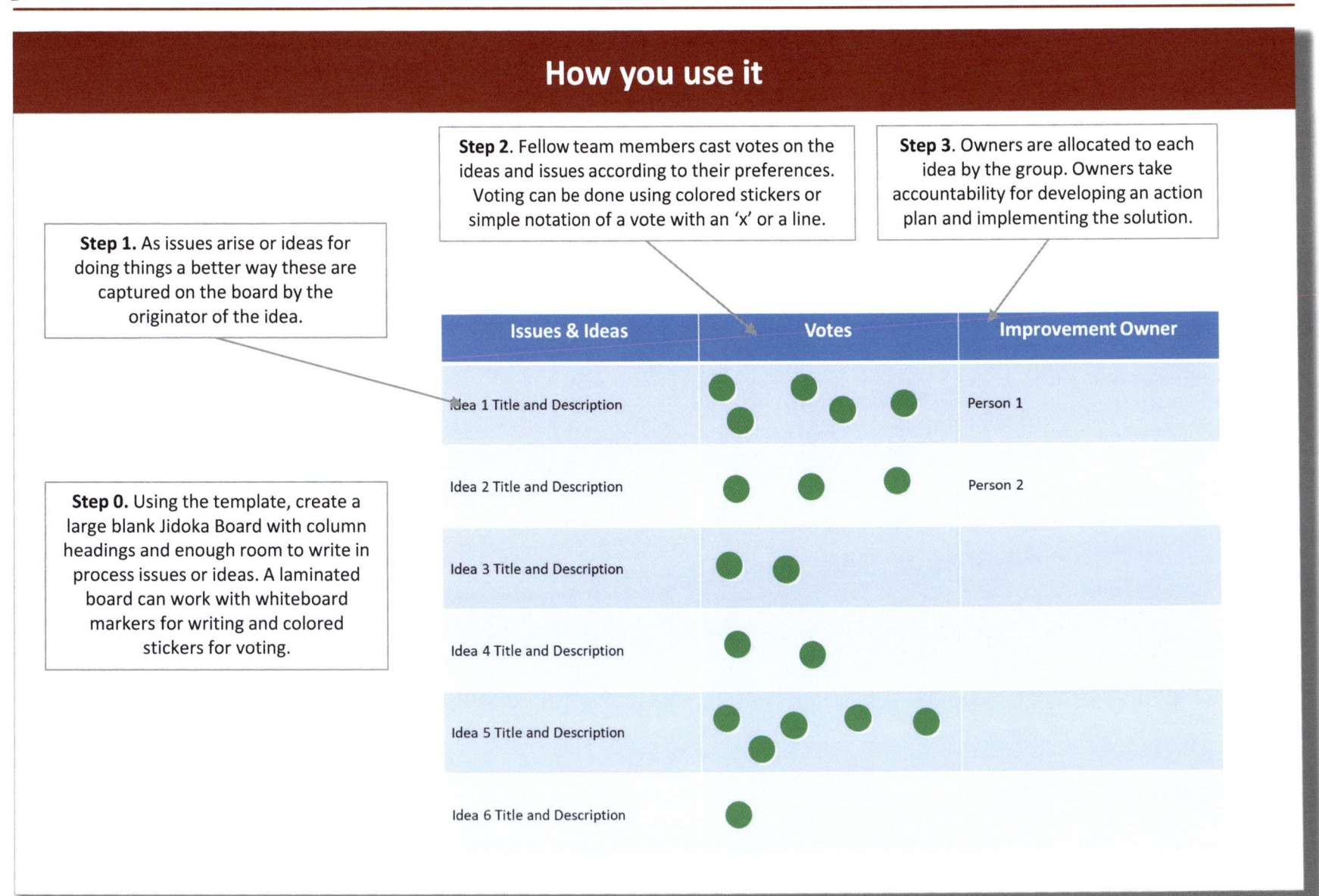

Jidoka Board – Method

How you use it

Step 1. As issues arise or ideas for doing things a better way these are captured on the board by the originator of the idea.

Step 2. Fellow team members cast votes on the ideas and issues according to their preferences. Voting can be done using colored stickers or simple notation of a vote with an 'x' or a line.

Step 3. Owners are allocated to each idea by the group. Owners take accountability for developing an action plan and implementing the solution.

Step 0. Using the template, create a large blank Jidoka Board with column headings and enough room to write in process issues or ideas. A laminated board can work with whiteboard markers for writing and colored stickers for voting.

Issues & Ideas	Votes	Improvement Owner
Idea 1 Title and Description	●●●●● ●	Person 1
Idea 2 Title and Description	●●●	Person 2
Idea 3 Title and Description	●●	
Idea 4 Title and Description	●	
Idea 5 Title and Description	●●●●●	
Idea 6 Title and Description	●	

Jidoka Board – Template

Issues & Ideas	Votes	Improvement Owner
Idea 1 Title and Description	●●●●●	Person 1
Idea 2 Title and Description	●●●	Person 2
Idea 3 Title and Description	●●	
Idea 4 Title and Description	●●	
Idea 5 Title and Description	●●●●●	
Idea 6 Title and Description	●	

“EXPERT TOOLKIT — MAKE A GREATER IMPACT”

Pain Point Analysis Template

A proven approach for representing, assessing and prioritizing the critical issues impacting a business process

Pain Point Analysis – Overview

What is it

Pain Point Analysis is a method for assessing the issues impacting the performance of a business process by considering the relative weighting of process issues across two dimensions. The analyst can choose the most relevant dimensions, however a typical combination is *impact* or *severity* combined with *volume* or *frequency*. An alternate to *volume / frequency* in some situations is *detectability*.

When to use it

Pain Point Analysis is a useful tool when assessing the current state performance of a business process and seeking to identify areas to focus remediation activity based on the likely return on effort. In other words, where will improvement time and resources reduce the most process pain. Effective use of the method is reliant on having stakeholders with suitable knowledge of process' current performance as well as the availability of relevant process performance data (e.g. volumes, error rates)

Why use it

Typically, processes will underperform across a range of areas – and a structured method for determining where to prioritize effort is critical to any process improvement exercise. Using Pain Point Analysis, a business analyst can guide an organization to agree on where maximum pain is being experienced and therefore where it is most essential to focus improvement effort and resources. Following Pain Point Analysis, Solution Ideation and Assessment are used to asses effort, feasibility and risk of solutions.

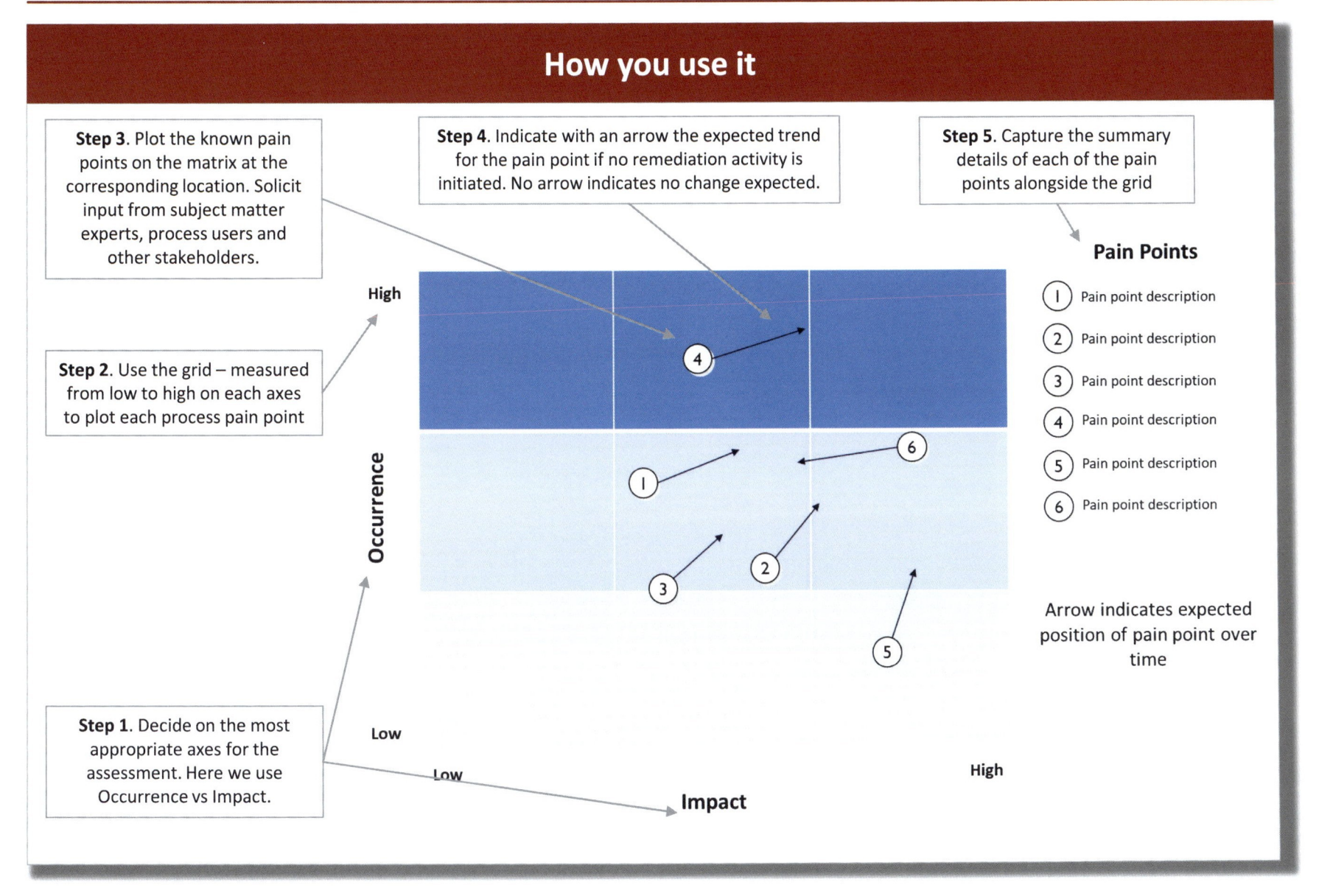

Pain Point Analysis – Method

How you use it

Step 1. Decide on the most appropriate axes for the assessment. Here we use Occurrence vs Impact.

Step 2. Use the grid – measured from low to high on each axes to plot each process pain point

Step 3. Plot the known pain points on the matrix at the corresponding location. Solicit input from subject matter experts, process users and other stakeholders.

Step 4. Indicate with an arrow the expected trend for the pain point if no remediation activity is initiated. No arrow indicates no change expected.

Step 5. Capture the summary details of each of the pain points alongside the grid

Pain Points

1. Pain point description
2. Pain point description
3. Pain point description
4. Pain point description
5. Pain point description
6. Pain point description

Arrow indicates expected position of pain point over time

Axes: Occurrence (vertical, Low to High) vs Impact (horizontal, Low to High)

Pain Point Analysis – Template

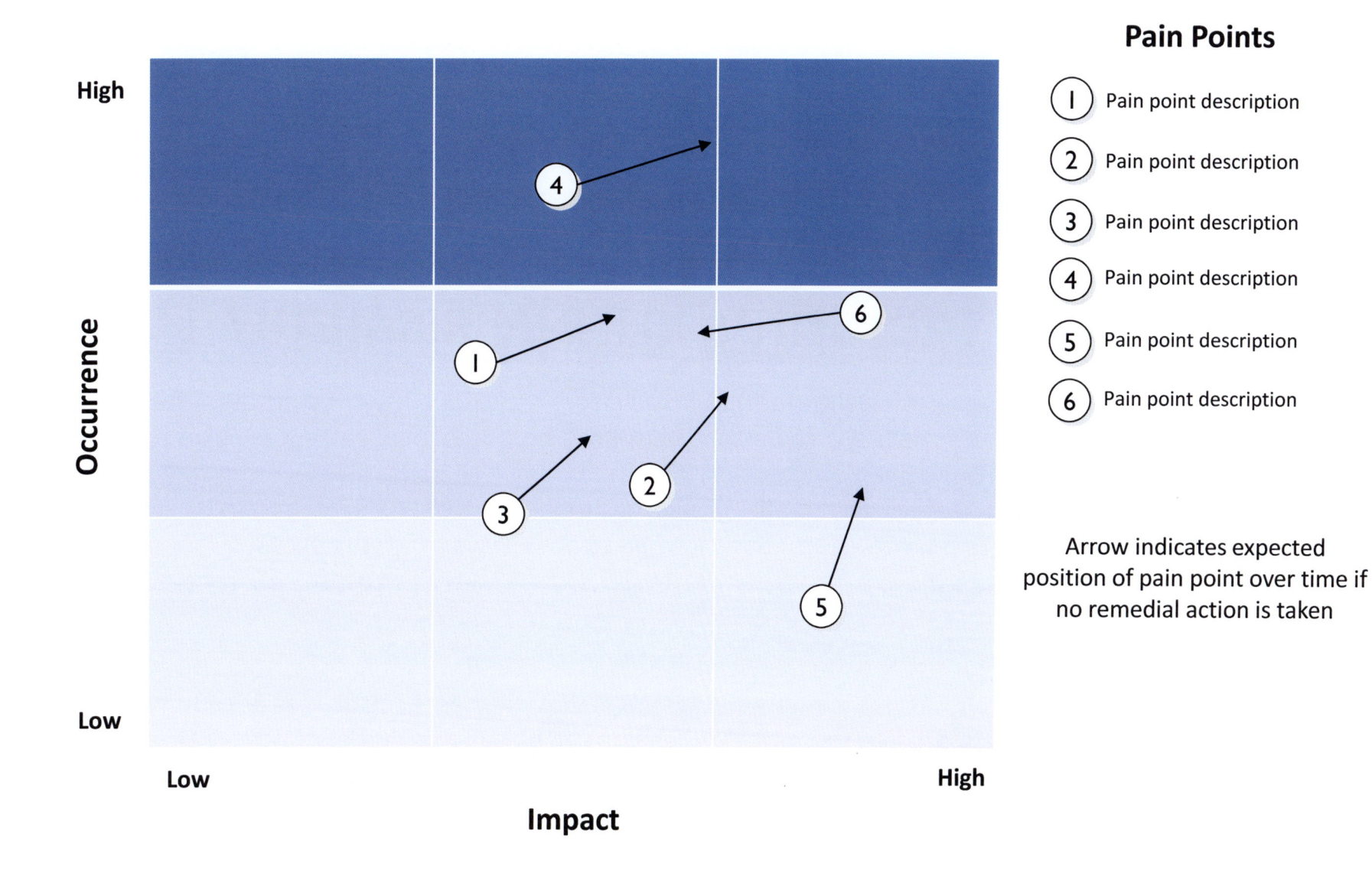

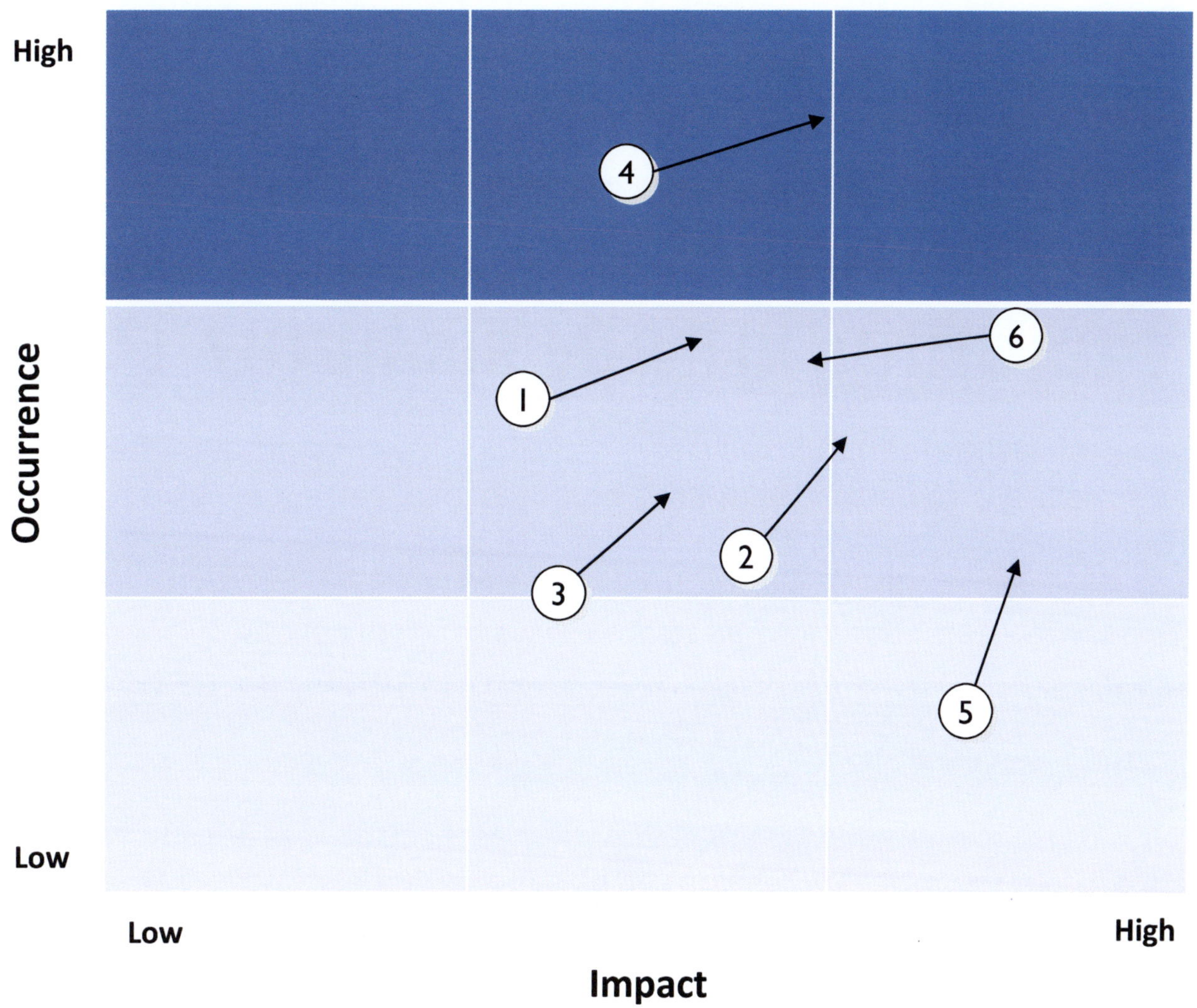
High
Low
Occurrence
Low
High
Impact
1
2
3
4
5
6

Pain Points

1. Pain point description
2. Pain point description
3. Pain point description
4. Pain point description
5. Pain point description
6. Pain point description

Arrow indicates expected position of pain point over time if no remedial action is taken

PEST Analysis Matrix Template

A proven method for assessing market trends and defining strategic choices to capitalize on those trends

PEST Analysis Matrix – Overview

What is it

The PEST Analysis Matrix is a framework for outlining the critical market trends impacting an organization, how they manifest as Opportunities or Threats and what Strategies could be adopted in order to capitalize on the market trends.

When to use it

The PEST Analysis Matrix Template should be used as part of strategic analysis exercise that adopts the PEST approach. The Template is helpful at synthesizing the key points pertinent to market trend analysis and in a format that can easily be included in a market assessment report. The Template is intended to be a summary information capture template that can be supplemented with more in-depth analysis worksheets where required.

Why use it

The PEST Analysis Matrix Template is concise and adaptable, providing a structured and logical mechanism for laying out the key market trends, impacts and strategies. It is a useful template for collating the essential information when conducting a strategic market analysis – this information can then, in turn, be summarized for communicating the most relevant trends and strategies to executive stakeholders.

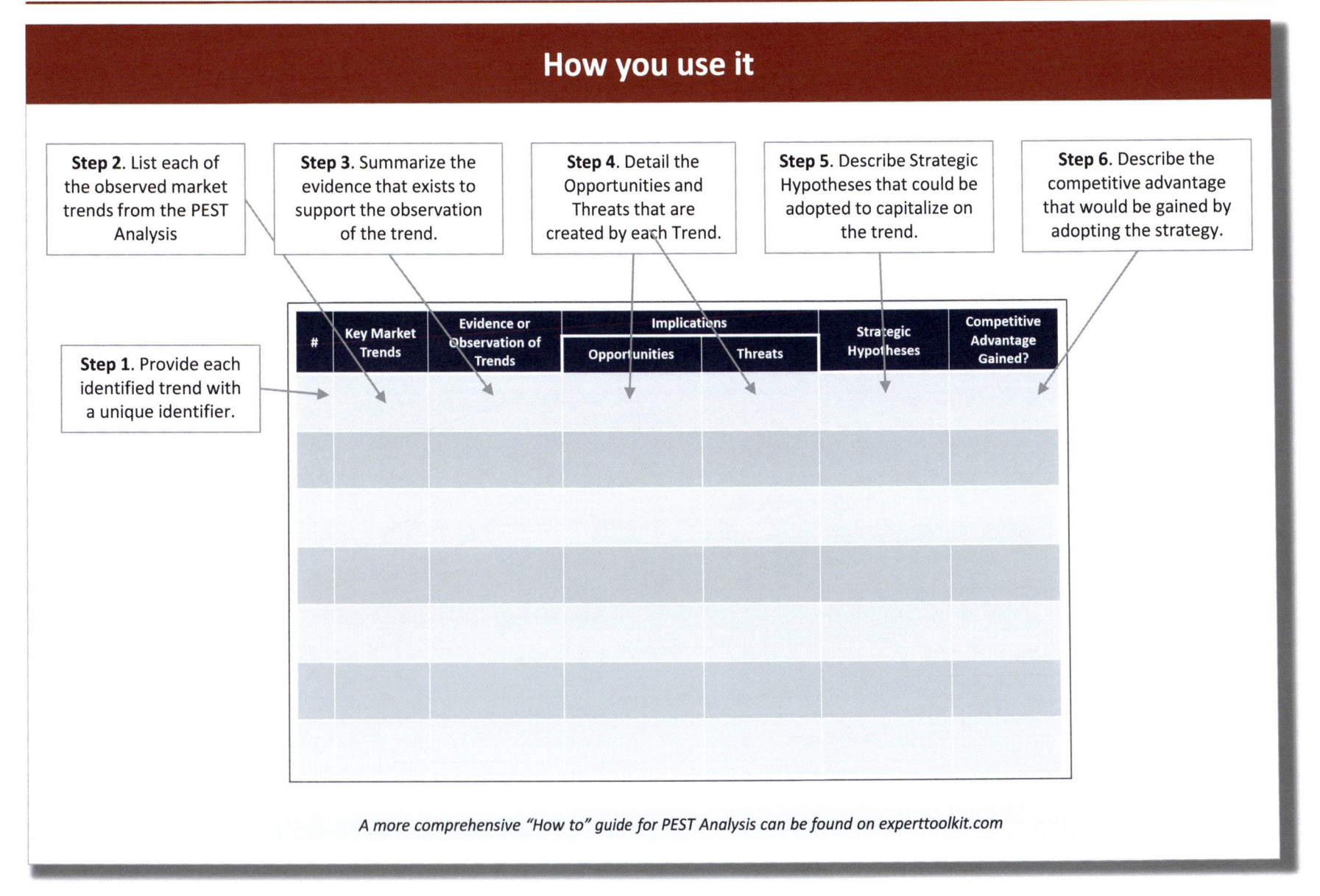

PEST Analysis Matrix – Method

How you use it

Step 1. Provide each identified trend with a unique identifier.

Step 2. List each of the observed market trends from the PEST Analysis

Step 3. Summarize the evidence that exists to support the observation of the trend.

Step 4. Detail the Opportunities and Threats that are created by each Trend.

Step 5. Describe Strategic Hypotheses that could be adopted to capitalize on the trend.

Step 6. Describe the competitive advantage that would be gained by adopting the strategy.

#	Key Market Trends	Evidence or Observation of Trends	Implications		Strategic Hypotheses	Competitive Advantage Gained?
			Opportunities	Threats		

A more comprehensive "How to" guide for PEST Analysis can be found on experttoolkit.com

PEST Analysis Matrix – Template

#	Key Market Trends	Evidence or Observation of Trends	Implications		Strategic Hypotheses	Competitive Advantage Gained?
			Opportunities	Threats		

Process Flow Analysis Template

A structured template for summarizing process flow, key issues and improvement opportunities

Process Flow Analysis – Overview

What is it

The process flow analysis template is a proven, structured approach for outlining the flow of an end to end process in addition to its performance issues and opportunities for improvement. The template allows for all of the key attributes of a process to be captured (including inputs, outputs, steps, resources and description) in addition to the areas experience pain.

When to use it

This template is ideally suited for use at the conclusion of process analysis when key information is needing to be summarized and presented to an executive audience or other stakeholders. It is most applicable when the flow of a "left to right" process is relevant to the analysis and discussion. Note that the template includes 4 process flow steps, more can be added by using additional pages.

Why use it

This template is effective at conveying the key items relating to the process in terms of context, flow, attributes, issues and improvement opportunities. It is proven to work with executive audiences and a wide array of stakeholders needing to understand challenges facing an operational environment, the ideas for improvement and garnering support for transformation.

Process Flow Analysis – Method

How you use it

Step 1. Identify the input to each discrete step in the process.

Step 2. List the resources that are involved in supporting the process – these could be human.

Step 3. Name the step or task that is performed in this part of the process.

Step 4. Describe the step or task that is performed.

Step 5. Identify the outputs of the process step.

Step 6. Summarize the key issues that are experienced as part of this step in the process.

Step 7. Summarize the improvement opportunities that arise and would address the issues.

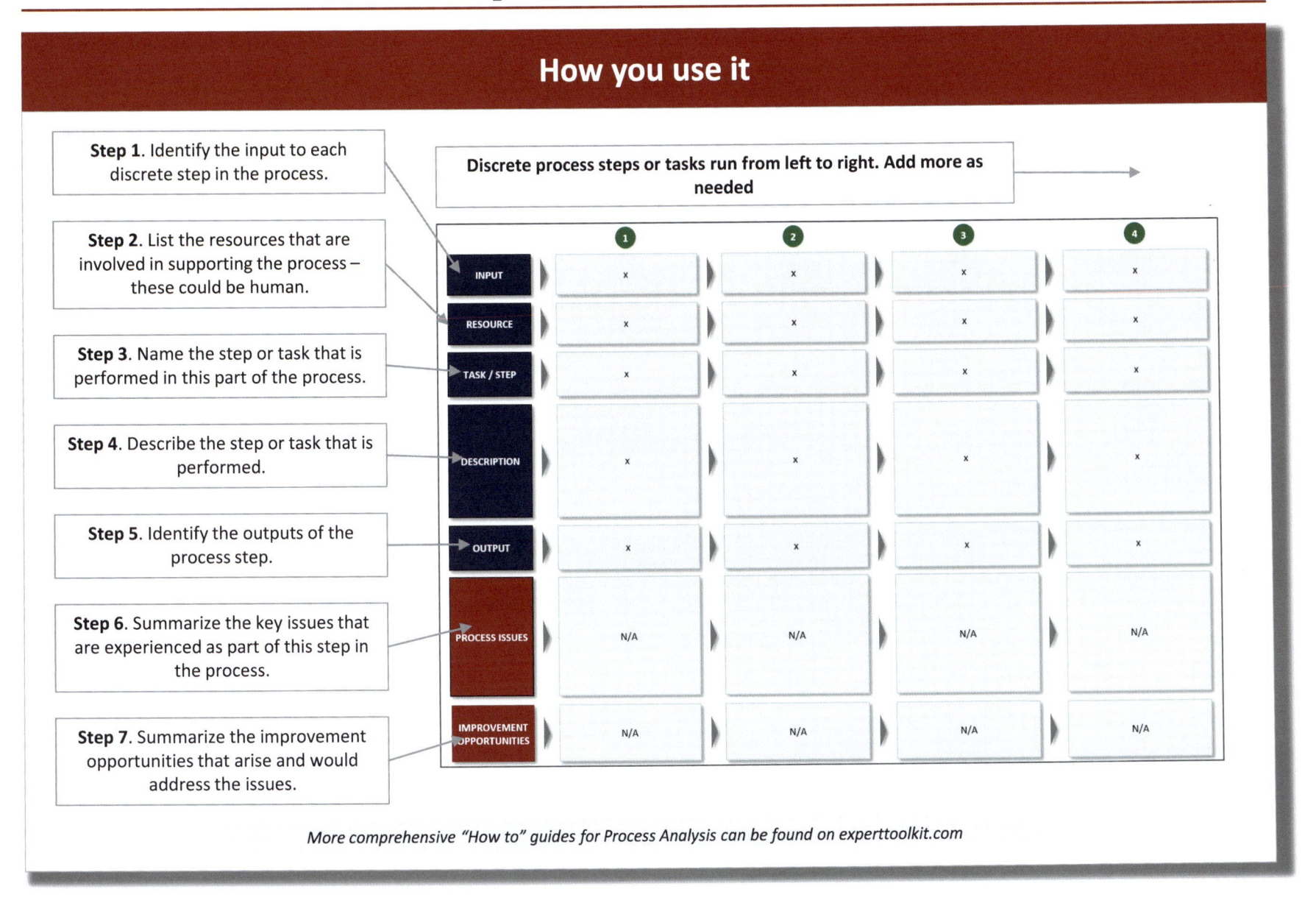

Discrete process steps or tasks run from left to right. Add more as needed

	1	2	3	4
INPUT	x	x	x	x
RESOURCE	x	x	x	x
TASK / STEP	x	x	x	x
DESCRIPTION	x	x	x	x
OUTPUT	x	x	x	x
PROCESS ISSUES	N/A	N/A	N/A	N/A
IMPROVEMENT OPPORTUNITIES	N/A	N/A	N/A	N/A

More comprehensive "How to" guides for Process Analysis can be found on experttoolkit.com

Process Flow Analysis – Template

	1	2	3	4
INPUT	x	x	x	x
RESOURCE	x	x	x	x
TASK / STEP	x	x	x	x
DESCRIPTION	x	x	x	x
OUTPUT	x	x	x	x
PROCESS ISSUES	N/A	N/A	N/A	N/A
IMPROVEMENT OPPORTUNITIES	N/A	N/A	N/A	N/A

Process Issues Summary Template

A structured template for outlining key process issues and challenges

Process Issues Summary – Overview

What is it

The process issues summary template is concise format for summarizing the key roles, steps and tasks that are involved in executing a process from end-to-end *and* the critical issues that are currently impacting the performance of the process.

When to use it

Use this template at the conclusion of a rigorous process analysis exercise when you are needing to summarize the key attributes of the process and the key issues that have been identified. It is ideally suited to conveying the key details to an executive audience or group of stakeholders who require some explanation of the process mechanics as well as the issues that are being encountered.

Why use it

This template is effective at conveying what needs to be conveyed in terms of process context and process issues. It is proven to work with executive audiences and a wide array of stakeholders needing to understand challenges facing an operational environment and therefore securing their support for improvement or transformation via process change.

Process Issues Summary – Method

How you use it

Step 1. List the roles that are involved in supporting the process from end to end.

Step 2. List the key tasks or process steps that are involved in delivering the end to end process.

Step 3. Describe in detail the steps involved in performing the Task.

Step 4. Document the key issues that are observed or identified for each Task.

Step 5. Use numbered notations to link the issues to the process steps affected.

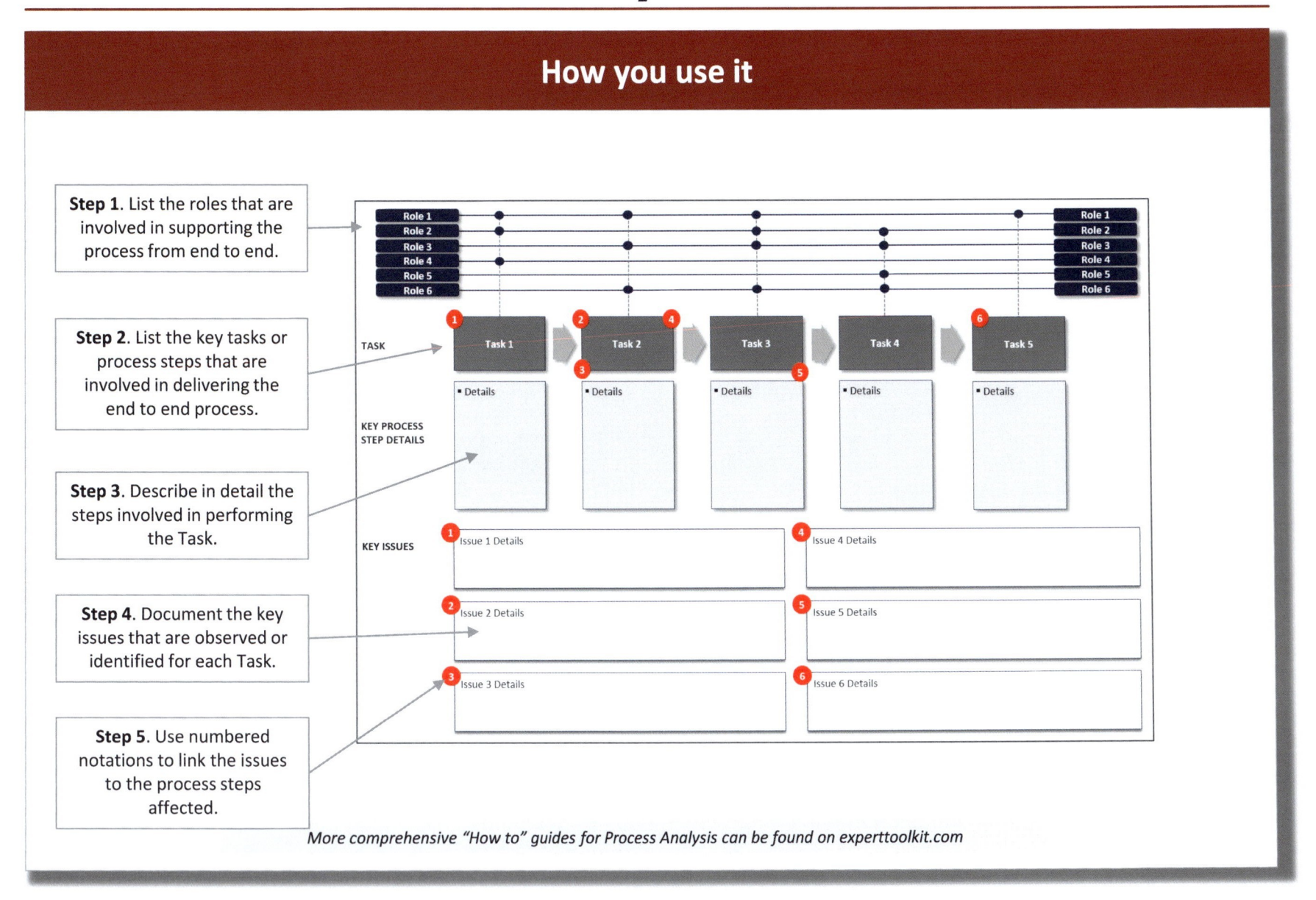

More comprehensive "How to" guides for Process Analysis can be found on experttoolkit.com

Process Issues Summary – Template

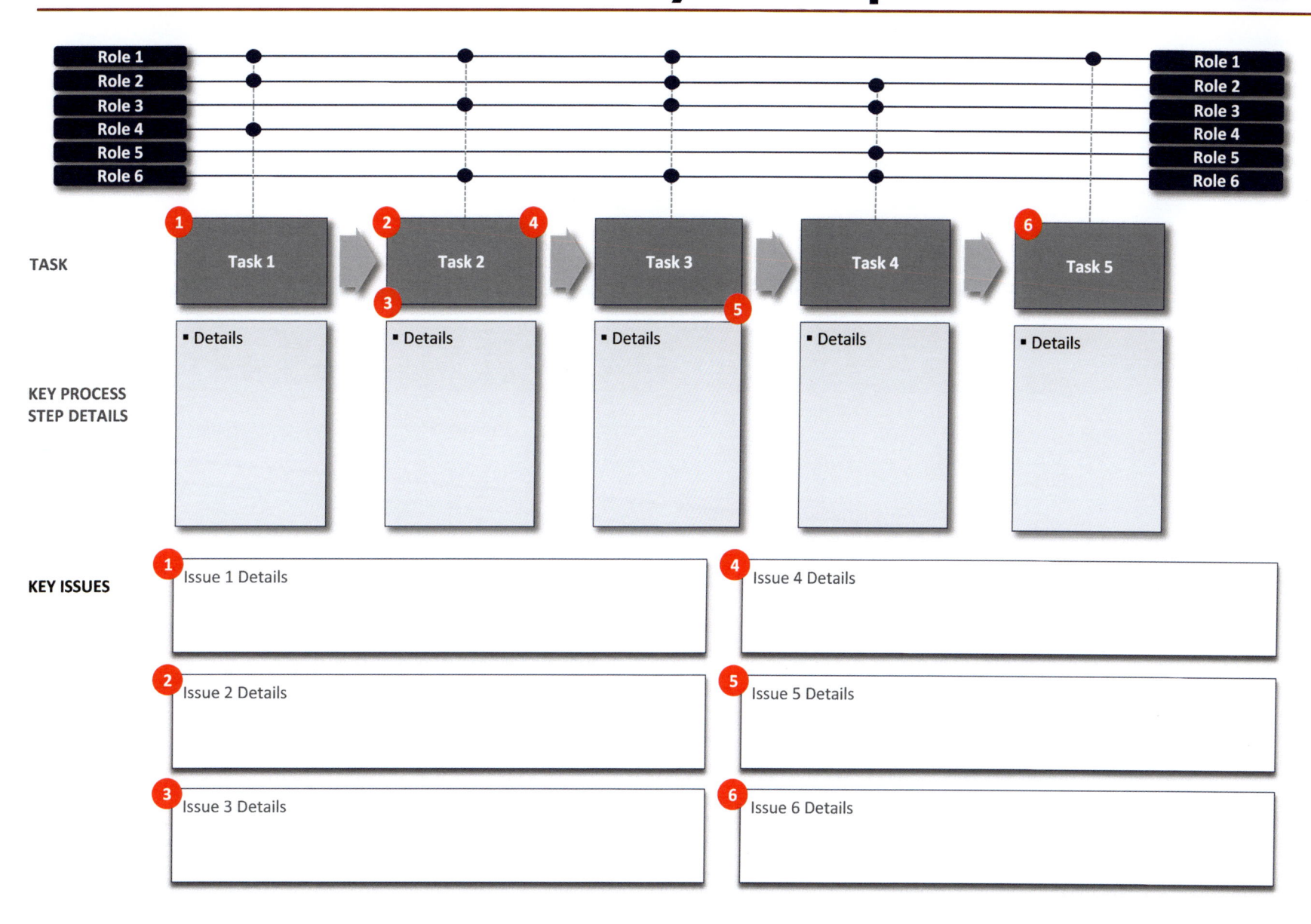

Role 1 | Role 1
Role 2 | Role 2
Role 3 | Role 3
Role 4 | Role 4
Role 5 | Role 5
Role 6 | Role 6

TASK

1. Task 1
2. Task 2
4. (Task 2)
3. Task 3
5. (Task 3)
Task 4
6. Task 5

KEY PROCESS STEP DETAILS

- Details (Task 1)
- Details (Task 2)
- Details (Task 3)
- Details (Task 4)
- Details (Task 5)

KEY ISSUES

1. Issue 1 Details
2. Issue 2 Details
3. Issue 3 Details
4. Issue 4 Details
5. Issue 5 Details
6. Issue 6 Details

Project Status Report

A concise and proven format for providing executive project status updates to key stakeholders

Project Status Report – Overview

What is it

The Project Status Report Template is a concise and clear layout for reporting regular status updates to sponsors and other stakeholders for a business analysis, improvement or transformation initiative.

When to use it

Use the template on a regular basis (weekly is recommended) during a business analysis, improvement or transformation project to provide updates and progress reports to sponsors and stakeholders.

Why use it

In any business initiative it is imperative to provide regular and concise updates to stakeholders with information on scope, activities, deliverables, risks, issues and progress. This template is proven to be effective at providing these updates.

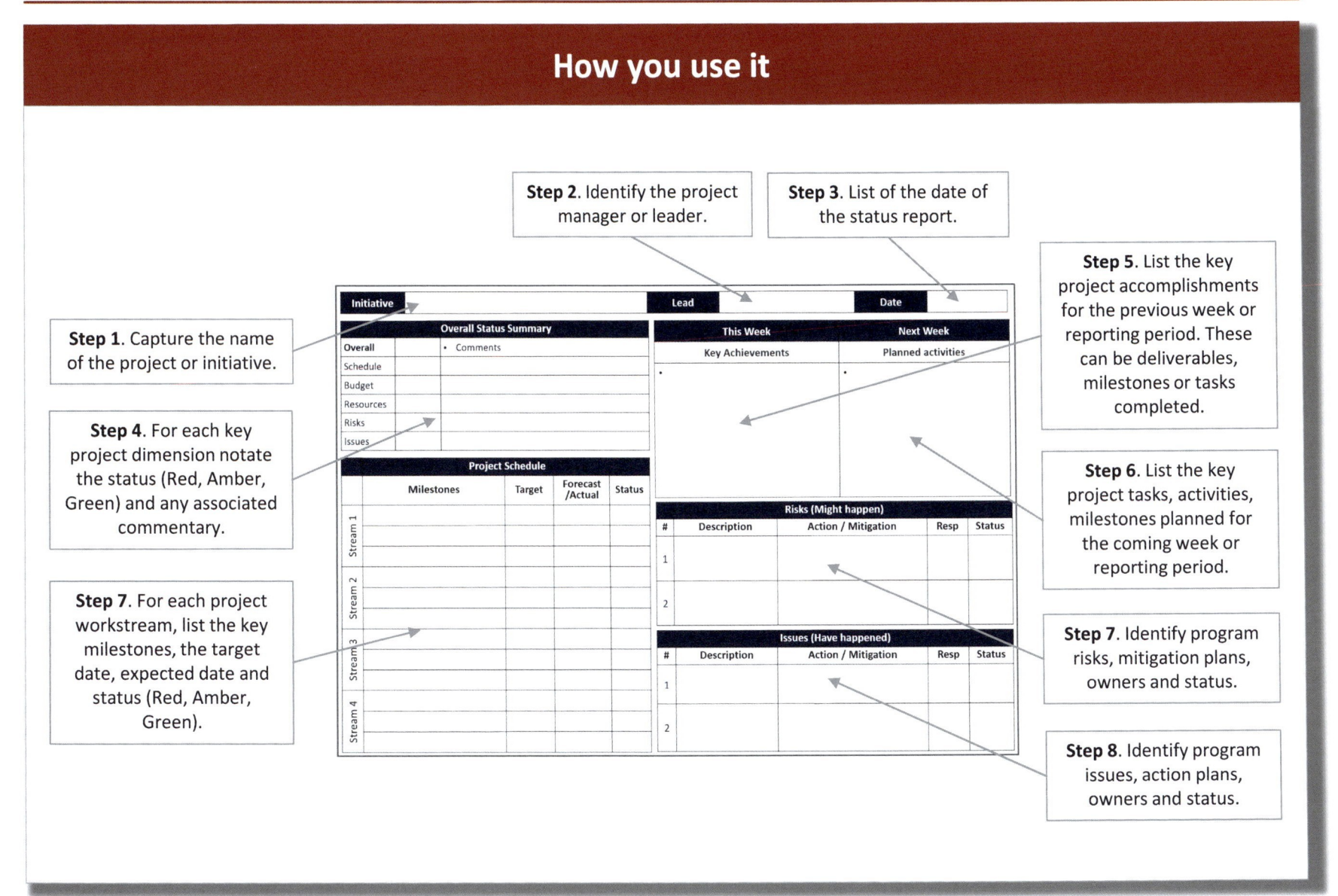

Project Status Report – Method

How you use it

Step 1. Capture the name of the project or initiative.

Step 2. Identify the project manager or leader.

Step 3. List of the date of the status report.

Step 4. For each key project dimension notate the status (Red, Amber, Green) and any associated commentary.

Step 5. List the key project accomplishments for the previous week or reporting period. These can be deliverables, milestones or tasks completed.

Step 6. List the key project tasks, activities, milestones planned for the coming week or reporting period.

Step 7. For each project workstream, list the key milestones, the target date, expected date and status (Red, Amber, Green).

Step 7. Identify program risks, mitigation plans, owners and status.

Step 8. Identify program issues, action plans, owners and status.

Project Status Report – Template

Initiative		Lead		Date	

Overall Status Summary

Overall	
	• Comments
Schedule	
Budget	
Resources	
Risks	
Issues	

Project Schedule

	Milestones	Target	Forecast /Actual	Status
Stream 1				
Stream 2				
Stream 3				
Stream 4				

This Week — Key Achievements

•

Next Week — Planned activities

•

Risks (Might happen)

#	Description	Action / Mitigation	Resp	Status
1				
2				

Issues (Have happened)

#	Description	Action / Mitigation	Resp	Status
1				
2				

RACI Template

A structured business analysis technique for assessing and allocating workload across teams and individuals

RACI – Overview

What is it

RACI helps to clarify what activities & functions need to be done and who needs to do them. RACI development is a systematic process involving the identification of functions to be accomplished and clarification of roles and levels of participation for the activities. RACI is useful at clarifying the allocation of workload across teams and identifying inefficiencies in current workload allocation models. RACI development is meant to be collaborative – facilitating group involvement for design and buy-in.

When to use it

RACI is a useful tool in a number of business analysis and improvement scenarios: The distribution of workload across a team is sub-optimal; A team, function or business unit is reorganized and a method is needed to verify workload coverage and clarify responsibilities; Staffing changes necessitate team and individual workload coverage reviews; Functional procedures and accountabilities need clarifying and documenting.

Why use it

RACI is a very effective tool for identifying workload imbalances in teams. It can help to ensures that key functions and activities are not overlooked and that there is not surplus capacity. A RACI can help new team members rapidly identify their 'roles and responsibilities'. A RACI can provide a mechanism for discussion and resolving inter/intra team confusion around workload responsibilities. RACI is a simple way to document and communicate roles and responsibilities.

RACI – Method

How you use it

Step 1. Determine the task, job or function that needs a RACI developed

Step 2. Determine and list the activities and roles involved in that task or job and the individuals involved

Step 3. For each activity, assign Accountability and the appropriate amount of R's, C's and I's to accomplish the task (see next page for definitions)

Step 4. Ensure all of the roles / individuals understand the requirements of them and are capable and committed to delivering

Step 5. Analyze RACI matrix for issues, inefficiencies and opportunities to improve (see 2 pages over for insights)

Functional Roles
Roles and positions assigned to complete an activity

Task Name
Task 1

Activities	Project Director	Team Leader	Technical Architect	Business Analyst	Process Lead	Finance Lead
Activity 1			R	A		
Activity 2	A/R		C	I	C	
Activity 3			I		A/R	C
Activity 4			R		A	
Activity 5	I		A		R	
Activity 6	A	I			R	C
Activity 7		A	C	R		I

A more comprehensive "How to" guide for the RACI can be found on experttoolkit.com

RACI – Method

How you use it

Step 3. Definitions

Responsible
- Someone who performs an activity and is responsible for the action being completed. "R"s can be shared across team members.

Accountable
- The individual who is ultimately accountable for the activity or decision – and includes yes/no and veto power. Only one "A" can be assigned to any activity/decision.

Consulted
- Individuals that need to be consulted prior to a final decision or before/after an activity is performed. "C" individuals participate in two-way communication.

Informed
- Individuals who needs to be informed after a decision or action is taken. "I" people receive one-way communication.

RACI – Method

How you use it

Step 5. Insights

	What to look for	What it might mean
Horizontal	Lots of Rs	Too many people involved
	No Rs or As	Activity is not getting done or doesn't need doing
	More than one A	Uncertainty
	Lots of Cs	Too many people involved
	Lots of Is	Too many people being advised
Vertical	Lots of Rs	Too much work
	No empty spaces	Too much work or involvement
	No Rs or As	Activity is not required
	Too many As	Accountability not at the right level

RACI – Template

Task / Function										
Activities / Decisions										

Root Cause Analysis Template

A proven business analysis method for getting to the heart of operational performance problems

Root Cause Analysis – Overview

What is it

The Fishbone Root Cause Analysis Method is a technique for analyzing business problems (symptoms) and drilling down to discover the true underlying root causes for the problem. It is a qualitative technique and relies on the participation of stakeholders who have knowledge of the operational environment and can therefore provide input into current problems and their potential causes.

When to use it

The fishbone method and tool is ideally suited to situations where brainstorming among a group of individuals is necessary to explore symptoms, possible root causes with the aim of prioritizing areas requiring further analysis, investigation, quantification and solution development. It is particularly useful in the development of hypotheses which can then be further tested with more rigorous, quantitative data analysis. It is particularly useful when combined with the 5 Whys Method.

Why use it

Root Cause Analysis digs down to the real problem - the 'root cause'. The process helps to break down what can appear to be an impossible-to-solve issue into smaller, more easily handled elements. It facilitates a structured discussion around possible root causes and allows targeted solution ideation to commence. It also helps to look beyond what may appear to be the issue, in order to identify the real driver of the problem.

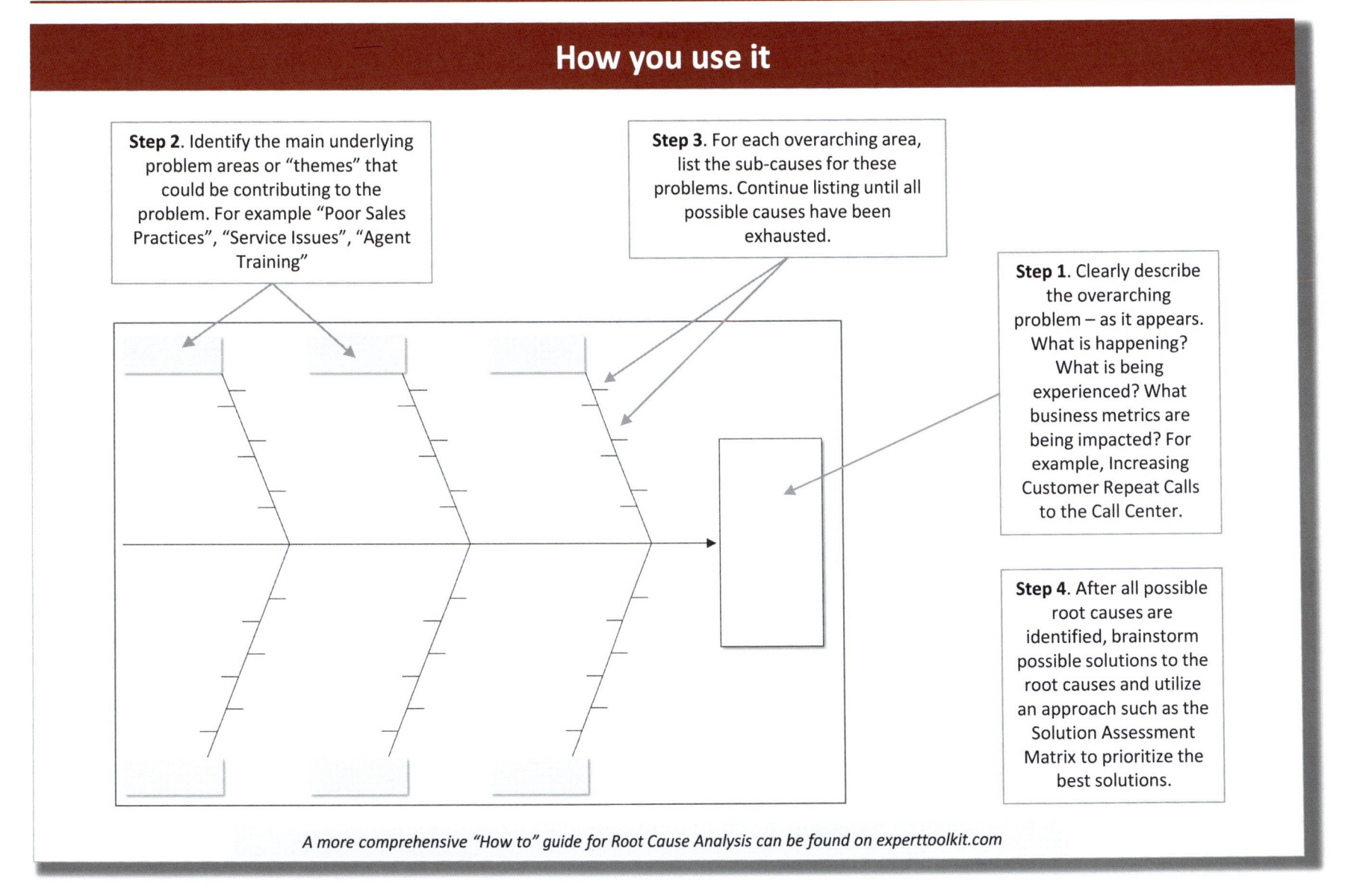

Root Cause Analysis – Method

How you use it

Step 1. Clearly describe the overarching problem – as it appears. What is happening? What is being experienced? What business metrics are being impacted? For example, Increasing Customer Repeat Calls to the Call Center.

Step 2. Identify the main underlying problem areas or "themes" that could be contributing to the problem. For example "Poor Sales Practices", "Service Issues", "Agent Training"

Step 3. For each overarching area, list the sub-causes for these problems. Continue listing until all possible causes have been exhausted.

Step 4. After all possible root causes are identified, brainstorm possible solutions to the root causes and utilize an approach such as the Solution Assessment Matrix to prioritize the best solutions.

A more comprehensive "How to" guide for Root Cause Analysis can be found on experttoolkit.com

Root Cause Analysis – Template

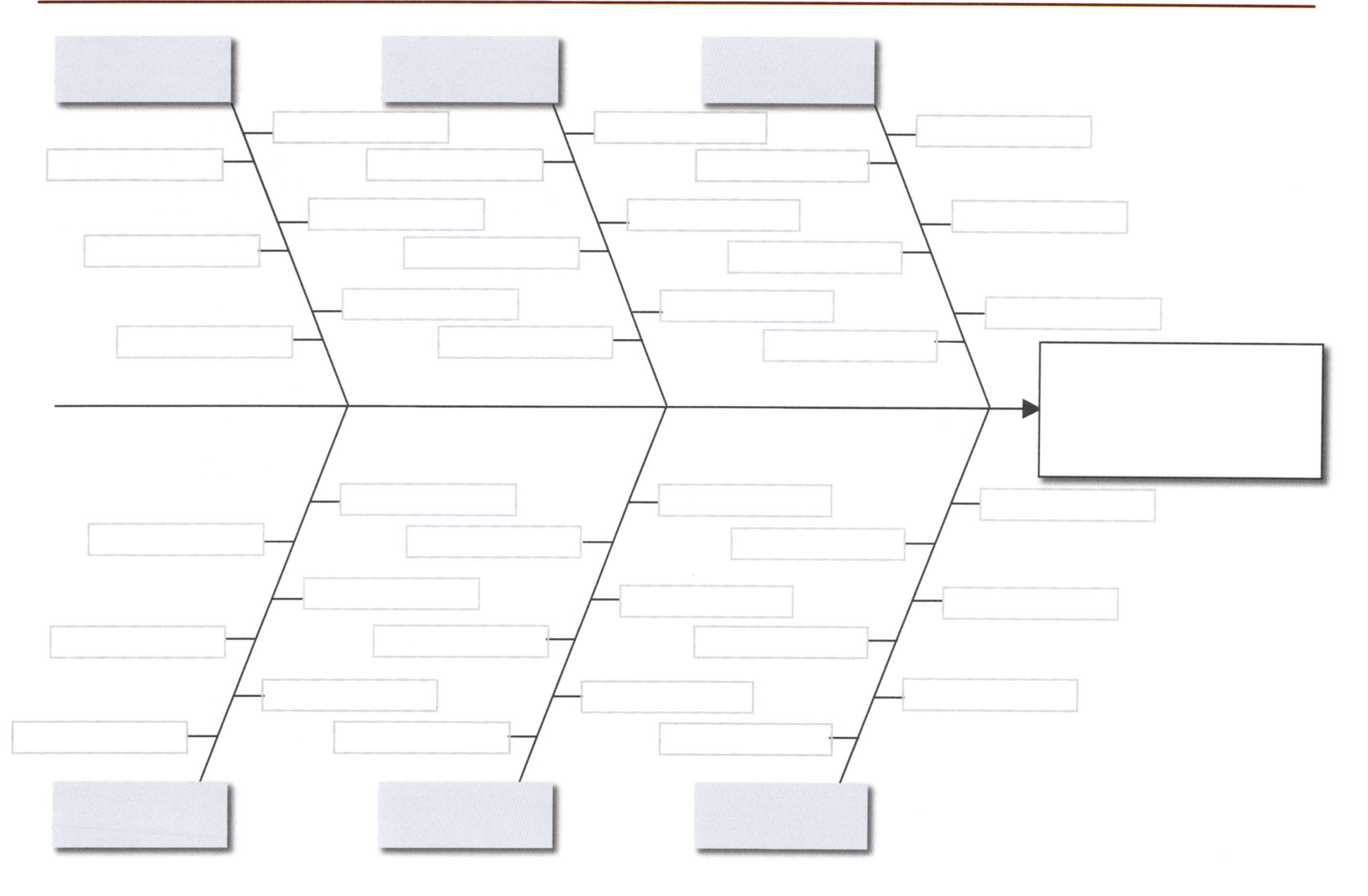

SIPOC Template

A useful tool for understanding the boundaries, actors and inputs that make up a customer-facing process

SIPOC – Overview

What is it

SIPOC stands for "Suppliers, Inputs, Process, Outputs, Customers". It is a fairly simple method for capturing and laying out the critical elements, actors, inputs and steps associated with delivering value to a customer through an end-to-end business process. It is primarily used for process understanding, scoping and high level problem diagnosis.

When to use it

SIPOC is best used in situations where a process or value chain is utilized to deliver customer value – and it is performing sub-optimally or is poorly understood by key stakeholders. It is especially useful in a group setting (such as a workshop) for establishing a baseline level of understanding for a complex process or value chain that involves multiple actors and steps to deliver an outcome to a customer. It is also a useful tool for clarifying scope boundaries, and roles and responsibilities across a complex process.

Why use it

SIPOC can be used to bring understanding and clarity to a value chain that takes "raw ingredients" from suppliers and produces outputs and value for a customer. Having a clear and common understanding of key process elements and boundaries is a good starting point for more comprehensive process analysis and value chain diagnosis utilizing more analytical methods.

SIPOC – Method

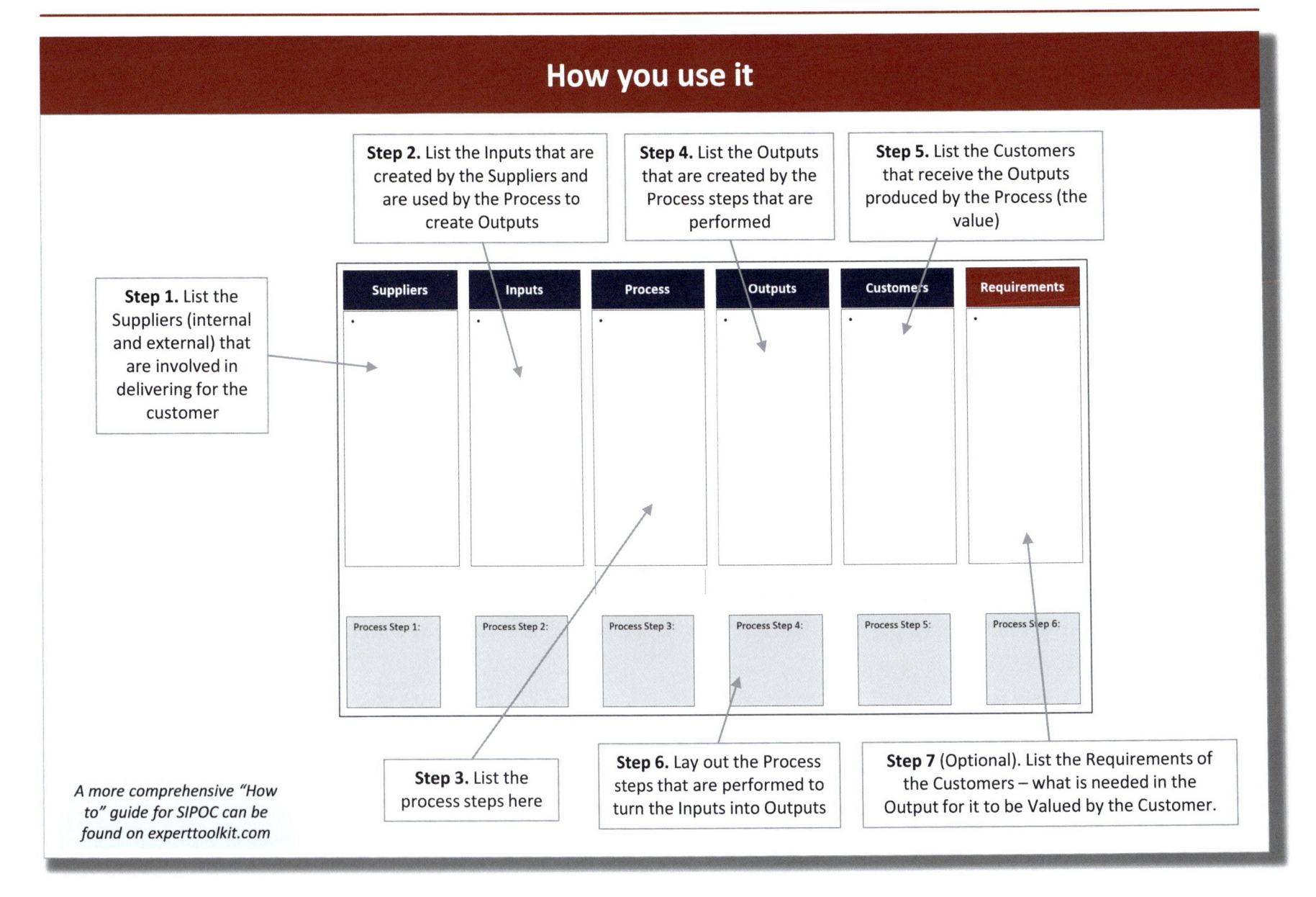

How you use it

Step 1. List the Suppliers (internal and external) that are involved in delivering for the customer

Step 2. List the Inputs that are created by the Suppliers and are used by the Process to create Outputs

Step 4. List the Outputs that are created by the Process steps that are performed

Step 5. List the Customers that receive the Outputs produced by the Process (the value)

Suppliers	Inputs	Process	Outputs	Customers	Requirements
·	·	·	·	·	·

| Process Step 1: | Process Step 2: | Process Step 3: | Process Step 4: | Process Step 5: | Process Step 6: |

Step 3. List the process steps here

Step 6. Lay out the Process steps that are performed to turn the Inputs into Outputs

Step 7 (Optional). List the Requirements of the Customers – what is needed in the Output for it to be Valued by the Customer.

A more comprehensive "How to" guide for SIPOC can be found on experttoolkit.com

SIPOC – Template

Suppliers	Inputs	Process	Outputs	Customers	Requirements
•	•	•	•	•	•

| Process Step 1: | Process Step 2: | Process Step 3: | Process Step 4: | Process Step 5: | Process Step 6: |

Solution Assessment Method

A proven approach for assessing the value and risk associated with potential business improvement solutions

Solution Assessment – Overview

What is it

The Solution Assessment Method is a proven approach for evaluating potential business improvement solutions and initiatives across a range of essential dimensions. The approach provides an objective lens when reviewing potential solutions that are identified to address business performance issues and their underlying root causes. The method is highly adaptable, easily customized to suit the specific application and accommodate different assessment criteria and weightings.

When to use it

The Solution Assessment Method is best suited once current state analysis has been conducted and a clear, accurate view of business performance issues, pain points are understood and potential solutions have been ideated. With the potential solutions that have been brainstormed or proposed, the Solution Assessment Method can be utilized to evaluate and prioritize the solutions with the aim of selecting the solutions which deliver the greatest business value with the least risk.

Why use it

The Solution Assessment Method is proven, flexible, adaptable and easy to use. It is intuitive for stakeholders involved in the process and for those who get to see and endorse the outcomes. The technique brings the right level of objectivity to what can be a political and subjective exercise, but without bogging down a business improvement program in overly complex and time wasting analysis.

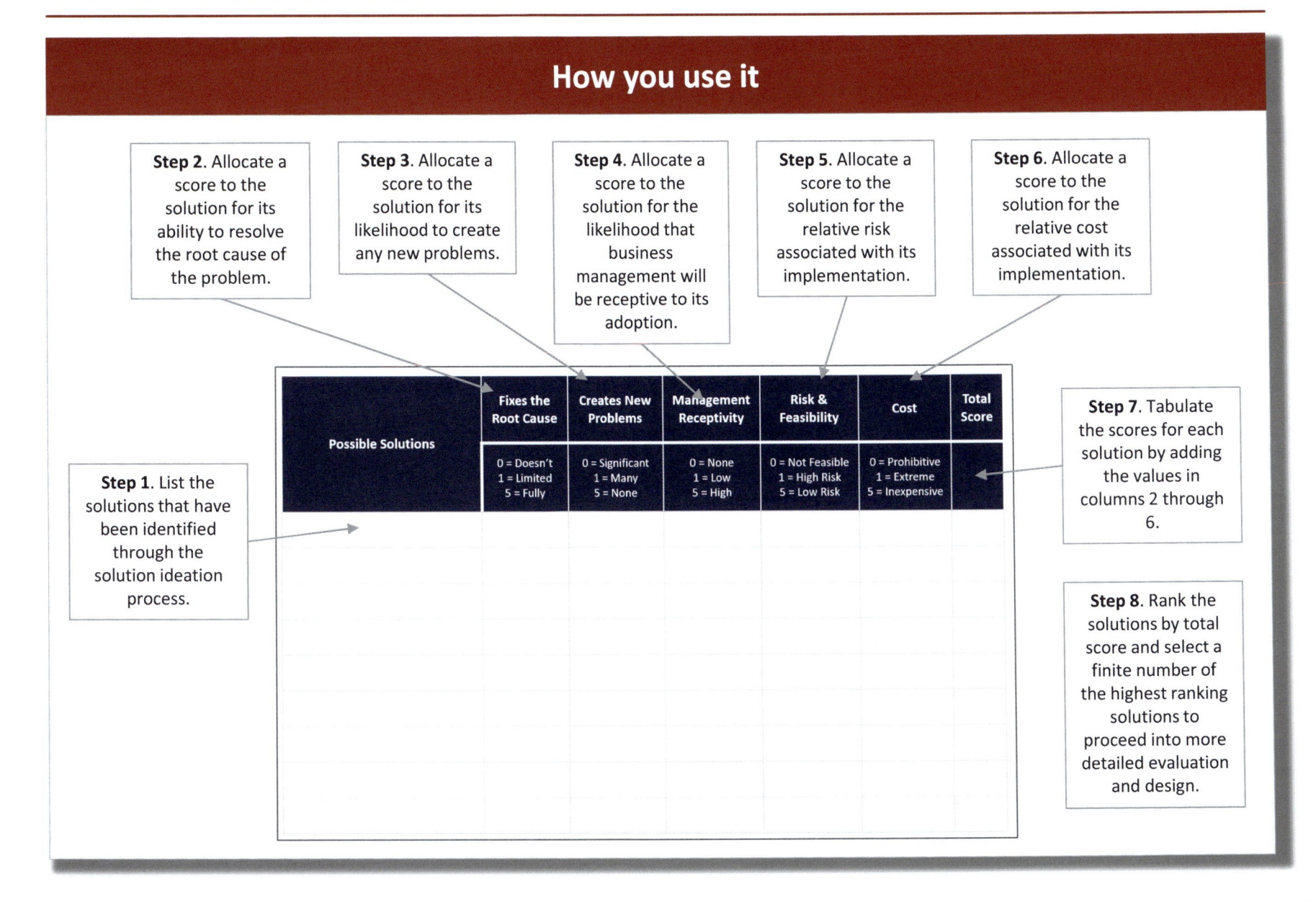

Solution Assessment – Method

How you use it

Step 1. List the solutions that have been identified through the solution ideation process.

Step 2. Allocate a score to the solution for its ability to resolve the root cause of the problem.

Step 3. Allocate a score to the solution for its likelihood to create any new problems.

Step 4. Allocate a score to the solution for the likelihood that business management will be receptive to its adoption.

Step 5. Allocate a score to the solution for the relative risk associated with its implementation.

Step 6. Allocate a score to the solution for the relative cost associated with its implementation.

Step 7. Tabulate the scores for each solution by adding the values in columns 2 through 6.

Step 8. Rank the solutions by total score and select a finite number of the highest ranking solutions to proceed into more detailed evaluation and design.

Possible Solutions	Fixes the Root Cause	Creates New Problems	Management Receptivity	Risk & Feasibility	Cost	Total Score
	0 = Doesn't 1 = Limited 5 = Fully	0 = Significant 1 = Many 5 = None	0 = None 1 = Low 5 = High	0 = Not Feasible 1 = High Risk 5 = Low Risk	0 = Prohibitive 1 = Extreme 5 = Inexpensive	

Solution Assessment – Template

Possible Solutions	Fixes the Root Cause	Creates New Problems	Management Receptivity	Risk & Feasibility	Cost	Total Score
	0 = Doesn't 1 = Limited 5 = Fully	0 = Significant 1 = Many 5 = None	0 = None 1 = Low 5 = High	0 = Not Feasible 1 = High Risk 5 = Low Risk	0 = Prohibitive 1 = Extreme 5 = Inexpensive	

Solution Ideation & Ranking

A structured and proven approach for brainstorming and prioritizing business improvement initiatives

Solution Ideation & Ranking – Overview

What is it

Solution Ideation and Ranking is a proven, structured approach for brainstorming and prioritizing potential business improvement initiatives. The method utilizes a scoring system to measure the positive impact of potential business improvement projects against a set of targeted business metrics. The metrics should be chosen based on identified areas within the business where performance improvement is desired and the metrics are confirmed measures of associated performance improvement in the area.

When to use it

This method is useful when exploring potential initiatives to drive business improvement. It is best used after current state analysis has been performed and there is general agreement on what areas within the business are in need of performance improvement. The method is effective in workshop settings and the steps outlined on the following page can be used by a competent facilitator with an audience of stakeholders to arrive at a good outcome – a finite set of prioritized initiatives to assess further.

Why use it

The Solution Ideation and Ranking Method brings a level of structure and objectivity to what can sometimes be a subjective and emotional process – choosing which initiatives to prioritize. Led by a competent business analyst or facilitator, this technique is very useful at taking a long list of possible ideas and paring it down to a much shorter list of initiatives that can evaluated further. The method is also effective at soliciting executive endorsement for prioritization – given the structured process applied.

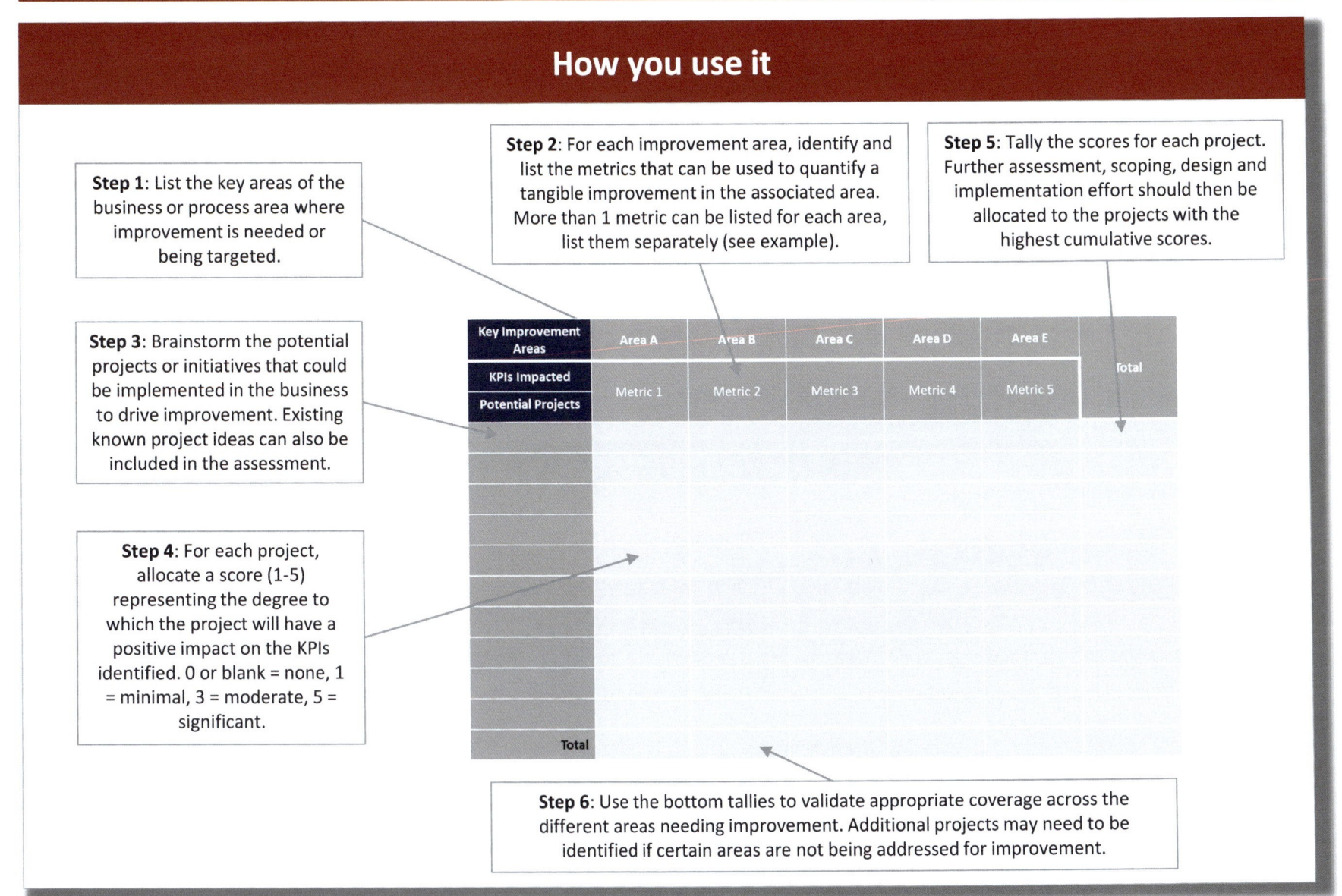

Solution Ideation & Ranking – Method

How you use it

Step 1: List the key areas of the business or process area where improvement is needed or being targeted.

Step 2: For each improvement area, identify and list the metrics that can be used to quantify a tangible improvement in the associated area. More than 1 metric can be listed for each area, list them separately (see example).

Step 3: Brainstorm the potential projects or initiatives that could be implemented in the business to drive improvement. Existing known project ideas can also be included in the assessment.

Step 4: For each project, allocate a score (1-5) representing the degree to which the project will have a positive impact on the KPIs identified. 0 or blank = none, 1 = minimal, 3 = moderate, 5 = significant.

Step 5: Tally the scores for each project. Further assessment, scoping, design and implementation effort should then be allocated to the projects with the highest cumulative scores.

Step 6: Use the bottom tallies to validate appropriate coverage across the different areas needing improvement. Additional projects may need to be identified if certain areas are not being addressed for improvement.

Key Improvement Areas	Area A	Area B	Area C	Area D	Area E	Total
KPIs Impacted	Metric 1	Metric 2	Metric 3	Metric 4	Metric 5	
Potential Projects						
Total						

Solution Ideation & Ranking – Template

Key Improvement Areas	Area A	Area B	Area C	Area D	Area E	Total
KPIs Impacted	Metric 1	Metric 2	Metric 3	Metric 4	Metric 5	
Potential Projects						
Total						

Solution Ideation & Ranking – Example

Key Improvement Areas	Growth	Customer Satisfaction		Costs		Total
KPIs Impacted / **Potential Projects**	Revenue	NPS	Complaints	Time to Market	Headcount	
Project 1	1	2	2			5
Project 2		1	2	4		**7**
Project 3		3	1		3	**7**
Project 4		3		2		5
Project 5					4	4
Project 6	2		4		5	**11**
Project 7		1			5	6
Project 8	2		3			5
Project 9		3	2	4		**9**
Project 10		4		2		6
Total	5	17	14	12	17	

Swim Lane Process Map Template

A proven approach for laying out a process in order to provide clarity around accountabilities, steps, decisions and flows.

Swim Lane Process Map – Overview

What is it

The Swim Lane Process Map is a proven, logical and concise method for laying out a business or operational process in a way that provides clarity on core elements such as process actors, decision points, process steps and sequential flows. The approach and the format of the process map also accommodate additional notations and highlights to be added to draw attention to specific areas of interest, such as a process deficiencies, process volume data or opportunities for improvement.

When to use it

The Swim Lane Process Map is effective in two distinct business analysis situations. Firstly, it is effective at laying out a current state business process, highlighting key issues and socializing the process amongst stakeholders for awareness and agreement. Secondly, the same format is well suited for capturing a proposed future state – with emphasis given to recommended or proposed process changes and improvements to address identified gaps in the current state process.

Why use it

The Swim Lane Process Map is effective at capturing and conveying the core elements of any process being analyzed. It is simple, logical and minimizes the risk that important call outs within a process will get lost in a overly convoluted process diagram. A good process map should be readily understood by any business professional – and those with knowledge of the actual process should be able to confidently confirm that the process map represents reality. This tool enables this to occur.

Swim Lane Process Map – Method

How you use it

Step 1. Name the overarching process being mapped and the sub-process being documented.

Step 2. List the roles that are involved in the process vertically down the page.

Step 3. Use boxes to indicate process steps, tasks or activities – ensuring they are positioned in the correct role lane and that the sequence flows from left to right.

Step 4. Use diamonds to indicate decision points involved in the process flow.

Step 5. Use ovals to indicate inputs or outputs that are involved in each process step.

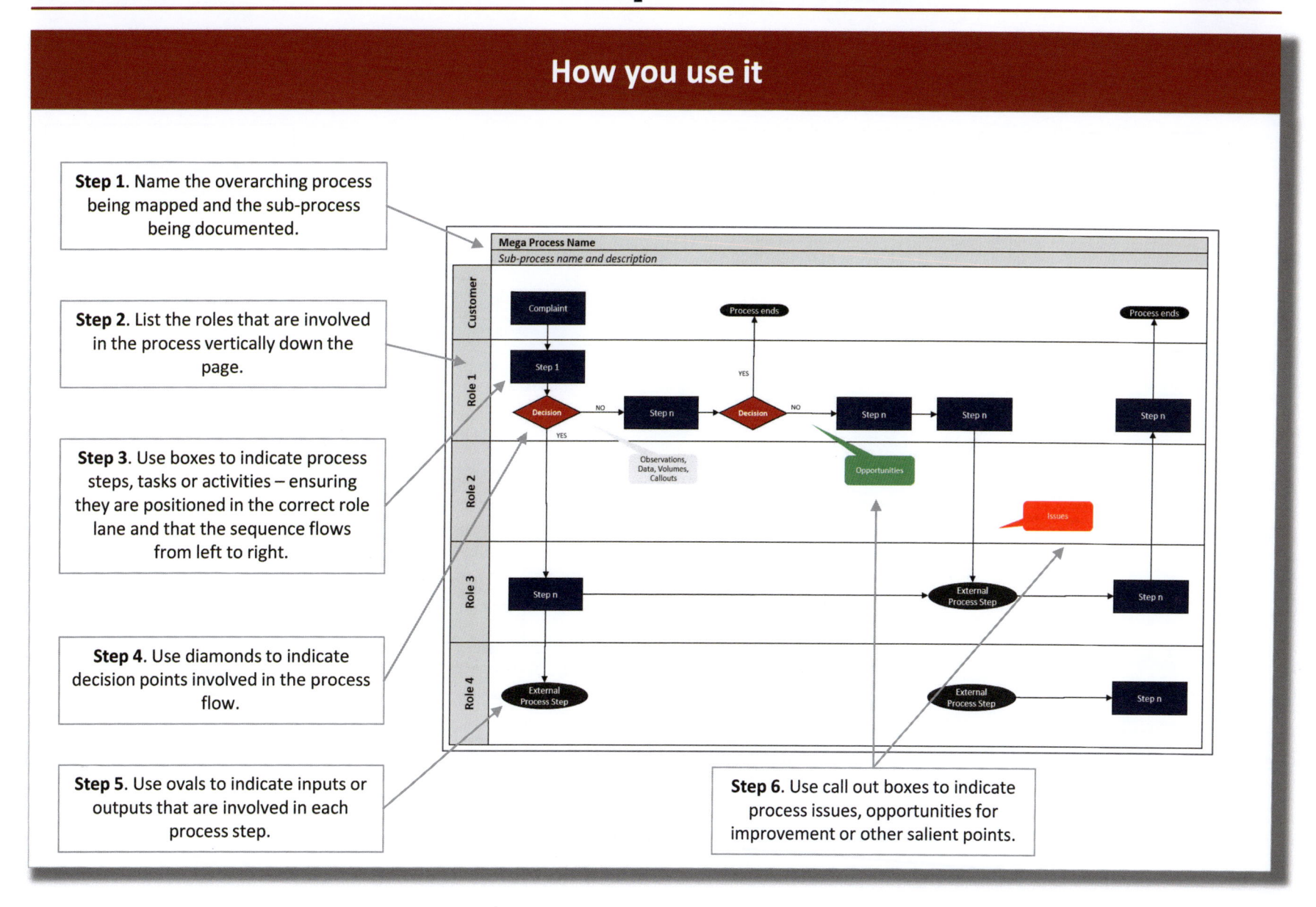

Step 6. Use call out boxes to indicate process issues, opportunities for improvement or other salient points.

Swim Lane Process Map – Template

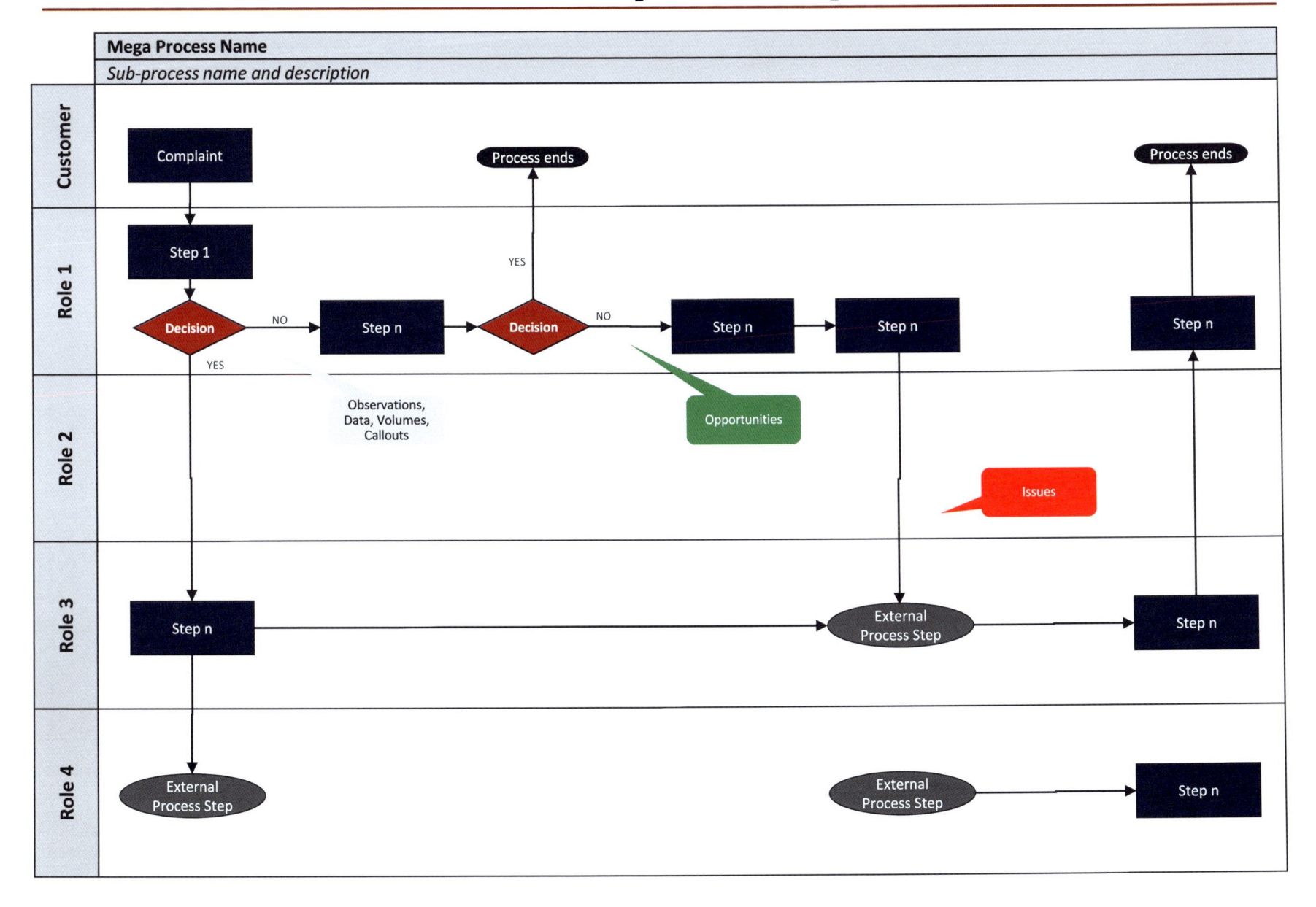

Mega Process Name
Sub-process name and description

Customer	Complaint → ... Process ends ... Process ends
Role 1	Step 1 → Decision —NO→ Step n → Decision —NO→ Step n → Step n ... Step n (YES from Decision 2 → Process ends; YES from Decision 1 goes down to Role 3)
Role 2	Observations, Data, Volumes, Callouts — Opportunities — Issues
Role 3	Step n → ... → External Process Step → Step n
Role 4	External Process Step ... External Process Step → Step n

The ABCD Tool

A feedback tool and continuous improvement method for lifting project team performance.

The ABC Tool – Overview

What is it

The ABC Tool is method for conducting team debriefs and capturing essential performance feedback information to take forward. A = Accomplishments, B = Benefits, C = Concerns and D = Do Next. The ABC Tool is a continuous improvement mechanism for teams to consistently reflect on their performance, an event or milestone that just happened or the project as a whole.

When to use it

Using the four categories identified above, a team captures key points reflecting on an event that has just occurred (such as a meeting or workshop) or at key milestones during a project (mid-point, conclusion, major deliverable). The ABCD Tool can be used as often as is suitable, and should be used in open, transparent forum with all participants and team members having equal opportunity to raise points and contribute.

Why use it

Project teams that regularly reflect on their performance and take targeted action are higher performing and deliver better results, more consistently. Surprisingly though, team performance reflection and constructive debriefs are not conducted on the vast majority of business projects (and most projects don't deliver their intended outcomes!). The ABC Tool is a simple, powerful mechanism for incorporating continuous improvement and constructive feedback into any project.

The ABC Tool – Method

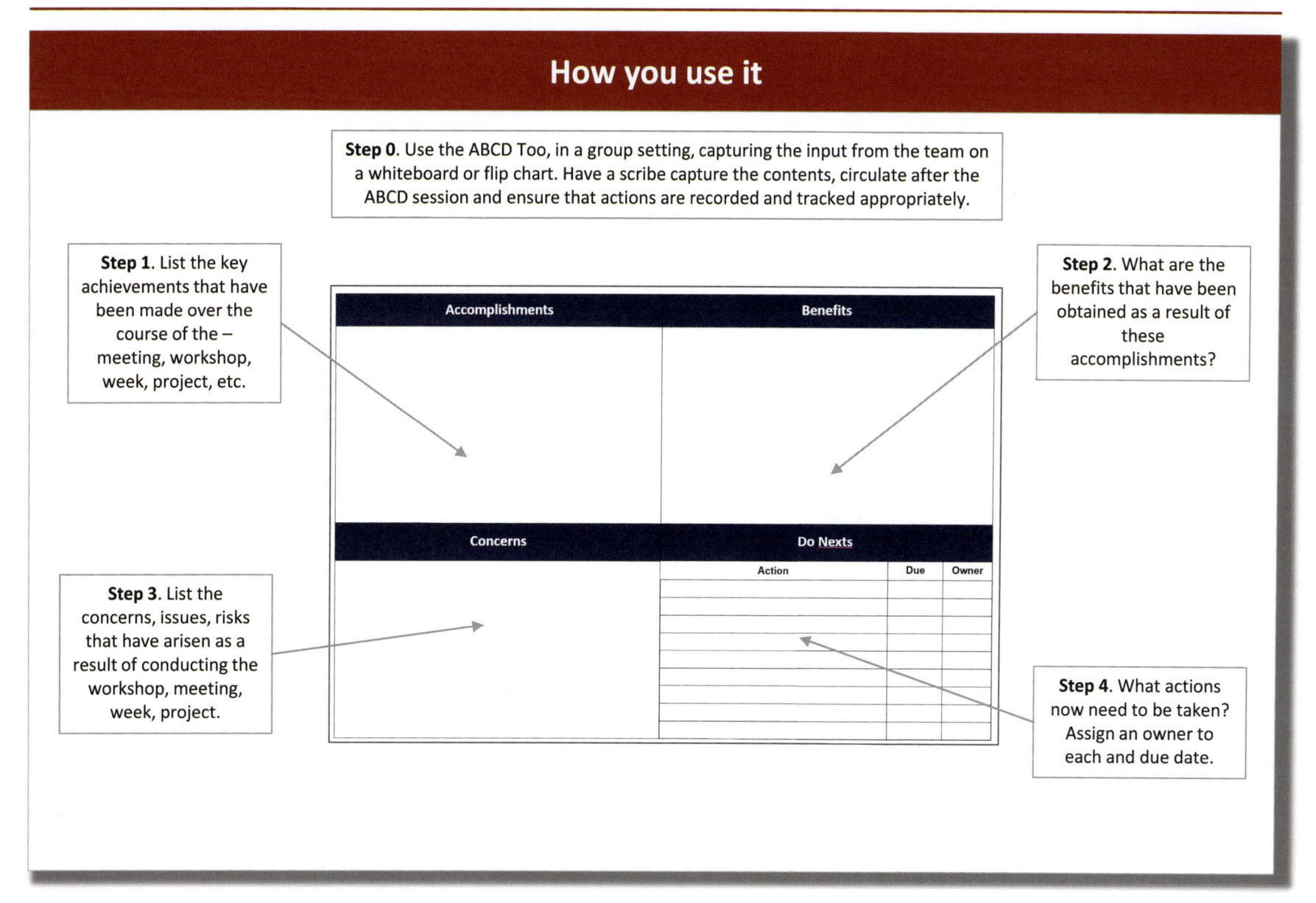

How you use it

Step 0. Use the ABCD Too, in a group setting, capturing the input from the team on a whiteboard or flip chart. Have a scribe capture the contents, circulate after the ABCD session and ensure that actions are recorded and tracked appropriately.

Step 1. List the key achievements that have been made over the course of the – meeting, workshop, week, project, etc.

Step 2. What are the benefits that have been obtained as a result of these accomplishments?

Step 3. List the concerns, issues, risks that have arisen as a result of conducting the workshop, meeting, week, project.

Step 4. What actions now need to be taken? Assign an owner to each and due date.

Accomplishments	Benefits

Concerns	Do Nexts		
	Action	Due	Owner

The ABC Tool – Template

Accomplishments	Benefits

Concerns

Do Nexts

Action	Due	Owner

Activity Accountability Plan

A structured method for specifying team member roles and responsibilities for delivery of a business improvement project

Activity Accountability Plan – Overview

What is it

The Activity Accountability Plan is an approach and framework for clearly outlining the "jobs that need to be done" as part of a business program and the roles that individuals need to play in order for those jobs to be successfully completed. It is an alternate approach to a typical project plan, by providing additional emphasis on ensuring individual roles and responsibilities for each task are clear in addition to timeframe expectations.

When to use it

The Activity Accountability Plan is ideally suited for use at the stage of a project where detailed planning is occurring and additional clarity is required regarding the role and responsibility of individual project team members and other key stakeholders. The plan can be developed in a workshop environment with the core project team and it can also be developed through an iterative fashion as project activities are determined and then accountability is assigned and refined.

Why use it

Clarity of objectives, plan, scope, timeframes and deliverables is essential for any business transformation or improvement project be successful. What's often overlooked however, is clarity of roles and responsibilities in relation to the scope of work. The Activity Accountability Plan provides a structured, simple mechanism to clearly specify work scope in addition to taking the extra step of identifying the role and responsibility of individuals for each work item.

Activity Accountability Plan

How you use it

Step 1. List the key activities, deliverables, tasks or milestones that must be completed as a part of a business initiative.

Step 2. For each RACI item, identify the appropriate individual for every task.

Step 3. Specify the weeks spanning the duration of the initiative.

Activities	R	A	C	I	Week 1	2	3	4	5	6	7	8	9	10	11	12
Activity details.	Initials	Initials	Initials	Initials												

Step 4. Draw in the bars to indicate the start, end and duration for each item.

Step 5. Utilize milestone icons also where necessary.

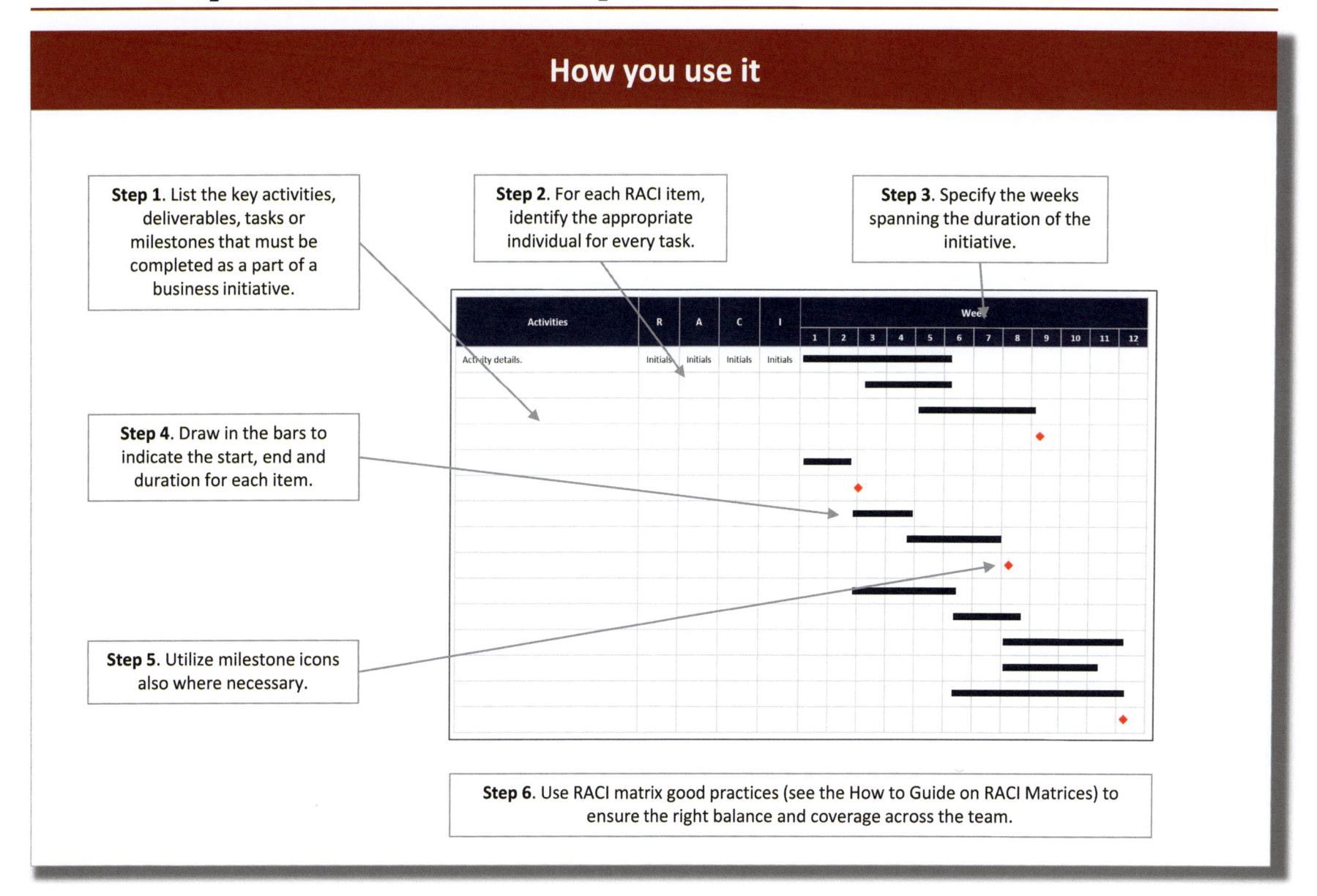

Step 6. Use RACI matrix good practices (see the How to Guide on RACI Matrices) to ensure the right balance and coverage across the team.

Activity Accountability Plan

Activities / Tasks / Deliverables	R	A	C	I	Week											
					1	2	3	4	5	6	7	8	9	10	11	12
Details	Initials	Initials	Initials	Initials												

Business Metrics Framework

A proven mechanism for specifying performance metrics to drive and measure transformation progress.

Business Metrics Framework – Overview

What is it

The Business Metrics Framework is a structured approach and template for defining future state business performance metrics in support of a business transformation or improvement program. The framework allows for key requirement and design information to be specified for metrics to then be agreed and progressed into development, deployment, reporting and tracking.

When to use it

The Business Metrics Framework should be used during the design and planning phase of a business transformation or improvement program. The ideal timing for metrics definition is after design of the key future state components is complete (such as operating model, high level processes, vision, objectives) – with the defined metrics providing the means to establish expected and motivational targets for the future state and track progress towards accomplishing these targets.

Why use it

Clear performance metrics are an essential part of any business looking to achieve operational excellence or transform performance and achieve improved results. The first step in establishing effective and aligned metrics is the specification of the requirements, targets and approach. This template is proven in multiple business environments and transformation settings to help organizations outline metrics necessary to motivate and manage transformation progress.

Business Metrics Framework – Method

How you use it

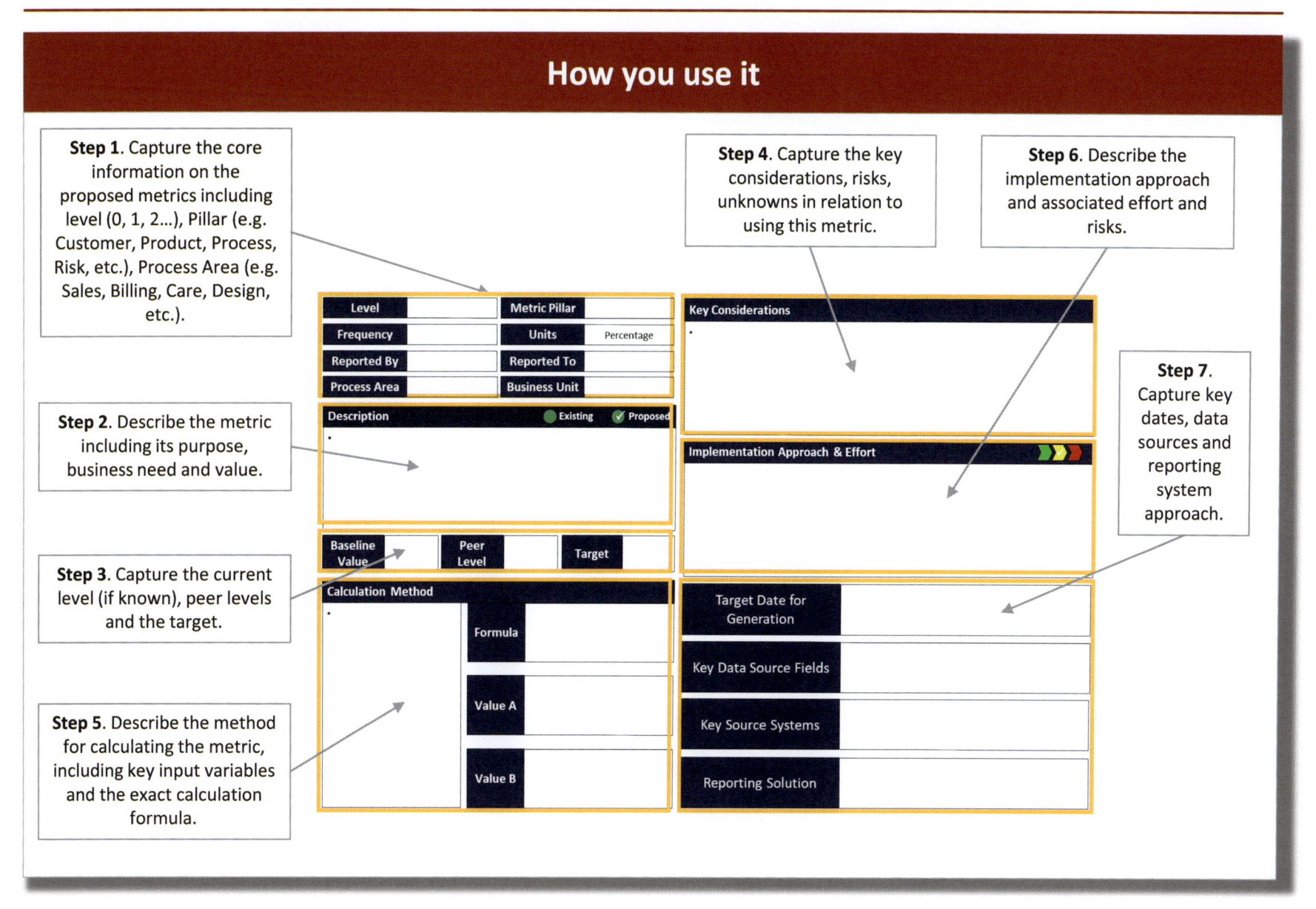

Step 1. Capture the core information on the proposed metrics including level (0, 1, 2...), Pillar (e.g. Customer, Product, Process, Risk, etc.), Process Area (e.g. Sales, Billing, Care, Design, etc.).

Step 2. Describe the metric including its purpose, business need and value.

Step 3. Capture the current level (if known), peer levels and the target.

Step 4. Capture the key considerations, risks, unknowns in relation to using this metric.

Step 5. Describe the method for calculating the metric, including key input variables and the exact calculation formula.

Step 6. Describe the implementation approach and associated effort and risks.

Step 7. Capture key dates, data sources and reporting system approach.

Template fields

- Level
- Metric Pillar
- Frequency
- Units: Percentage
- Reported By
- Reported To
- Process Area
- Business Unit
- Description (Existing / Proposed ✓)
- Baseline Value
- Peer Level
- Target
- Calculation Method
  - Formula
  - Value A
  - Value B
- Key Considerations
- Implementation Approach & Effort
- Target Date for Generation
- Key Data Source Fields
- Key Source Systems
- Reporting Solution

Business Metrics Framework – Template

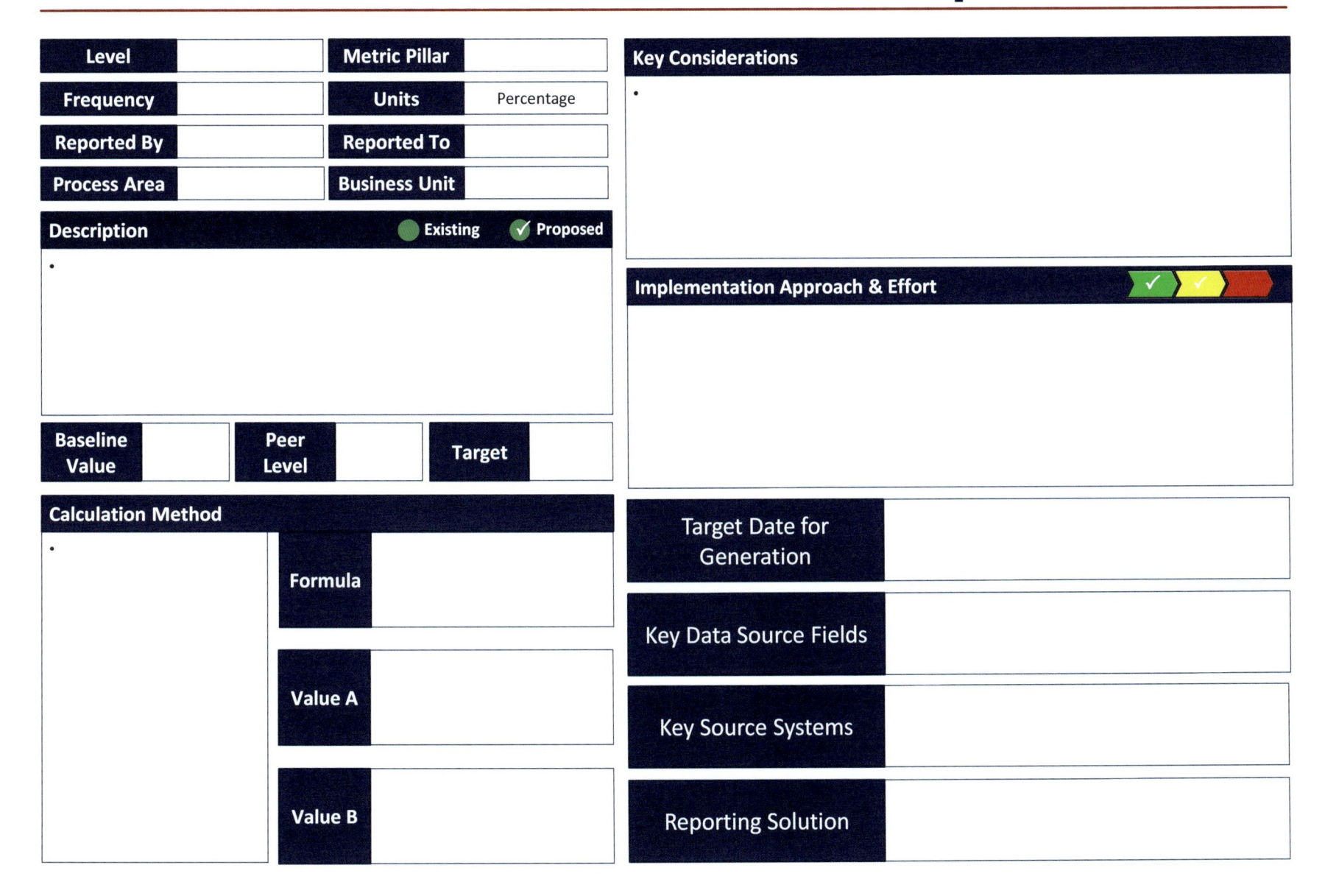

Level		Metric Pillar	
Frequency		**Units**	Percentage
Reported By		**Reported To**	
Process Area		**Business Unit**	

Description ● Existing ✓ Proposed

•

Baseline Value | **Peer Level** | **Target**

Calculation Method

•

- Formula
- Value A
- Value B

Key Considerations

•

Implementation Approach & Effort ✓ ✓

Target Date for Generation

Key Data Source Fields

Key Source Systems

Reporting Solution

Business Stakeholder Map

Understand, engage, influence and manage your business stakeholders with this proven mapping approach

Business Stakeholder Map – Overview

What is it

The Business Stakeholder Map is a method and framework for evaluating the disposition of business stakeholders (individuals and groups) in relation to a transformation program. The map allows stakeholders to be plotted to assess their relative degree of influence and support over a transformation program. Using this assessment, stakeholder engagement and communication activities can be initiated to help "move" stakeholders to the desired level of support relative to their influence.

When to use it

A Stakeholder Disposition Map should be developed at the commence of a transformation program – during the planning cycle and it should be continually refined and updated to include new stakeholders and adjust the changing disposition of existing stakeholders. As the stakeholder map is developed, stakeholder actions and disposition should be tracked using the Stakeholder Tracking Sheet.

Why use it

Business Transformation Program's succeed on the back of well managed and engaged stakeholders. Moreover, a critical and common root cause of transformation program failure is the failure to adequately understand and engage with key stakeholders across the spectrum. While simple in form, this template will help to keep awareness and focus around stakeholder engagement. This template should be used in conjunction with the other stakeholder mapping and management tools found on experttoolkit.com.

Business Stakeholder Map – Method (Option 1)

How you use it

Plot. Plot stakeholders (individuals or groups) on the map according to their disposition towards to the program.

Optional: Plot the desired disposition for each stakeholder (individuals or groups). Where do we want them to be?

Y-Axis. How much can the stakeholder influence the success of the program?

Track: Track stakeholder disposition, engagement and actions on the Stakeholder Tracking Sheet.

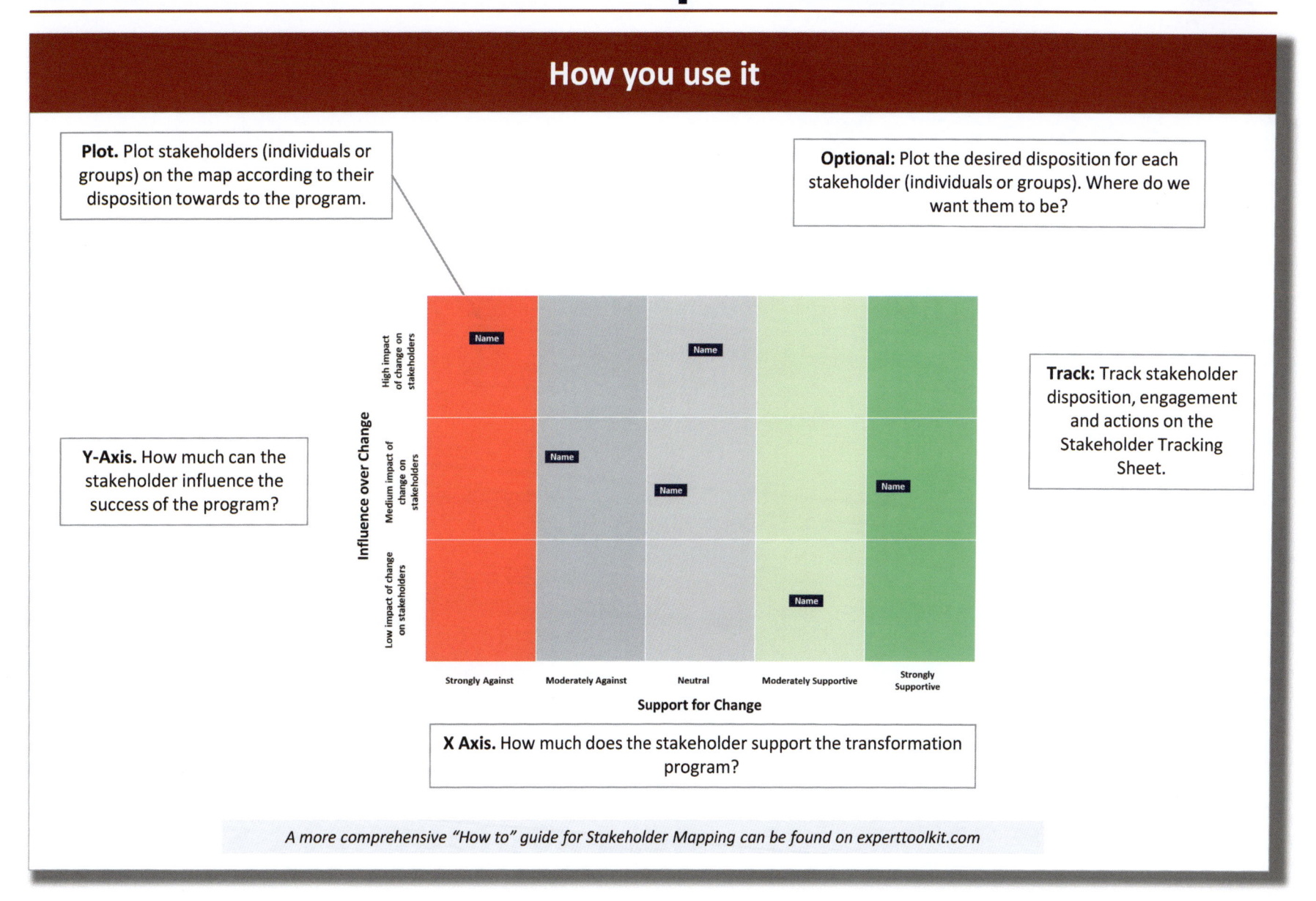

X Axis. How much does the stakeholder support the transformation program?

Y-axis (Influence over Change): High impact of change on stakeholders / Medium impact of change on stakeholders / Low impact of change on stakeholders

X-axis (Support for Change): Strongly Against / Moderately Against / Neutral / Moderately Supportive / Strongly Supportive

A more comprehensive "How to" guide for Stakeholder Mapping can be found on experttoolkit.com

Business Stakeholder Map – Template (Option 1)

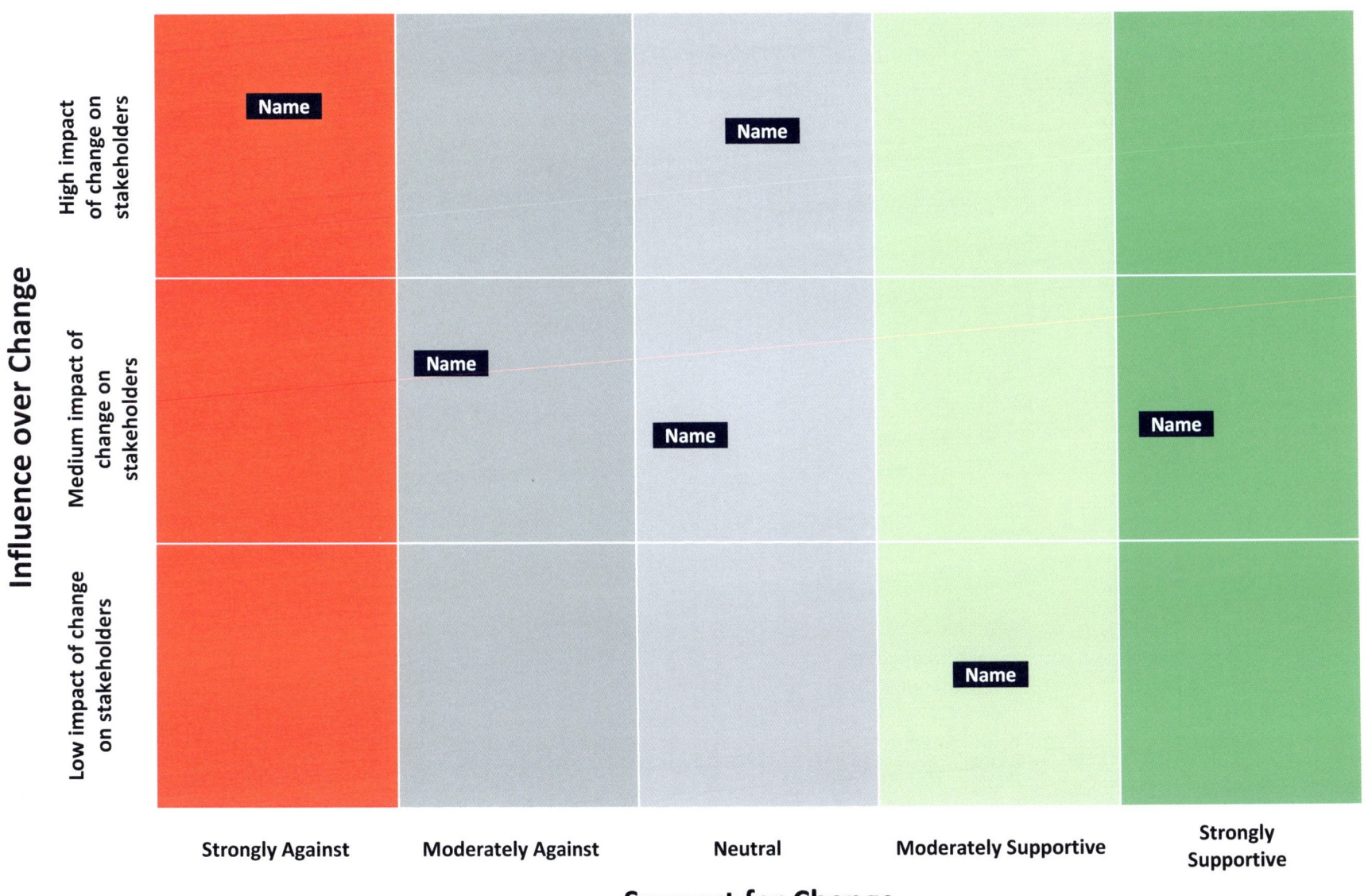

Influence over Change (y-axis, top to bottom): High impact of change on stakeholders / Medium impact of change on stakeholders / Low impact of change on stakeholders

Support for Change (x-axis): Strongly Against | Moderately Against | Neutral | Moderately Supportive | Strongly Supportive

Influence \ Support	Strongly Against	Moderately Against	Neutral	Moderately Supportive	Strongly Supportive
High impact	Name		Name		
Medium impact		Name	Name		Name
Low impact				Name	

Business Stakeholder Map – Method (Option 2)

How you use it

Plot. Plot stakeholders (individuals or groups) on the map according to their disposition towards to the program.

Optional: Plot the desired disposition for each stakeholder (individuals or groups). Where do we want them to be?

Y-Axis. How much can the stakeholder influence the success of the program?

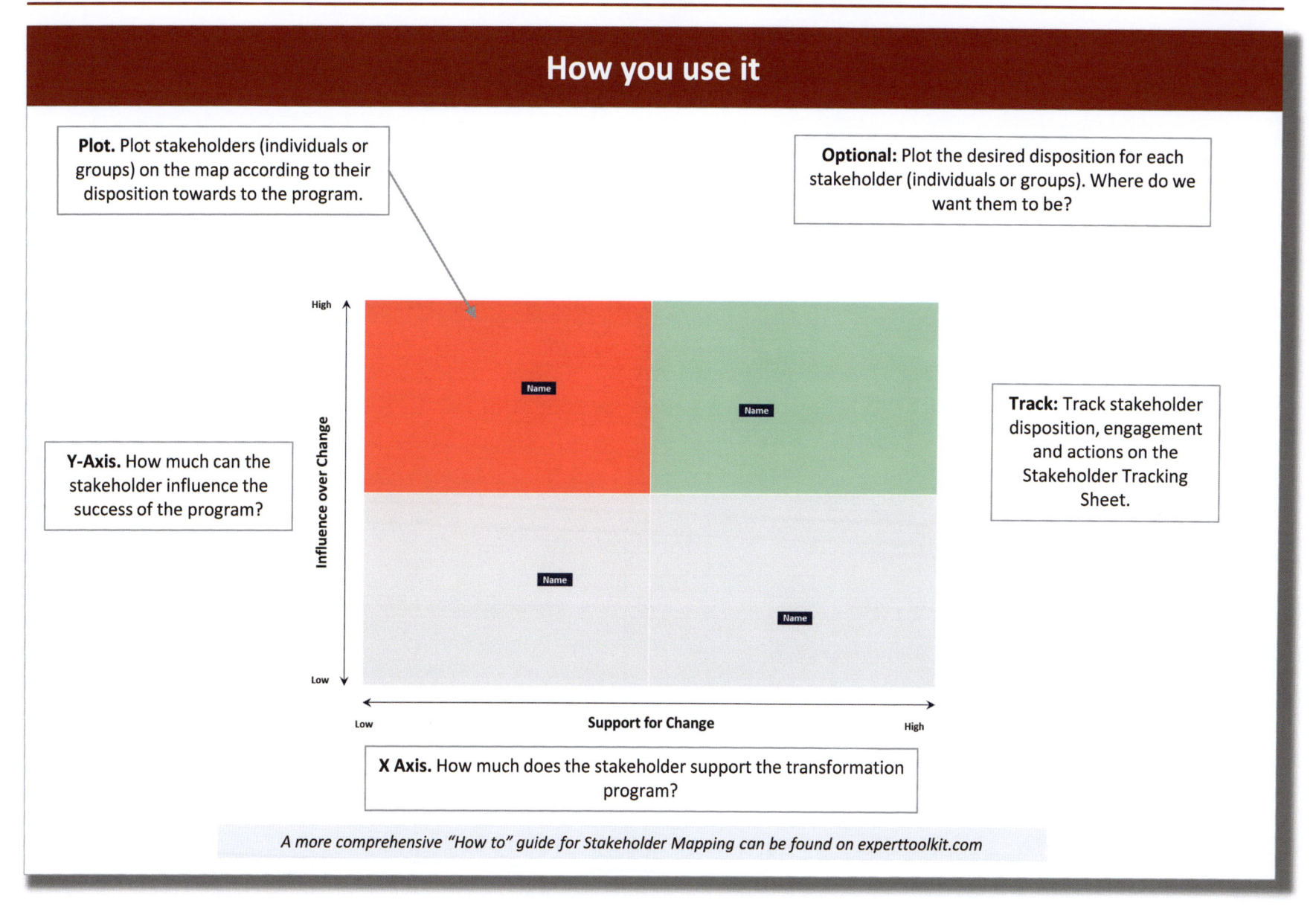

Track: Track stakeholder disposition, engagement and actions on the Stakeholder Tracking Sheet.

X Axis. How much does the stakeholder support the transformation program?

Axes: Influence over Change (Low to High) vs. Support for Change (Low to High)

A more comprehensive "How to" guide for Stakeholder Mapping can be found on experttoolkit.com

Business Stakeholder Map – Template (Option 2)

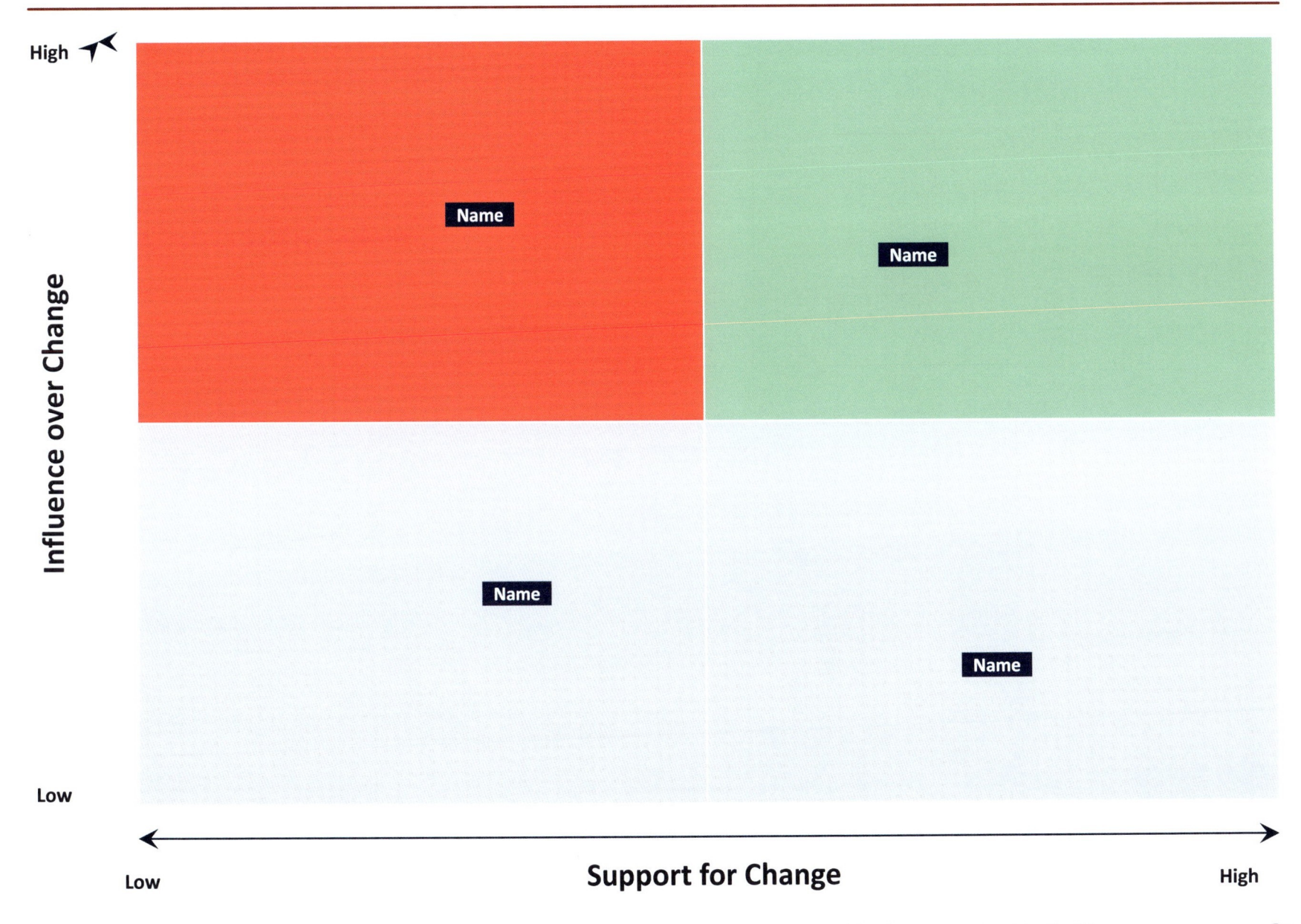

	Low Support for Change	High Support for Change
High Influence over Change	Name	Name
Low Influence over Change	Name	Name

Additional: Name (center, low influence area)

- Y-axis: Influence over Change (Low → High)
- X-axis: Support for Change (Low → High)

Business Stakeholder Tracking Sheet
Effectively track, engage and influence key stakeholders to facilitate transformation program success

Business Stakeholder Tracking Sheet – Overview

What is it

The Business Stakeholder Tracking Sheet is a proven format for capturing the essential information regarding stakeholders that need to be engaged and managed in relation to a business transformation program. The template allows a Change Manager or Project Manager to capture and track key data and actions to help influence the disposition of stakeholders so as they will be supportive and accepting of a transformational change program.

When to use it

The Business Stakeholder Tracking Sheet should be used at the beginning and throughout the life of a business transformation program. At the commencement of a program it is helpful to establish as baseline in regards to stakeholder disposition and then use the Stakeholder Tracking Sheet to continually track actions and stakeholder disposition.

Why use it

Business Transformation Program's succeed on the back of well managed and engaged stakeholders. Moreover, a critical and common root cause of transformation program failure is the failure to adequately understand and engage with key stakeholders across the spectrum. While simple in form, this template will help to keep awareness and focus around stakeholder engagement. This template should be used in conjunction with the other stakeholder mapping and management tools found on experttoolkit.com.

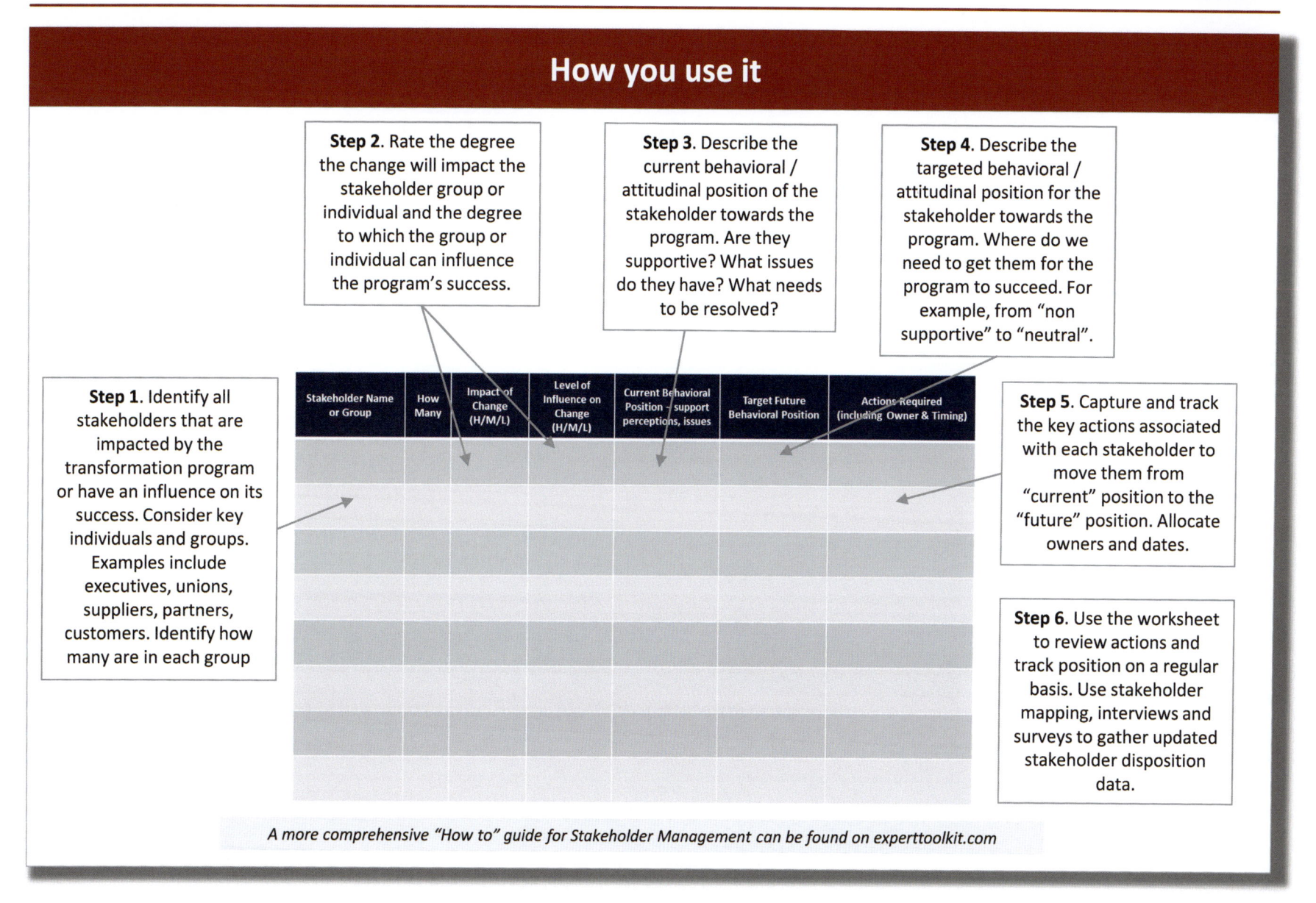

Business Stakeholder Tracking Sheet – Method

How you use it

Step 1. Identify all stakeholders that are impacted by the transformation program or have an influence on its success. Consider key individuals and groups. Examples include executives, unions, suppliers, partners, customers. Identify how many are in each group

Step 2. Rate the degree the change will impact the stakeholder group or individual and the degree to which the group or individual can influence the program's success.

Step 3. Describe the current behavioral / attitudinal position of the stakeholder towards the program. Are they supportive? What issues do they have? What needs to be resolved?

Step 4. Describe the targeted behavioral / attitudinal position for the stakeholder towards the program. Where do we need to get them for the program to succeed. For example, from "non supportive" to "neutral".

Step 5. Capture and track the key actions associated with each stakeholder to move them from "current" position to the "future" position. Allocate owners and dates.

Step 6. Use the worksheet to review actions and track position on a regular basis. Use stakeholder mapping, interviews and surveys to gather updated stakeholder disposition data.

Stakeholder Name or Group	How Many	Impact of Change (H/M/L)	Level of Influence on Change (H/M/L)	Current Behavioral Position – support perceptions, issues	Target Future Behavioral Position	Actions Required (including Owner & Timing)

A more comprehensive "How to" guide for Stakeholder Management can be found on experttoolkit.com

Business Stakeholder Tracking Sheet – Template

Stakeholder Name or Group	How Many	Impact of Change (H/M/L)	Level of Influence on Change (H/M/L)	Current Behavioral Position – support perceptions, issues	Target Future Behavioral Position	Actions Required (including Owner & Timing)

Business Transformation Guiding Principles

Align stakeholders around the key principles that are essential to the design and delivery of a business transformation program

Transformation Guiding Principles – Overview

What is it

The Transformation Guiding Principles Template is a structure for defining and capturing a set of guiding principles that can be utilized to shape and inform the design and delivery of a major business transformation program. The principles captured should represent a set of agreements, givens, attributes or "design criteria" that can be used to make critical decisions and shape the design of the end-state operating model and transformation program.

When to use it

The Transformation Guiding Principles Template should be used after a business vision or transformation vision has been developed, but prior to the creation of future state operating models. The principles agreed-to and captured will then guide the design of the operating models. The guiding principles should be developed in a collaborative fashion (such as a workshop, or series of workshops) with input and buy-in from a wide range of stakeholders. Once documented the principles should be socialized widely and referred to often – particularly in situations where critical design decisions are required to be made.

Why use it

A compelling, clear transformation vision and robust future state design that has buy-in from necessary stakeholders is critical to any business transformation. Establishing a set of guiding principles is a proven mechanism for developing a strong design that delivers on the vision and needs of the business – thus setting up the transformation program for success from the outset.

Transformation Guiding Principles – Method

How you use it

Step 1. Capture the Business Transformation Vision which has been defined to set the future state aspiration.

Step 2. Identify and capture the key dimensions relevant to the transformation program – for the purpose of documenting guiding principles.

Step 3. Capture the guiding principles for each dimension. Guiding principles should be used to inform "how" the transformation is execute and "what" the transformation delivers (the end state)

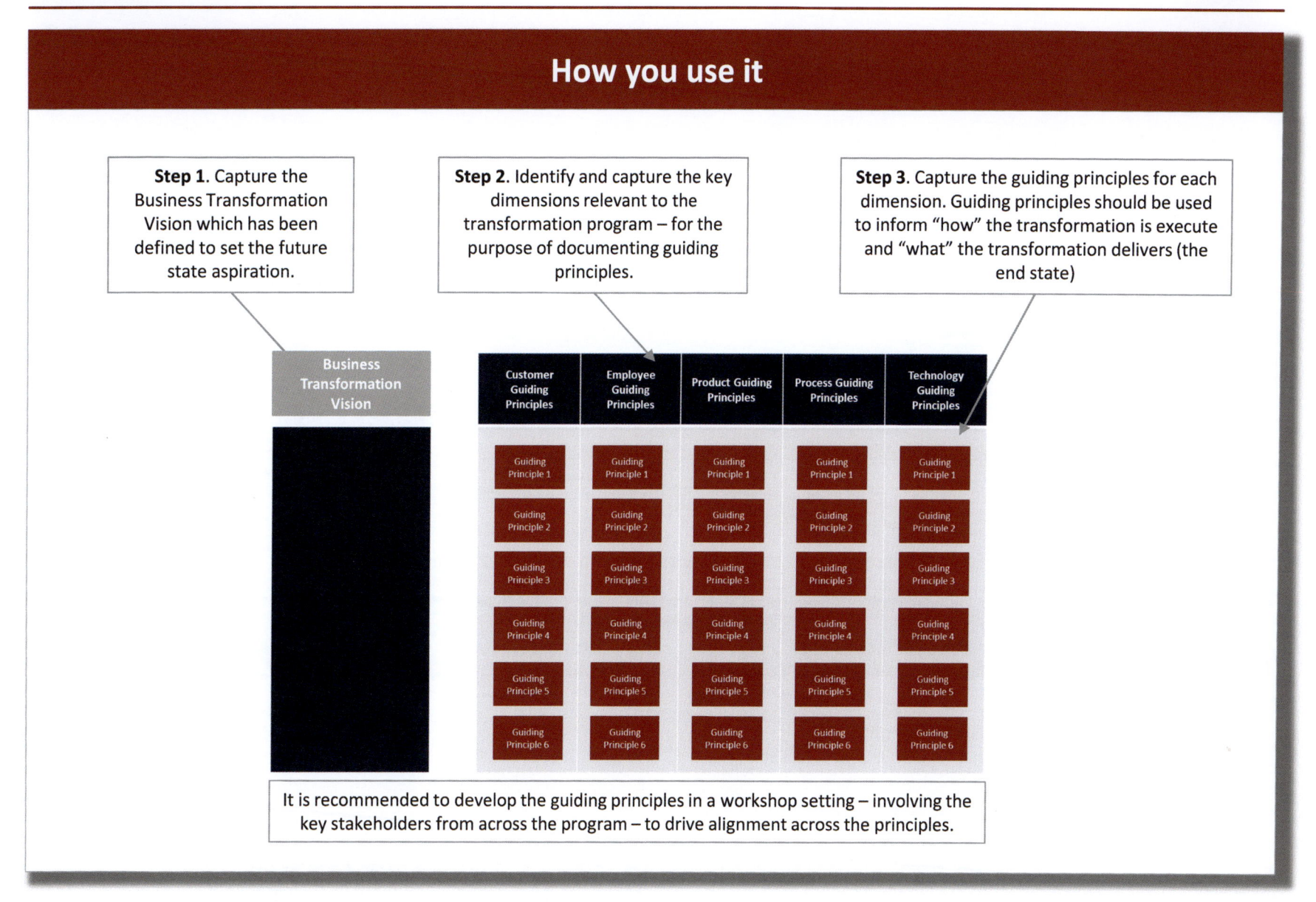

Business Transformation Vision	Customer Guiding Principles	Employee Guiding Principles	Product Guiding Principles	Process Guiding Principles	Technology Guiding Principles
	Guiding Principle 1	Guiding Principle 1	Guiding Principle 1	Guiding Principle 1	Guiding Principle 1
	Guiding Principle 2	Guiding Principle 2	Guiding Principle 2	Guiding Principle 2	Guiding Principle 2
	Guiding Principle 3	Guiding Principle 3	Guiding Principle 3	Guiding Principle 3	Guiding Principle 3
	Guiding Principle 4	Guiding Principle 4	Guiding Principle 4	Guiding Principle 4	Guiding Principle 4
	Guiding Principle 5	Guiding Principle 5	Guiding Principle 5	Guiding Principle 5	Guiding Principle 5
	Guiding Principle 6	Guiding Principle 6	Guiding Principle 6	Guiding Principle 6	Guiding Principle 6

It is recommended to develop the guiding principles in a workshop setting – involving the key stakeholders from across the program – to drive alignment across the principles.

Transformation Guiding Principles – Template

Business Transformation Vision	Customer Guiding Principles	Employee Guiding Principles	Product Guiding Principles	Process Guiding Principles	Technology Guiding Principles
	Guiding Principle 1	Guiding Principle 1	Guiding Principle 1	Guiding Principle 1	Guiding Principle 1
	Guiding Principle 2	Guiding Principle 2	Guiding Principle 2	Guiding Principle 2	Guiding Principle 2
	Guiding Principle 3	Guiding Principle 3	Guiding Principle 3	Guiding Principle 3	Guiding Principle 3
	Guiding Principle 4	Guiding Principle 4	Guiding Principle 4	Guiding Principle 4	Guiding Principle 4
	Guiding Principle 5	Guiding Principle 5	Guiding Principle 5	Guiding Principle 5	Guiding Principle 5
	Guiding Principle 6	Guiding Principle 6	Guiding Principle 6	Guiding Principle 6	Guiding Principle 6

Transformation Guiding Principles – Example

Business Transformation Vision

To be the best telecommunications company by advocacy, innovation and service.

We will accomplish our vision by:

- Delivering innovative customer solutions with exceptional quality.
- Providing a world-class customer experience.
- Creating a work environment that supports creativity, excellence and personal growth.

Customer Guiding Principles	Employee Guiding Principles	Product Guiding Principles	Process Guiding Principles	Technology Guiding Principles
Right First Time	Understood & Valued	Modular	Closed Loop	Cloud First
Know Me	Visible Leadership	Just Works	Scalable	Service Oriented
Single View	Collaborative	Quality First	Error Proof	Simple
Privacy Privacy Privacy	Right Tools & Training	Managed Portfolio	Controlled	Digital First
At the Center	Customer Oriented	Profitable	Measured	
Listen	Bias for Action			

Business Transformation Recommendation Template

A structured format for capturing and presenting business improvement or transformation recommendations

Business Transformation Recommendation Template – Overview

What is it

The Business Transformation Recommendation Template is a simple and straight-forward layout for capturing and presenting business transformation or improvement recommendations. The format facilitates essential information for each recommendation being captured, including rationale, implications and considerations. The format is ready-to-use and proven to work effectively in many business settings, however it is easily customized to suit the needs of the user and the specific transformation context.

When to use it

The Business Transformation Recommendation Template is best used at the conclusion of a diagnostic exercise when improvement recommendations and solutions are being formulated. The template is very effective when used to convey recommendations to senior executive stakeholder audiences and garnering their buy-in before moving into more detailed transformation design. The template should be used in conjunction with other tools and templates – including solution assessment, initiative prioritization and transformation map.

Why use it

The Business Transformation Recommendation Template makes it easy to present the critical information for business recommendations to key stakeholder groups. Don't waste time with formats, and layouts – this template is one that works and allows you to focus on populating it with the details that are essential when presenting any sound business recommendation and linking it back to underlying strategic of performance issues.

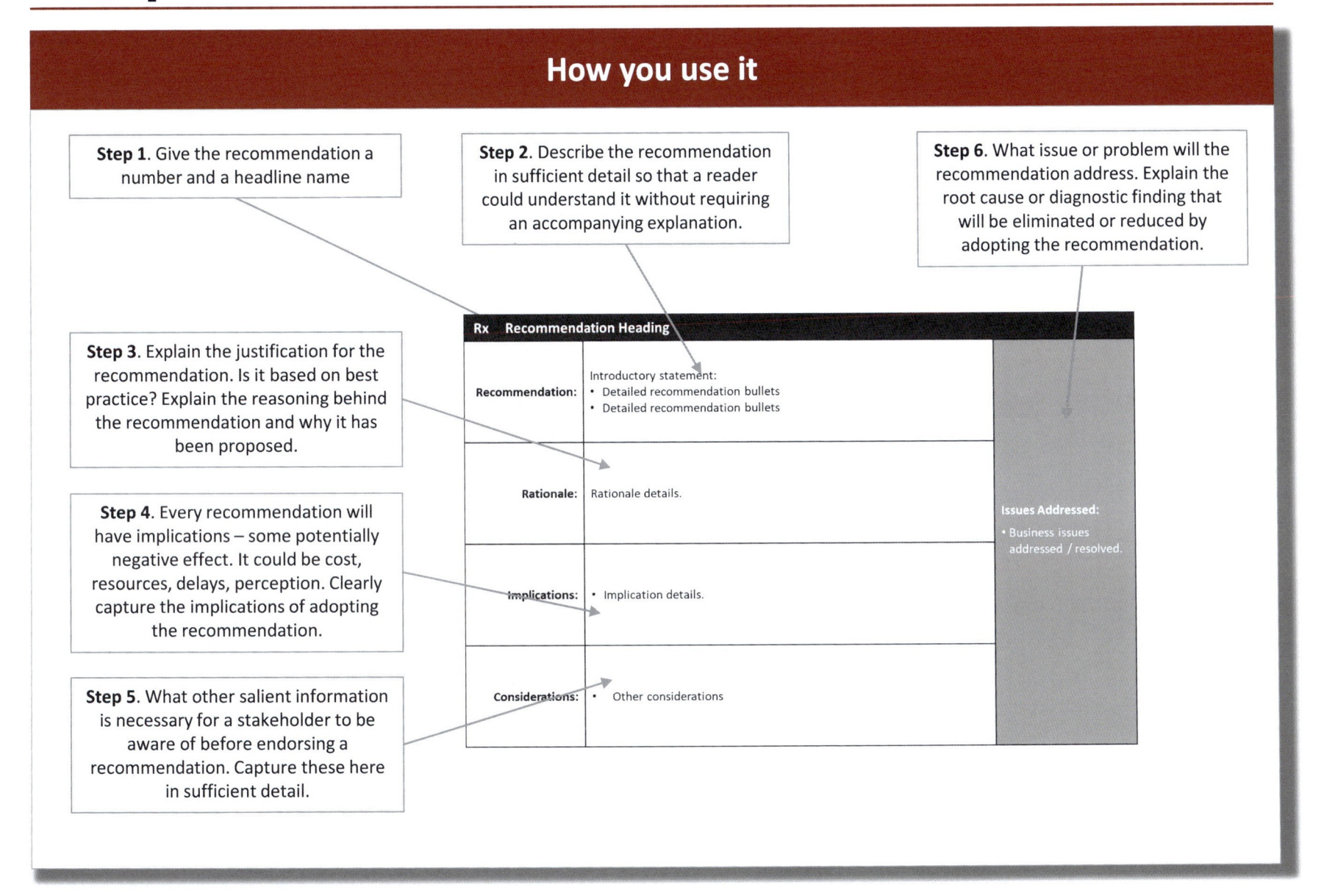

Business Transformation Recommendation Template – Method

How you use it

Step 1. Give the recommendation a number and a headline name

Step 2. Describe the recommendation in sufficient detail so that a reader could understand it without requiring an accompanying explanation.

Step 3. Explain the justification for the recommendation. Is it based on best practice? Explain the reasoning behind the recommendation and why it has been proposed.

Step 4. Every recommendation will have implications – some potentially negative effect. It could be cost, resources, delays, perception. Clearly capture the implications of adopting the recommendation.

Step 5. What other salient information is necessary for a stakeholder to be aware of before endorsing a recommendation. Capture these here in sufficient detail.

Step 6. What issue or problem will the recommendation address. Explain the root cause or diagnostic finding that will be eliminated or reduced by adopting the recommendation.

Rx	Recommendation Heading	
Recommendation:	Introductory statement: • Detailed recommendation bullets • Detailed recommendation bullets	**Issues Addressed:** • Business issues addressed / resolved.
Rationale:	Rationale details.	
Implications:	• Implication details.	
Considerations:	• Other considerations	

Business Transformation Recommendation Template – Template

Rx	Recommendation Heading	
Recommendation:	Introductory statement: • Detailed recommendation bullets • Detailed recommendation bullets	**Issues Addressed:** • Business issues addressed / resolved.
Rationale:	Rationale details.	
Implications:	• Implication details.	
Considerations:	• Other considerations	

Business Transformation Framework

A proven, step-by-step framework for defining, guiding and governing any business transformation program

Business Transformation Framework – Overview

What is it

The Business Transformation Framework is a 5-component framework (or methodology) intended to inform and assist with the design and delivery of a business transformation program. It begins with the "Transformation Vision" and concludes with "Metrics and Governance" to oversee execution and measure the success of delivery and accomplishment of the vision. For each step in the framework, tools and techniques are recommended for conducting the step effectively.

When to use it

The Business Transformation Framework provides a structured method for any team, unit, function or organization looking to transform. It can be used to guide the transformation approach based on good practices, allowing room for customization to suit the specific needs of the organization. It is not intended to be a formulaic recipe for completing a transformation, as every transformation is different. However, in the hands of a competent practitioner the framework will provide a strong transformation enabler.

Why use it

Transformations are typically complex, challenging and highly susceptible to failure. Starting out on a business transformation journey with a clear understanding of the ingredients for success is critical. The 5 steps in this framework, while not exhaustive, outline the essential elements that should be incorporated into the design and delivery of any transformation program in order for it to be successful and sustainable.

Business Transformation Framework

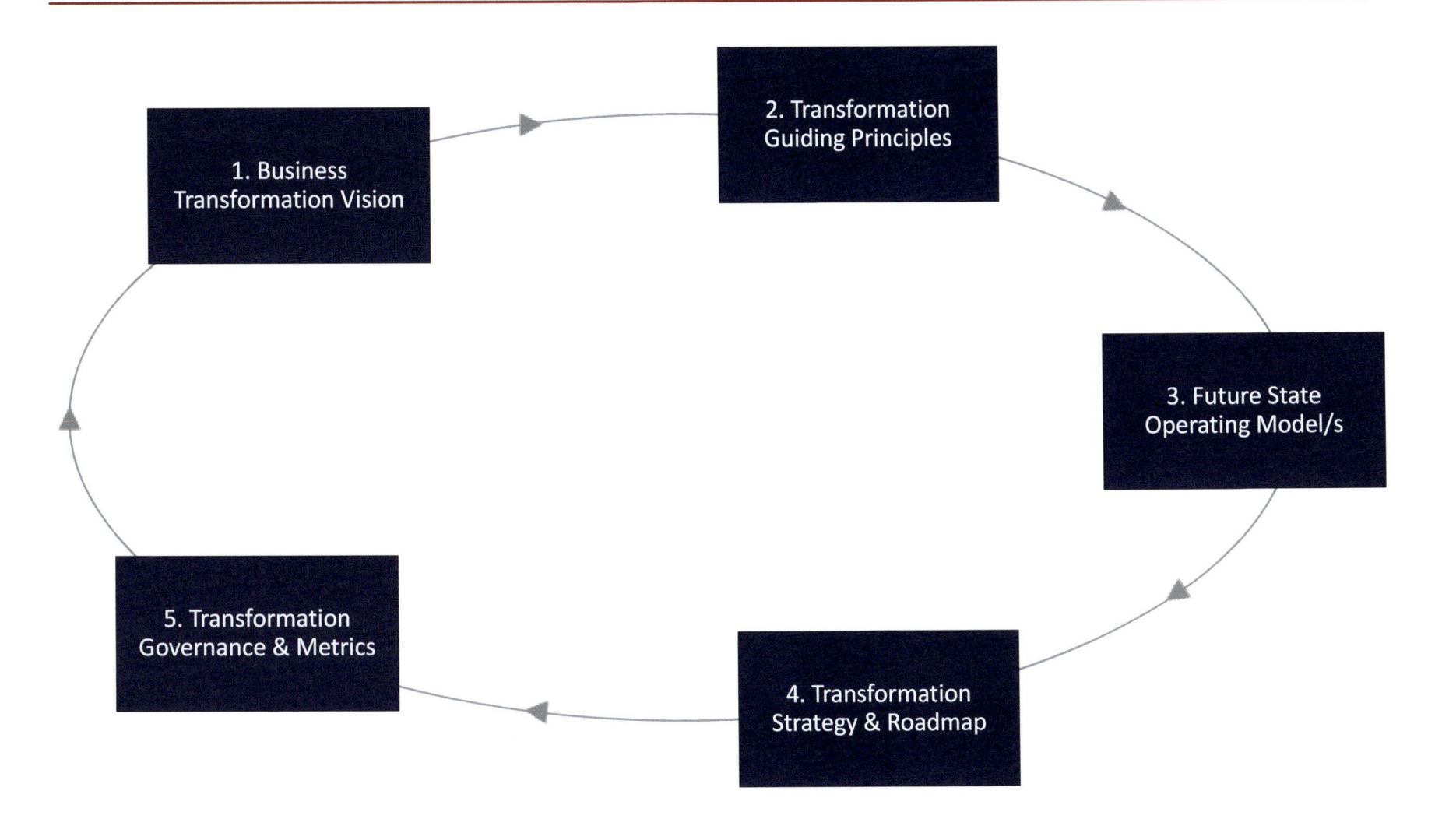

1. Business Transformation Vision
2. Transformation Guiding Principles
3. Future State Operating Model/s
4. Transformation Strategy & Roadmap
5. Transformation Governance & Metrics

Business Transformation Framework – Method

How you use it

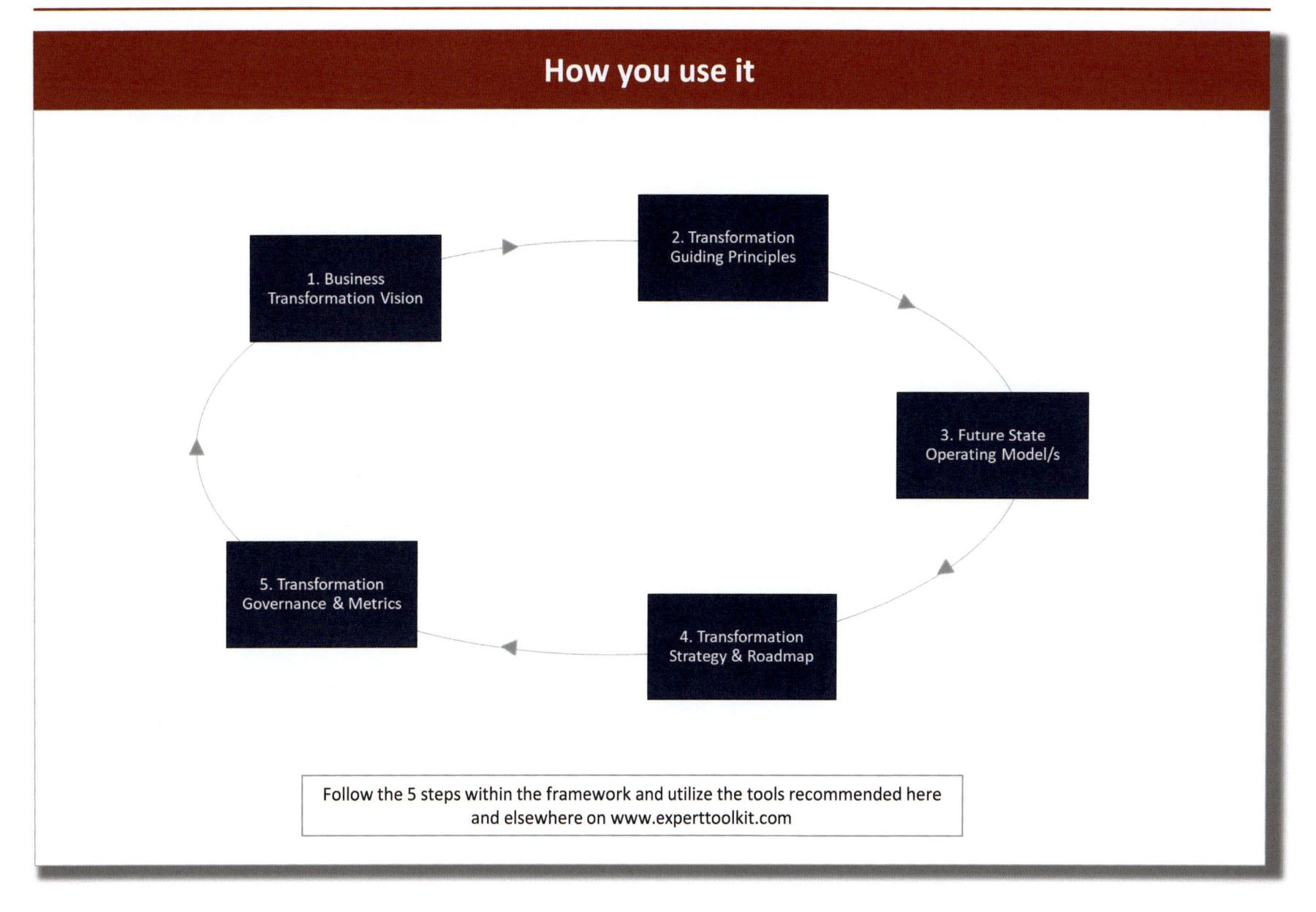

1. Business Transformation Vision
2. Transformation Guiding Principles
3. Future State Operating Model/s
4. Transformation Strategy & Roadmap
5. Transformation Governance & Metrics

Follow the 5 steps within the framework and utilize the tools recommended here and elsewhere on www.experttoolkit.com

Business Transformation Framework

1. Business Transformation Vision	Define the vision for the future state of the business and the vision for the transformation that needs to be undertaken.

Key Tools

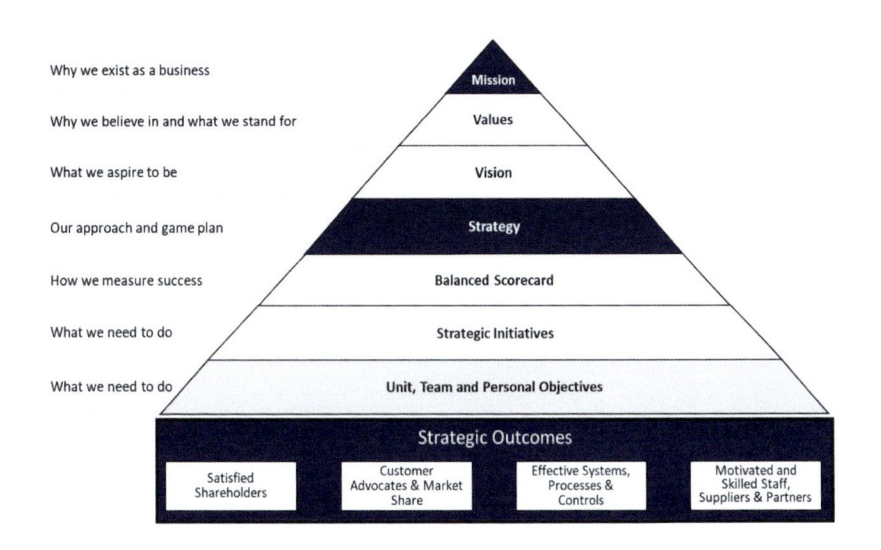

Strategy Pyramid

- Why we exist as a business — **Mission**
- Why we believe in and what we stand for — **Values**
- What we aspire to be — **Vision**
- Our approach and game plan — **Strategy**
- How we measure success — **Balanced Scorecard**
- What we need to do — **Strategic Initiatives**
- What we need to do — **Unit, Team and Personal Objectives**

Strategic Outcomes
- Satisfied Shareholders
- Customer Advocates & Market Share
- Effective Systems, Processes & Controls
- Motivated and Skilled Staff, Suppliers & Partners

Business Transformation Vision Template

Customer: Simple (Easy to do business with), Partner (Help me achieve my goals), No Surprises (Deliver what you promised), Quality (Don't let me down)

Leadership: Motivate (We empower our staff by living our values), Respect (We actively listen and respect others), Strength (We lead with clarity and direction), Inclusive (We are supportive and accepting of all), Serve (We are leaders who serve)

Mission: We exist to enable people to connect anywhere, anytime with anyone.

Vision: To be the best telecommunications company by advocacy, innovation and service.

We will accomplish our vision by:
- Delivering innovative customer solutions with exceptional quality.
- Providing a world-class customer experience.
- Creating a work environment that supports creativity, excellence and personal growth.

Culture: Innovative (New ideas thrive), Fun & Positive (A work environment we enjoy), Team Spirit (We support each other), Accountability (We deliver for each other), Integrity (We always do what is right)

Business Transformation Framework

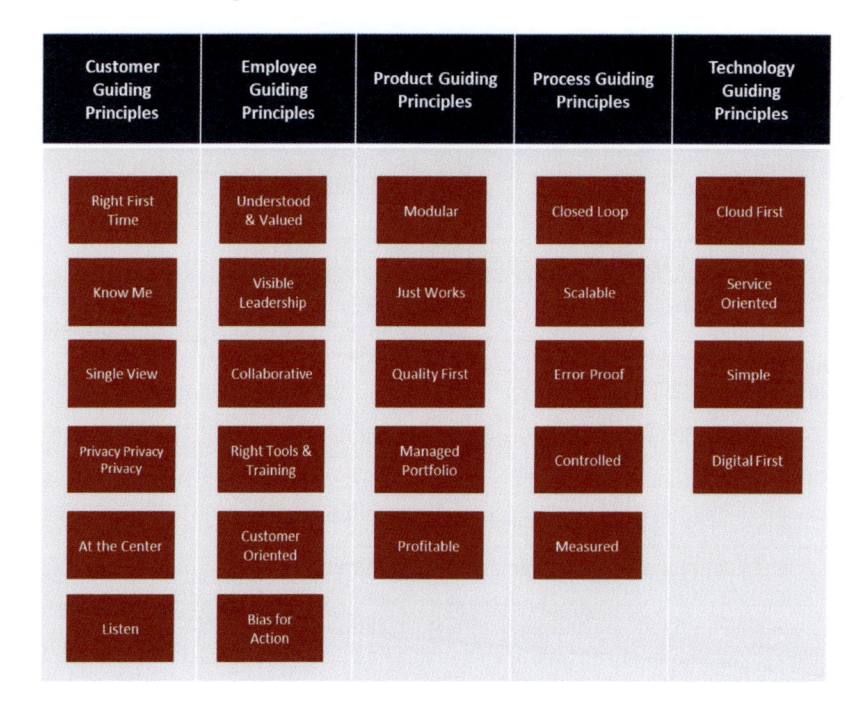

2. Transformation Guiding Principles

Outline a set of clear principles to help guide the design of the future state and the transformation program. Principles should be defined across dimensions that are most relevant to the business and the transformation being undertaken. Examples include Employee, Customer, Product, Process, Policy, Markets, Regulatory, Technology, Governance.

Key Tools

Business Transformation Vision	Customer Guiding Principles	Employee Guiding Principles	Product Guiding Principles	Process Guiding Principles	Technology Guiding Principles
To be the best telecommunications company by advocacy, innovation and service. We will accomplish our vision by: - Delivering innovative customer solutions with exceptional quality. - Providing a world-class customer experience. - Creating a work environment that supports creativity, excellence and personal growth.	Right First Time	Understood & Valued	Modular	Closed Loop	Cloud First
	Know Me	Visible Leadership	Just Works	Scalable	Service Oriented
	Single View	Collaborative	Quality First	Error Proof	Simple
	Privacy Privacy Privacy	Right Tools & Training	Managed Portfolio	Controlled	Digital First
	At the Center	Customer Oriented	Profitable	Measured	
	Listen	Bias for Action			

Transformation Guiding Principles Template

Business Transformation Framework

3. Future State Operating Model/s

Design the necessary future state operating models to clearly articulate the "what, how and who" of the business. Utilize an organizational impact assessment to understand the change that needs to occur to move from the current state to the future state.

Key Tools

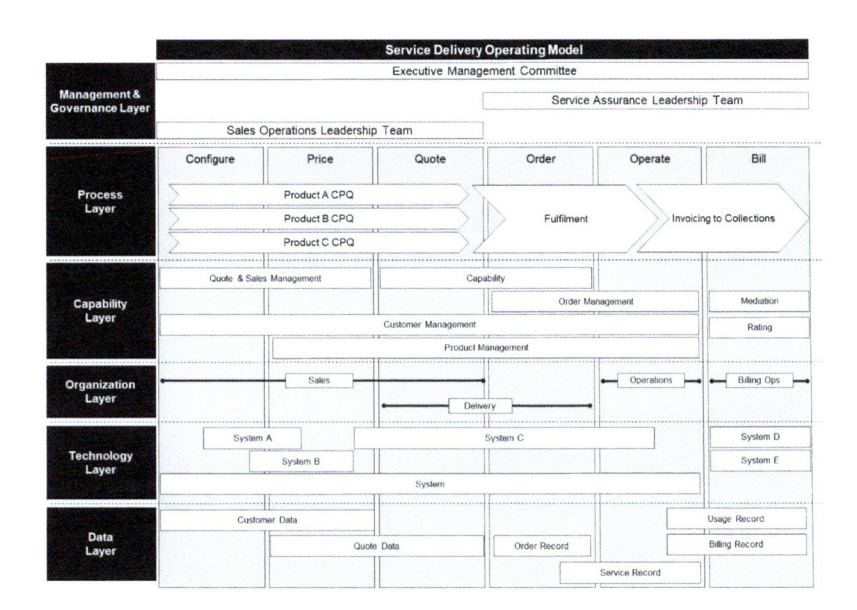

Operating Model Template

Organizational Impact Assessment

Business Transformation Framework

4. Transformation Roadmap & Change Strategy

Identify and prioritize the initiatives that need to be defined and delivered to deliver on the transformation vision and realize the operating model. Assess the stakeholders critical to executing these initiatives and implement effective stakeholder communications and management.

Key Tools

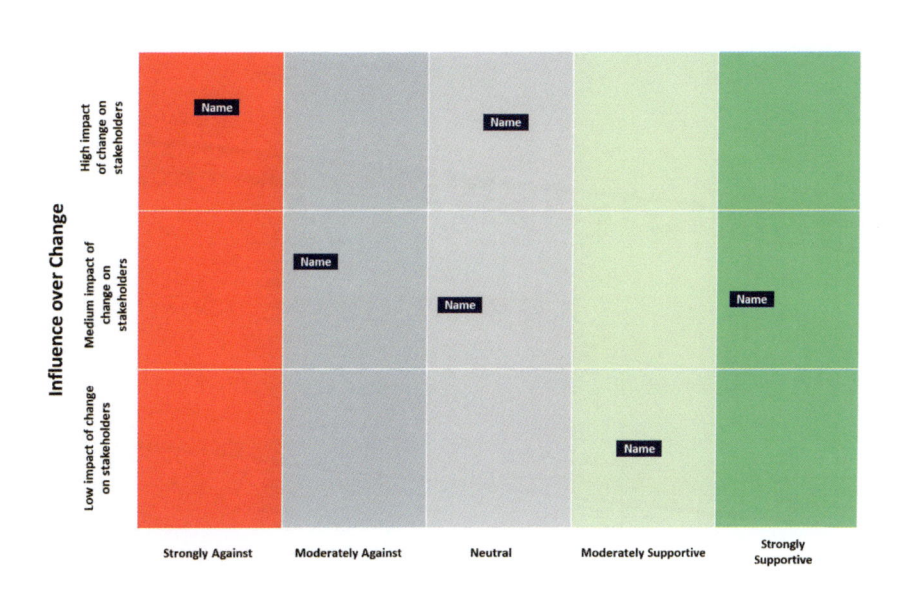

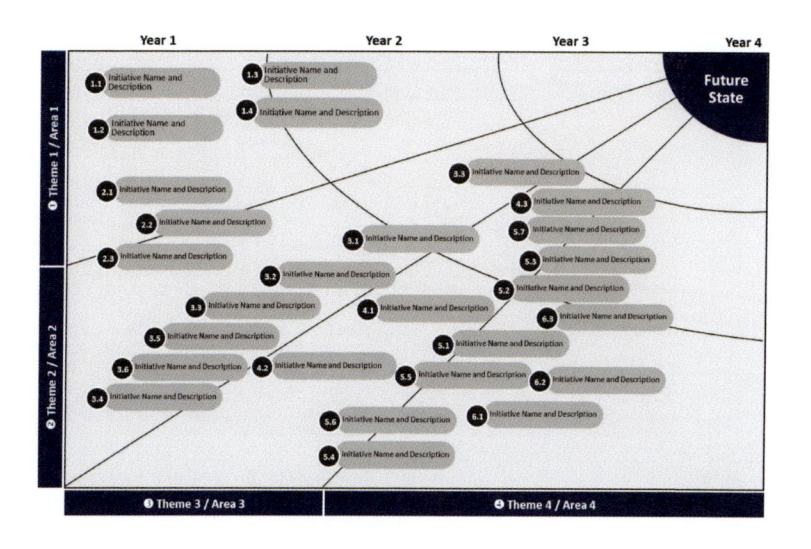

Stakeholder Disposition Map

Transformation Roadmap

Business Transformation Framework

5. Transformation Governance & Metrics	Implement governance mechanisms, tools and processes to manage the transformation and clearly define and operationalize measures that can be used to track transformation progress and performance against the end state vision.

Key Tools

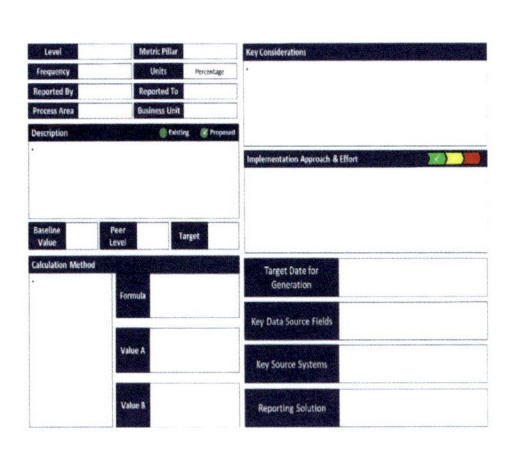

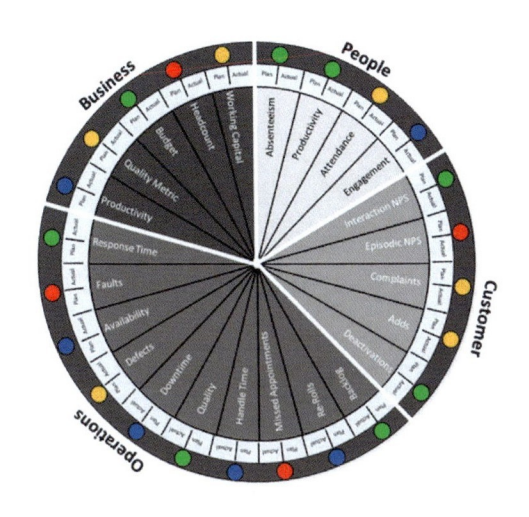

Business Metrics Definition **Balanced Scorecard** **Transformation Governance Tools**

Business Vision Framework

A proven, structured and highly customizable template for develop a strong vision for a business or transformation program

Business Vision Framework – Overview

What is it

The Business Vision Framework is structured format for outlining the key elements of a corporate or program vision and the related components necessary to accomplish that vision, including mission, values and objectives. It is a layout that allows creativity to focus on the essence of the vision, rather that "how do we lay it out". It is highly customizable and provides a very strong starting point for anyone working with a team to develop a vision for an entire organization, a program or a business unit.

When to use it

The Business Vision Framework can be used as part of a strategic planning or refresh cycle to develop a corporate vision, business unit vision or team vision. It can also be used to frame the vision and objectives for a business transformation program. When used in this way, aspects of the framework would be used to describe the end state (after the transformation has been delivered) and aspects could be used to describe transformation delivery priorities and behaviors that need to occur during the transformation program.

Why use it

Many a moment, day, week, month has been lost endeavoring to develop a strong vision, mission and objective statement with time wasted wrestling with "content" at the same time as "look and feel". The framework presented here presents an easy-to-use and proven structure for developing a great vision – allowing the focus and energy to be directed at the content, not the structure. The framework is very useful in a workshop environment and can be easily modified as the vision evolves.

Business Vision Framework – Method

How you use it

Step 1. Capture your program or organization's mission statement. This should be an inspirational, purpose-led statement that captures the core meaning of what the organization does every day.

Step 2. Capture your program or organization's vision statement. This statement should represent an end goal to strive towards. Where a mission is the purpose behind the journey, the vision is the destination.

Step 3. Identify 3-4 underlying objectives to put depth to the vision. These could be objectives on measures such as revenue, market share or more qualitative such as brand, customer perception, integrity.

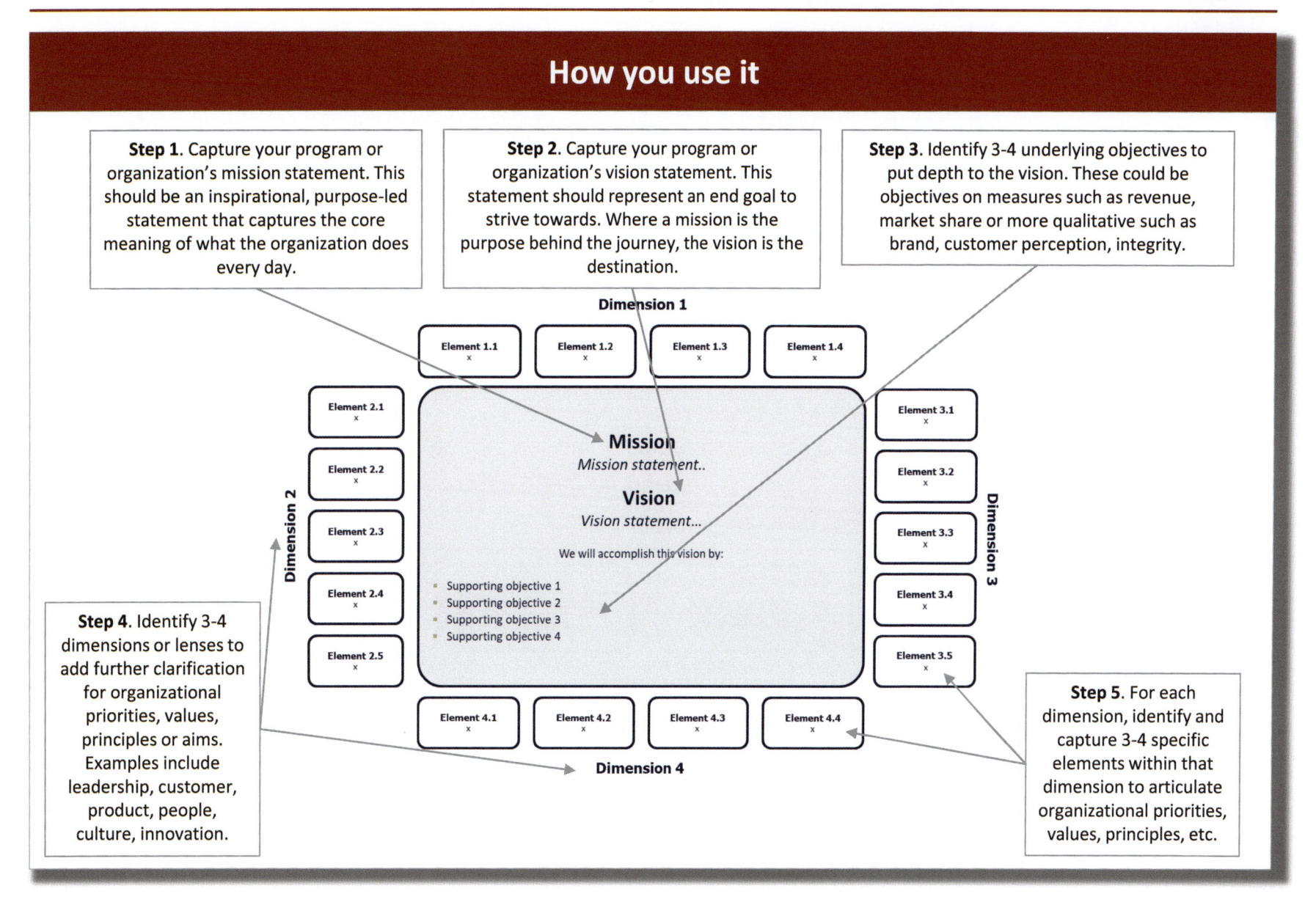

Step 4. Identify 3-4 dimensions or lenses to add further clarification for organizational priorities, values, principles or aims. Examples include leadership, customer, product, people, culture, innovation.

Step 5. For each dimension, identify and capture 3-4 specific elements within that dimension to articulate organizational priorities, values, principles, etc.

Dimension 1: Element 1.1 x, Element 1.2 x, Element 1.3 x, Element 1.4 x

Dimension 2: Element 2.1 x, Element 2.2 x, Element 2.3 x, Element 2.4 x, Element 2.5 x

Dimension 3: Element 3.1 x, Element 3.2 x, Element 3.3 x, Element 3.4 x, Element 3.5 x

Dimension 4: Element 4.1 x, Element 4.2 x, Element 4.3 x, Element 4.4 x

Mission
Mission statement..

Vision
Vision statement...

We will accomplish this vision by:
- Supporting objective 1
- Supporting objective 2
- Supporting objective 3
- Supporting objective 4

Business Vision Framework – Example

Customer

- **Simple** — Easy to do business with
- **Partner** — Help me achieve my goals
- **No Surprises** — Deliver what you promised
- **Quality** — Don't let me down

Leadership

- **Motivate** — We empower our staff by living our values
- **Respect** — We actively listen and respect others
- **Strength** — We lead with clarity and direction
- **Inclusive** — We are supportive and accepting of all
- **Serve** — We are leaders who serve

Culture

- **Innovative** — New ideas thrive
- **Fun & Positive** — A work environment we enjoy
- **Team Spirit** — We support each other
- **Accountability** — We deliver for each other
- **Integrity** — We always do what is right

Mission
We exist to enable people to connect anywhere, anytime with anyone.

Vision
To be the best telecommunications company by advocacy, innovation and service.

We will accomplish our vision by:

- Delivering innovative customer solutions with exceptional quality.
- Providing a world-class customer experience.
- Creating a work environment that supports creativity, excellence and personal growth.

Business Vision Framework – Template

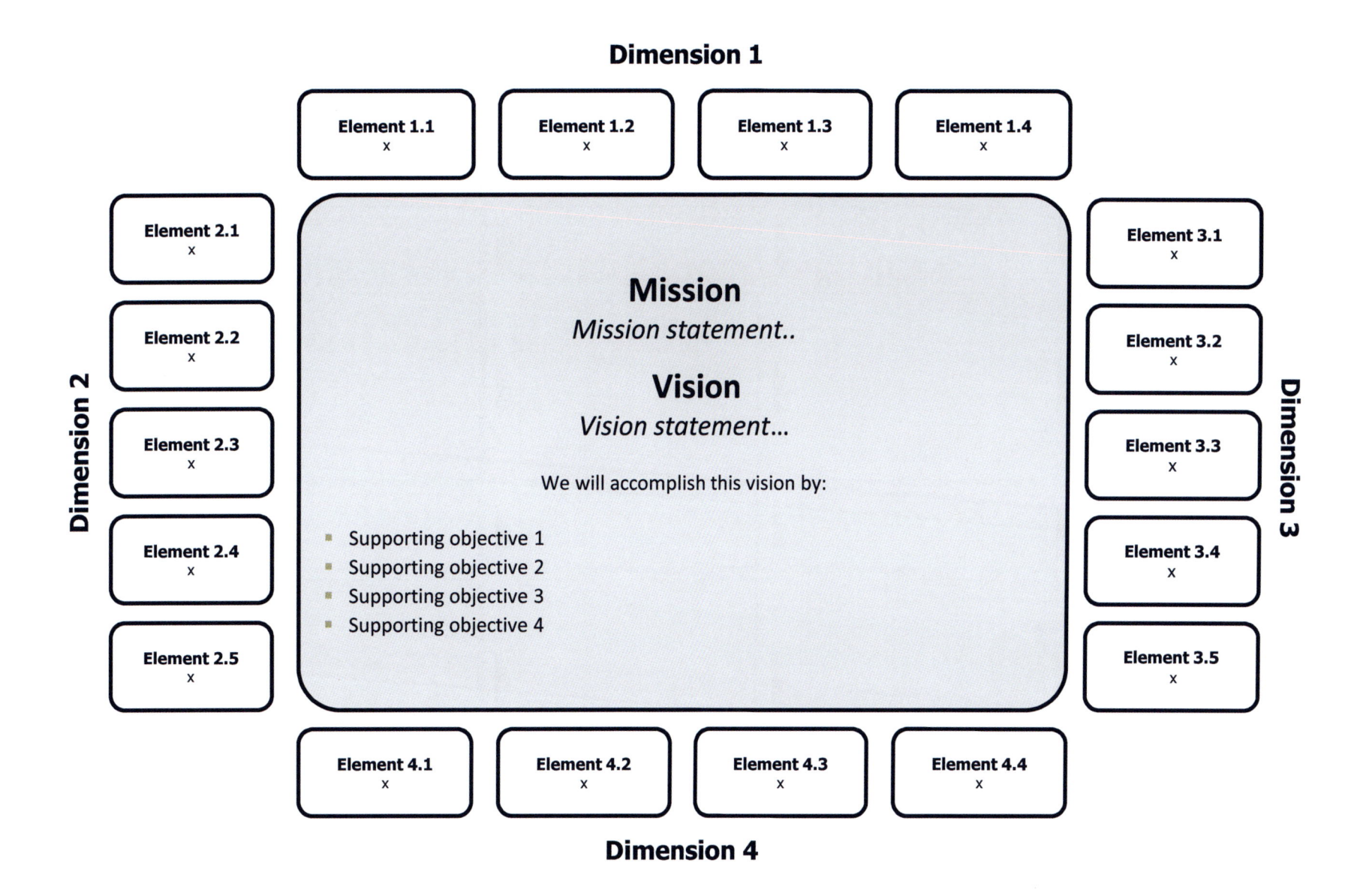

Dimension 1

| Element 1.1 x | Element 1.2 x | Element 1.3 x | Element 1.4 x |

Dimension 2

- Element 2.1 x
- Element 2.2 x
- Element 2.3 x
- Element 2.4 x
- Element 2.5 x

Dimension 3

- Element 3.1 x
- Element 3.2 x
- Element 3.3 x
- Element 3.4 x
- Element 3.5 x

Mission
Mission statement..

Vision
Vision statement…

We will accomplish this vision by:

- Supporting objective 1
- Supporting objective 2
- Supporting objective 3
- Supporting objective 4

Dimension 4

| Element 4.1 x | Element 4.2 x | Element 4.3 x | Element 4.4 x |

Communications Plan

Plan and deliver clear communications to business stakeholders to help manage transformational change

Communications Plan – Overview

What is it

The Communications Plan is a proven, effective template for structuring and planning communications with key stakeholders impacted by a business transformation program. It allows a project manager and change manager to plan and prepare for the key messages that need to be delivered to stakeholders over the course of a transformation program, with messages aligned in timing and content with the key activities and milestones of the program.

When to use it

The Communications Plan should be developed initially during the project planning phase and reviewed, kept current, updated regularly as the milestones and activities are adjusted and messages to stakeholders are refined and delivered. The best practice approach for effective use of the communications plan is for a regular meeting to be held between project sponsor, project manager, change manager and communications specialist to review plans, milestones, messages and communications.

Why use it

The value of effective communications in a transformation program cannot be overstated. It plays an essential role in the success of any program through the establishment of clear channels of communication and targeted messages to key stakeholders who need to be aware, engaged, accepting and adopting changes being delivered. This template is a proven framework for helping programs structure and manage their communications plan.

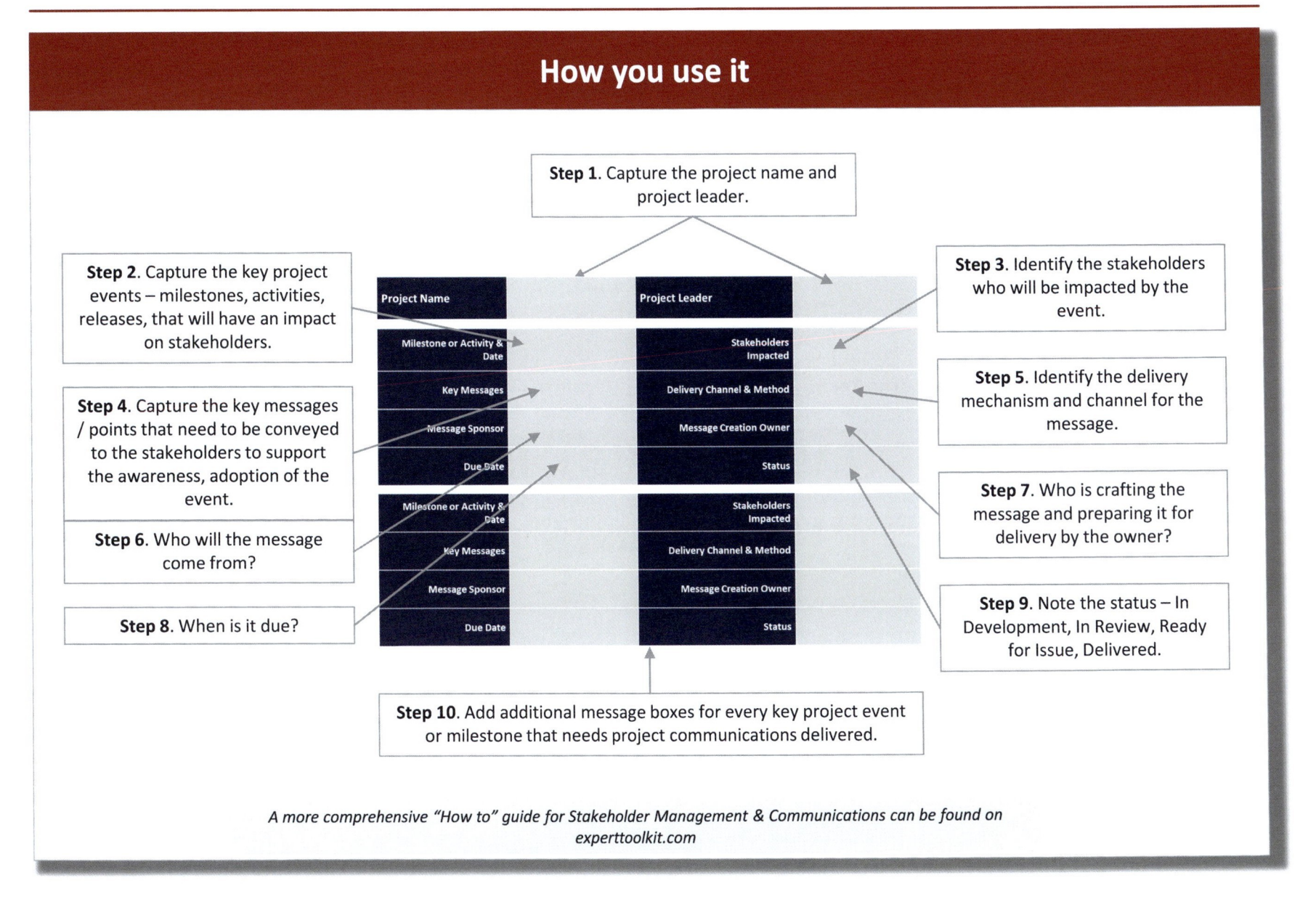

Communications Plan – Method

How you use it

Step 1. Capture the project name and project leader.

Step 2. Capture the key project events – milestones, activities, releases, that will have an impact on stakeholders.

Step 3. Identify the stakeholders who will be impacted by the event.

Step 4. Capture the key messages / points that need to be conveyed to the stakeholders to support the awareness, adoption of the event.

Step 5. Identify the delivery mechanism and channel for the message.

Step 6. Who will the message come from?

Step 7. Who is crafting the message and preparing it for delivery by the owner?

Step 8. When is it due?

Step 9. Note the status – In Development, In Review, Ready for Issue, Delivered.

Step 10. Add additional message boxes for every key project event or milestone that needs project communications delivered.

Project Name		Project Leader	
Milestone or Activity & Date		Stakeholders Impacted	
Key Messages		Delivery Channel & Method	
Message Sponsor		Message Creation Owner	
Due Date		Status	
Milestone or Activity & Date		Stakeholders Impacted	
Key Messages		Delivery Channel & Method	
Message Sponsor		Message Creation Owner	
Due Date		Status	

A more comprehensive "How to" guide for Stakeholder Management & Communications can be found on experttoolkit.com

Communications Plan – Template

Project Name		**Project Leader**	
Milestone or Activity & Date		**Stakeholders Impacted**	
Key Messages		**Delivery Channel & Method**	
Message Sponsor		**Message Creation Owner**	
Due Date		**Status**	
Milestone or Activity & Date		**Stakeholders Impacted**	
Key Messages		**Delivery Channel & Method**	
Message Sponsor		**Message Creation Owner**	
Due Date		**Status**	

Operating Model Template

A user-friendly, proven and configurable template for capturing and representing a business operating model

Operating Model Template – Overview

What is it

The Operating Model Template is framework for taking some of the mystery and struggle out of putting an operating model down on paper. People often find it difficult to draw a single-page operating model to suitably represent the current or future state of a business, organization or function. The Operating Model Template is aimed at making this easier by including the typical, core components of a good operating model and allowing the effort to go into modifying the model and populating the components to suit.

When to use it

The Operating Model Template can be used in two situations, primarily: 1) to articulate the current state of a business (to summarize the operation at the highest level in a current-state business analysis or review) or; 2) a target operating model which might be articulated as part of a transformation design phase, which would seek to clearly describe the future state aspirational state and structure of the business, process or organization. The template can be built during a workshop or in an offline mode.

Why use it

The Operating Model Template will save you time and frustration when looking to describe a business operating model. It is highly versatile in its application as well as being infinitely configurable to suit the needs of the situation. The Operating Model Template will work for all but the most complex operating model exercises and will allow the user to focus on the contents and engagement with stakeholders rather than worrying about "a good layout". This structure just works and works well.

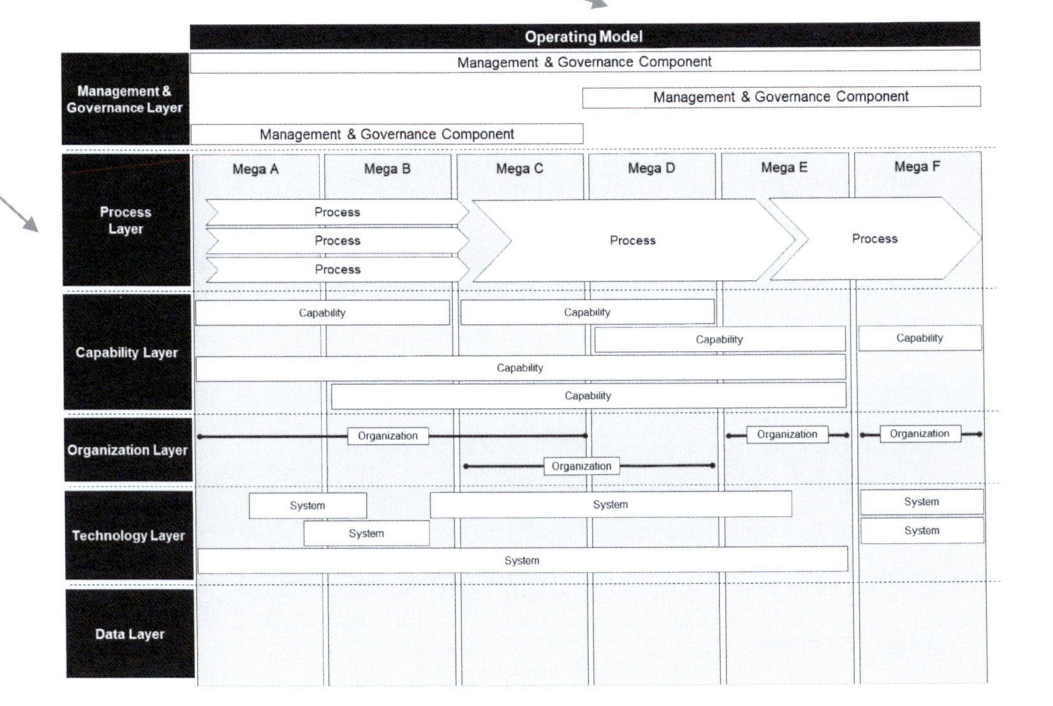

Operating Model Template – Method

How you use it

Step 1. Give the operating model a name, for example "Regional Manufacturing Operating Model"

Step 2. Choose the layers that are most applicable to the scope, context and purpose of the operating model. See below for other layer options. Order the layers in a logical sequence from "highest" or top level to "lowest".

Other Layer Options
- Product
- Customer
- Geography
- Market
- Division
- Region
- Channel
- Sector
- Supplier
- Knowledge
- Regulation

Operating Model

Management & Governance Layer	Management & Governance Component / Management & Governance Component / Management & Governance Component
Process Layer	Mega A, Mega B, Mega C, Mega D, Mega E, Mega F — Processes
Capability Layer	Capability (multiple)
Organization Layer	Organization (multiple)
Technology Layer	System (multiple)
Data Layer	

Operating Model Template – Method

How you use it

Step 3. Choose a primary layer to anchor the model. This layer should be segmented in relevant components which will then be used to inform how other layers of the operating model relate to the primary layer. In this example model, the process layer is the primary – which has been broken into 6 mega process steps and process flows added to these mega steps. The rest of the model will align to the mega process steps and process flows

Operating Model

Management & Governance Layer	Management & Governance Component (spanning); Management & Governance Component; Management & Governance Component
Process Layer	Mega A, Mega B, Mega C, Mega D, Mega E, Mega F — with Process flows across
Capability Layer	Capability blocks spanning various Megas
Organization Layer	Organization blocks across Megas
Technology Layer	System blocks across Megas
Data Layer	

Step 4. For each layer, add the components that make up that layer and align them appropriately with the primary layer and other related layers.

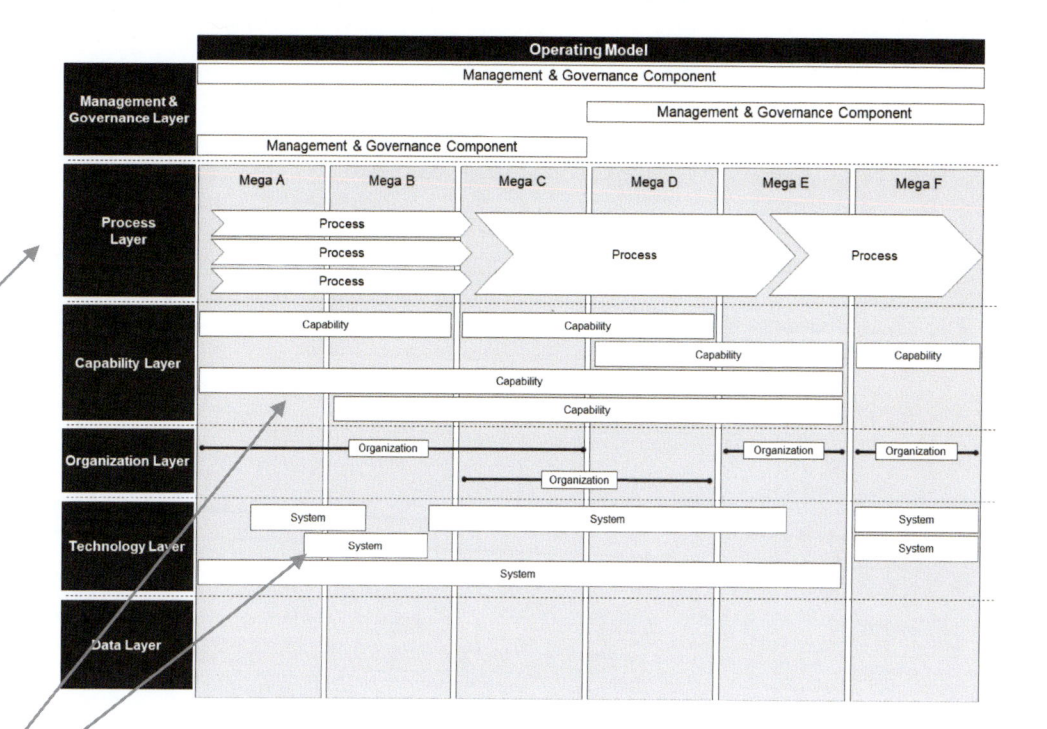

When looking at the model from top to bottom, it should be clear how the components work together as an integrated whole.

Subsequent panels / pages should be utilized where necessary to describe each layer and the components within each layer.

In this example, we can see the mega process steps (value chain) that is being delivered, how management oversees this value chain, what capabilities within the business support the value chain, what parts of the organization are involved and what systems and data elements.

Operating Model Template – Example

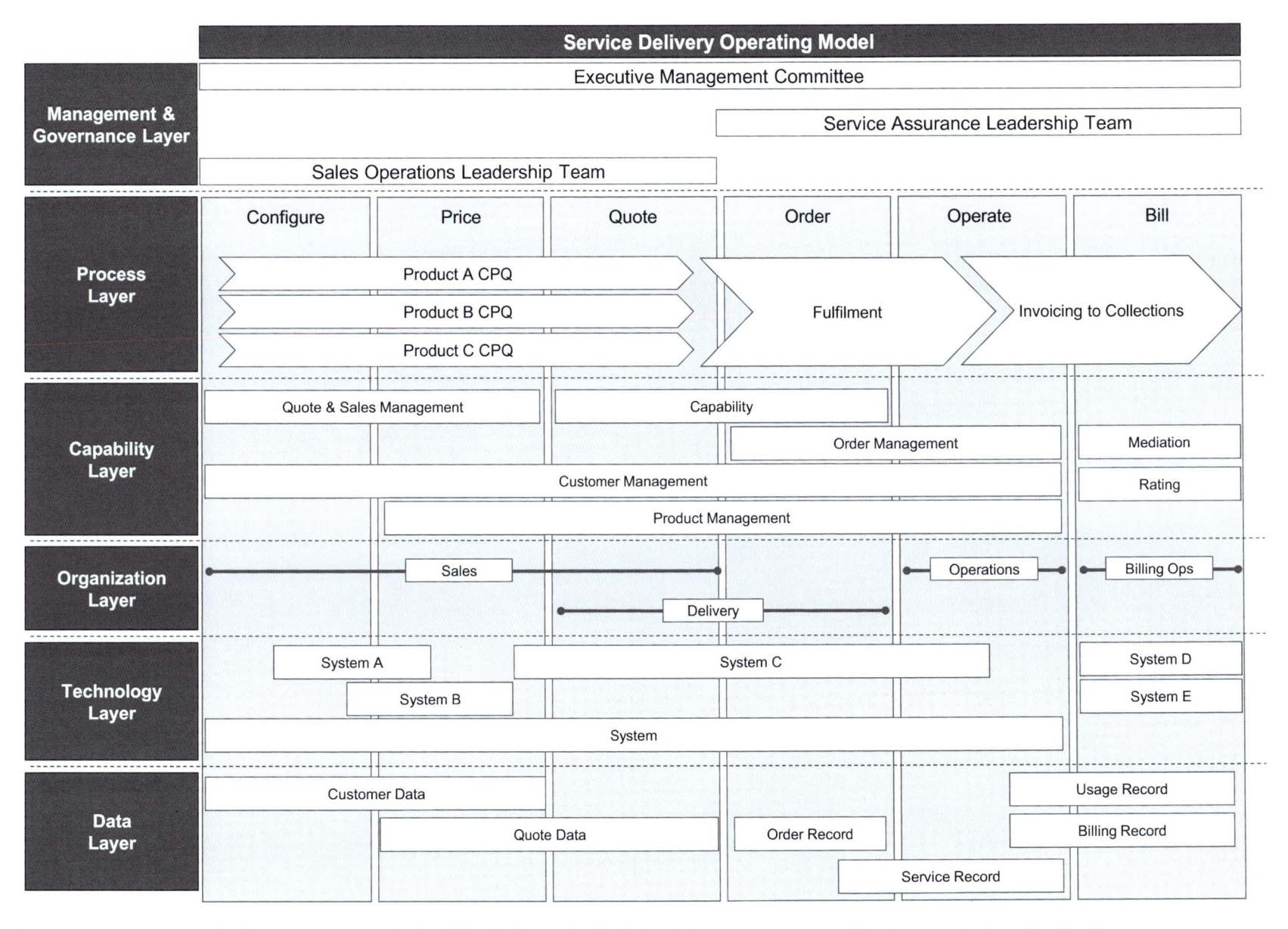

Service Delivery Operating Model

Management & Governance Layer	Executive Management Committee (spans all); Sales Operations Leadership Team (left); Service Assurance Leadership Team (right)					

Process Layer

Configure	Price	Quote	Order	Operate	Bill
Product A CPQ			Fulfilment		Invoicing to Collections
Product B CPQ					
Product C CPQ					

Capability Layer

- Quote & Sales Management (Configure–Quote)
- Capability (Order–Operate)
- Order Management (Order–Operate)
- Mediation (Bill)
- Customer Management (spans Configure–Operate)
- Rating (Bill)
- Product Management (spans Price–Operate)

Organization Layer

- Sales (Configure–Quote)
- Operations (Operate)
- Billing Ops (Bill)
- Delivery (Quote–Order)

Technology Layer

- System A (Configure–Price)
- System C (Quote–Operate)
- System D (Bill)
- System B (Price)
- System E (Bill)
- System (spans all)

Data Layer

- Customer Data (Configure–Price)
- Usage Record (Bill)
- Quote Data (Price–Quote)
- Order Record (Order)
- Billing Record (Bill)
- Service Record (Operate)

Operating Model Template – Template

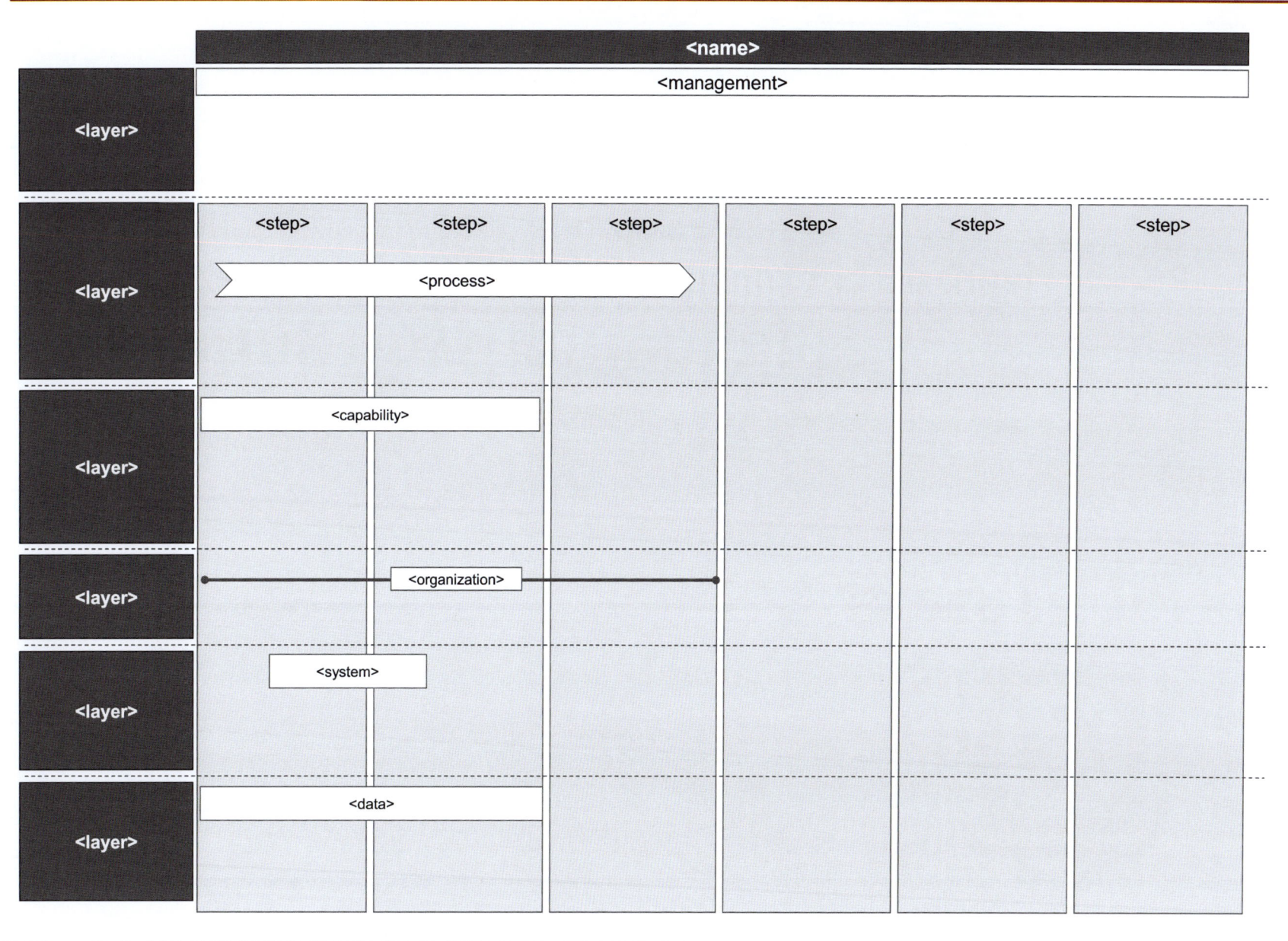

	<name>
<layer>	<management>

	<step>	<step>	<step>	<step>	<step>	<step>
<layer>	<process> →					
<layer>	<capability>					
<layer>	<organization>					
<layer>	<system>					
<layer>	<data>					

Operating Rhythm Template

A proven best-practice format for outlining the essential management meeting and reporting cycles in a high performance organization

Operating Rhythm Template – Overview

What is it

The Operating Rhythm Template is a proven layout for depicting the organization forums and meetings essential for driving organizational objectives. An Operating Rhythm should encapsulate the operating cadence of an organization, transformation program, division or discipline. Looked at holistically, a good operating rhythm will represent the "routine" of the business and should show how governance, management, controls, processes, functions, disciplines come together routinely to drive performance.

When to use it

The Operating Rhythm Template can be used to "insert" greater operational discipline into an existing business or unit – by designing the forums that need to occur to deliver the objectives of the business. It can also be used to review and streamline / rationalize existing forums. The Operating Rhythm Template can also be used as part of a business transformation program to show how a future state operating model (or components) will come to life through the regular cadence of forums and meeting bodies.

Why use it

Every business, division, function or transformation program should have a clear and optimized operating rhythm aimed at driving objectives and supporting "strategy to execution" effectively and efficiently. The Operating Rhythm Template is a proven format for driving operational excellence and helping leaders design a daily/weekly/monthly/quarterly/yearly cadence that is simple but effective.

Operating Rhythm Template – Method

How you use it

Step 1. Decide the appropriate layers that need to be covered by the operating rhythm. These can be organizational levels, functions, divisions.

Step 2. Decide how many operating frequencies need to be represented and capture these.

Step 3. Identify all forums and meetings that need to occur within the operating rhythm and for each one, indicate where it sits in terms of level (step 1) and frequency (step 2).

Step 4. For each forum, indicate the objective, chair and attendees.

Step 5. Indicate the information flows from one forum to another.

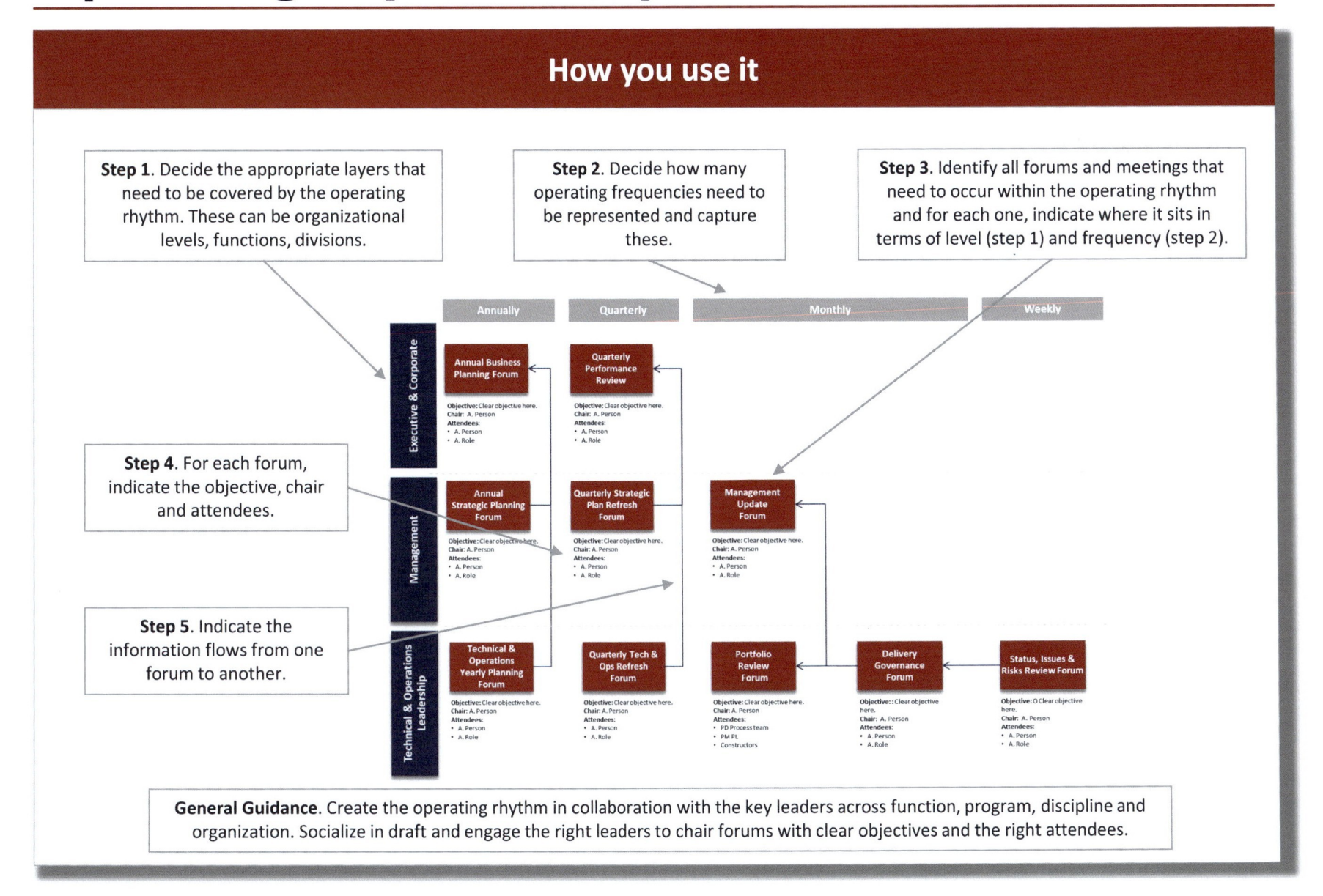

	Annually	Quarterly	Monthly	Weekly
Executive & Corporate	Annual Business Planning Forum	Quarterly Performance Review		
Management	Annual Strategic Planning Forum	Quarterly Strategic Plan Refresh Forum	Management Update Forum	
Technical & Operations Leadership	Technical & Operations Yearly Planning Forum	Quarterly Tech & Ops Refresh Forum	Portfolio Review Forum	Delivery Governance Forum / Status, Issues & Risks Review Forum

For each forum:
- **Objective:** Clear objective here.
- **Chair:** A. Person
- **Attendees:**
  - A. Person
  - A. Role

(Portfolio Review Forum attendees: PD Process team, PM PL, Constructors)

General Guidance. Create the operating rhythm in collaboration with the key leaders across function, program, discipline and organization. Socialize in draft and engage the right leaders to chair forums with clear objectives and the right attendees.

Operating Rhythm Template – Example

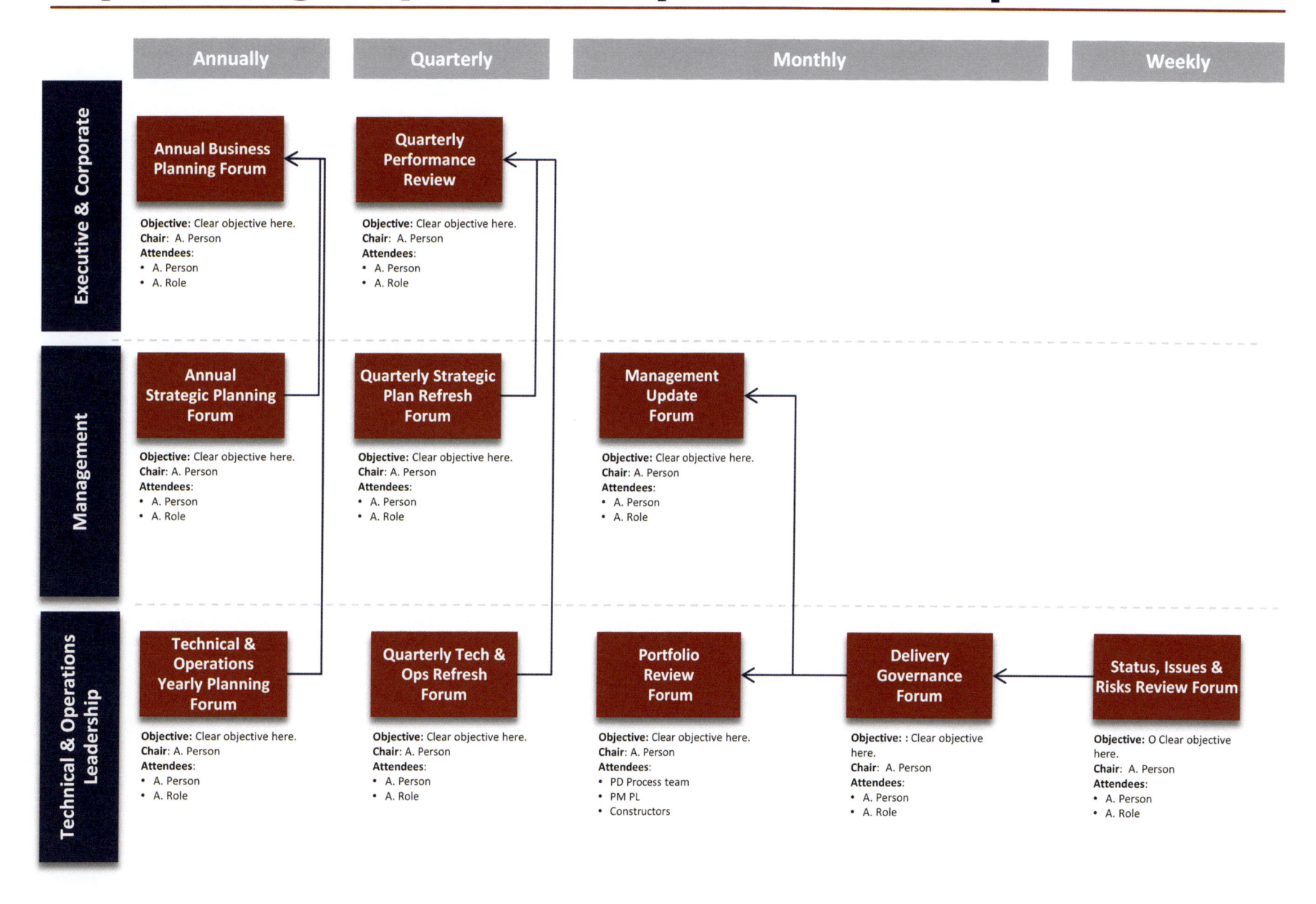

	Annually	Quarterly	Monthly	Weekly

Executive & Corporate

Annual Business Planning Forum
- **Objective:** Clear objective here.
- **Chair:** A. Person
- **Attendees:**
  - A. Person
  - A. Role

Quarterly Performance Review
- **Objective:** Clear objective here.
- **Chair:** A. Person
- **Attendees:**
  - A. Person
  - A. Role

Management

Annual Strategic Planning Forum
- **Objective:** Clear objective here.
- **Chair:** A. Person
- **Attendees:**
  - A. Person
  - A. Role

Quarterly Strategic Plan Refresh Forum
- **Objective:** Clear objective here.
- **Chair:** A. Person
- **Attendees:**
  - A. Person
  - A. Role

Management Update Forum
- **Objective:** Clear objective here.
- **Chair:** A. Person
- **Attendees:**
  - A. Person
  - A. Role

Technical & Operations Leadership

Technical & Operations Yearly Planning Forum
- **Objective:** Clear objective here.
- **Chair:** A. Person
- **Attendees:**
  - A. Person
  - A. Role

Quarterly Tech & Ops Refresh Forum
- **Objective:** Clear objective here.
- **Chair:** A. Person
- **Attendees:**
  - A. Person
  - A. Role

Portfolio Review Forum
- **Objective:** Clear objective here.
- **Chair:** A. Person
- **Attendees:**
  - PD Process team
  - PM PL
  - Constructors

Delivery Governance Forum
- **Objective:** : Clear objective here.
- **Chair:** A. Person
- **Attendees:**
  - A. Person
  - A. Role

Status, Issues & Risks Review Forum
- **Objective:** O Clear objective here.
- **Chair:** A. Person
- **Attendees:**
  - A. Person
  - A. Role

Organization Impact Assessment

A concise framework for assessing the impact of a transformation on an organization across 8 key dimensions

Organization Impact Assessment – Overview

What is it

The Organization Impact Assessment Template is a concise framework for assessing the extent to which an organization (group, team, function) will be impacted by a transformation program. It allows the user to assess the degree of impact across 8 key and proven dimensions. Based on this assessment, the user can then define strategies and tactics to ensure the organizational change is implemented successfully with changes understood, prepared for and risks mitigated effectively.

When to use it

The Organization Impact Assessment Template is best used after a future state operating model has been designed or after a future state organization architecture or design has been completed. The impact assessment can also be created iteratively, during operating model definition and to a greater level of detail and confidence once the organization design has been produced. It is also important to feed in the results of the organization impact assessment into the organization design process itself to ensure likely impacts are considered when looking to create an optimal design.

Why use it

When delivering any business transformation it is critical to understand the impacts to each and every business unit, function and team. With this knowledge, appropriate change management actions or design changes can be incorporated to ensure that the transformation is successful. This template is simple to use and will help any practitioner assess organizational impact across the 8 key dimensions.

Organization Impact Assessment – Method

How you use it

Step 1. For the current state organization, describe the organization across the 8 key dimensions. Provide clear descriptions for the organization as it currently stands across these areas.

Step 2. Across the same dimensions, describe how the future state organization will need to operate in order to be successful after the transformation.

Step 3. Indicate the degree of impact to the organization across each of the dimensions that will result from the change from current state to future state.

Step 4. Capture the actions that need to occur across each dimension in order to support a successful transformation.

Organizational Assessment Dimensions	As-Is	To-Be	Extent of Impact (H/M/L)	Transformation Actions Required
Communication Channels & Methods				
Key Reporting Lines				
Allocation of Resources				
Location of Resources				
Key Skill Areas				
Ways of Working & Culture				
Hand-Offs Between Teams and Groups				
Degree of Inter-Group Engagement & Cooperation				
Other Key Points				

Step 5. Repeat this exercise for all organizations / teams / units / functions impacted and capture actions in the change management strategy / plan.

Step 6. Where necessary, make design adjustments to minimize the extent or organizational impact expected.

Organization Impact Assessment – Template

Organizational Assessment Dimensions	As-Is	To-Be	Extent of Impact (H/M/L)	Transformation Actions Required
Communication Channels & Methods				
Key Reporting Lines				
Allocation of Resources				
Location of Resources				
Key Skill Areas				
Ways of Working & Culture				
Hand-Offs Between Teams and Groups				
Degree of Inter-Group Engagement & Cooperation				
Other Key Points				

Project Evaluation Template

A proven framework for capturing essential project information to facilitate planning and prioritization

Project Evaluation Template – Overview

What is it

The Project Evaluation Template is a proven, structured layout for specifying a program or project aimed at delivering performance improvement and benefits to a business. The template consists of a concise structure for capturing the information necessary to assess, prioritize and plan a portfolio of business improvement initiatives which may be delivered as part of a broader business transformation program or portfolio.

When to use it

The Project Evaluation Template is ideally suited for use at the conclusion of a business diagnostic exercise when a transformation program is being shaped and planned. These programs typically consist of multiple projects requiring investment commitment and prioritization. The template can also be used as part of a yearly performance improvement cycle to plan and prioritize the improvement initiatives that a business wishes to undertake in order to accomplish specific performance targets.

Why use it

To facilitate effective decision making, planning and prioritization of transformation initiatives (or business initiatives in general) it is essential to capture critical information – both qualitative and quantitative. This template helps facilitate uniform data capture across initiatives which allows a consistent lens to be applied for assessment purposes. This evaluation template can be used to gather the necessary information for initiatives to be assessed using the Transformation Initiative Prioritization Tool.

Project Evaluation Template – Method

How you use it

Step 0. For each project in a portfolio or program, complete this template.

Step 1. Capture the basic information on the project including sponsor, lead, impacted areas.

Step 2. Provide project background and a concise summary of the projects objectives.

Step 3. Summarize the project scope (key activities, deliverables, milestones), implementation approach and indicate the level of effort.

Step 4. Capture the key financial information including cost (CapEx, OpEx) and benefits.

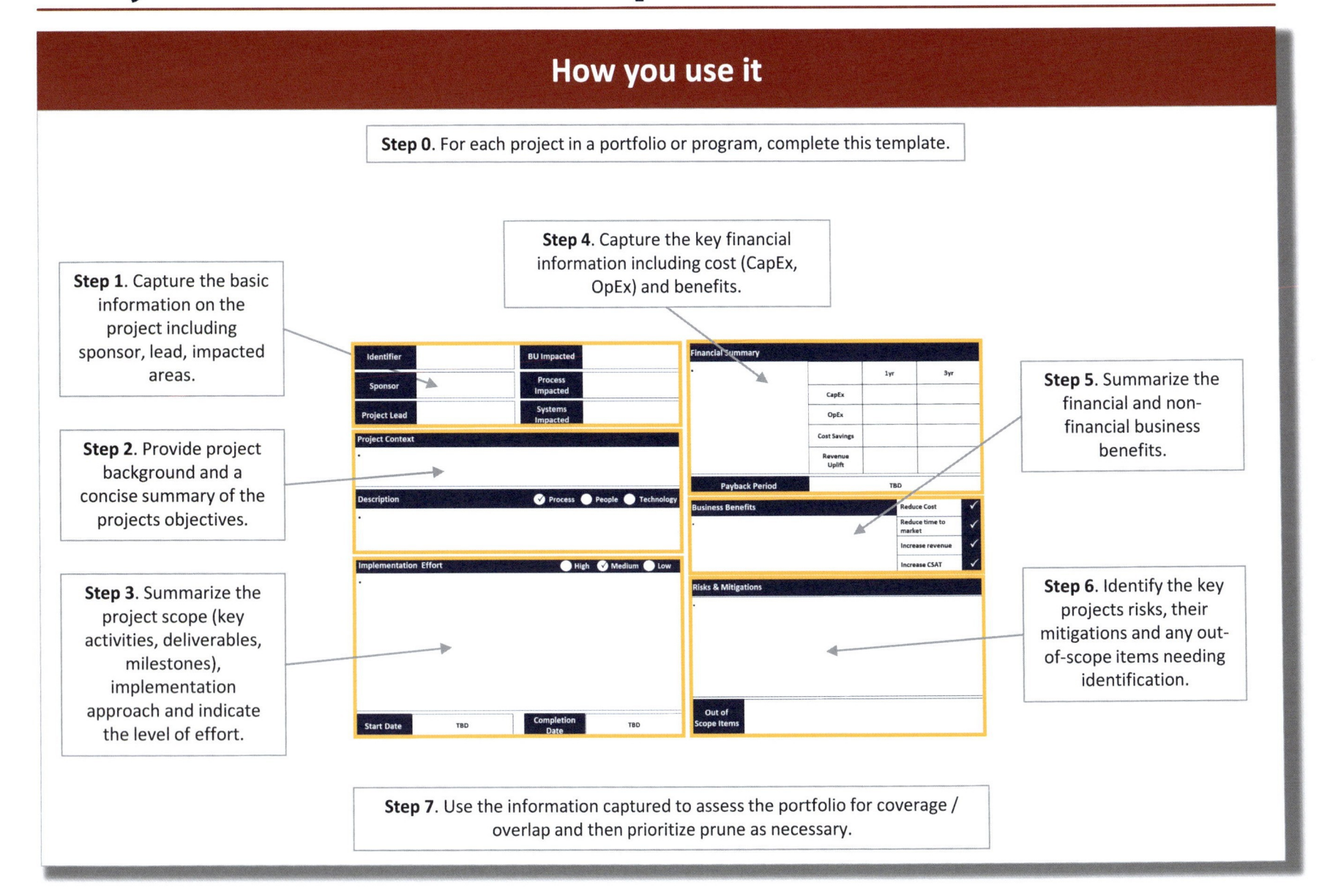

Step 5. Summarize the financial and non-financial business benefits.

Step 6. Identify the key projects risks, their mitigations and any out-of-scope items needing identification.

Step 7. Use the information captured to assess the portfolio for coverage / overlap and then prioritize prune as necessary.

Project Evaluation Template – Template

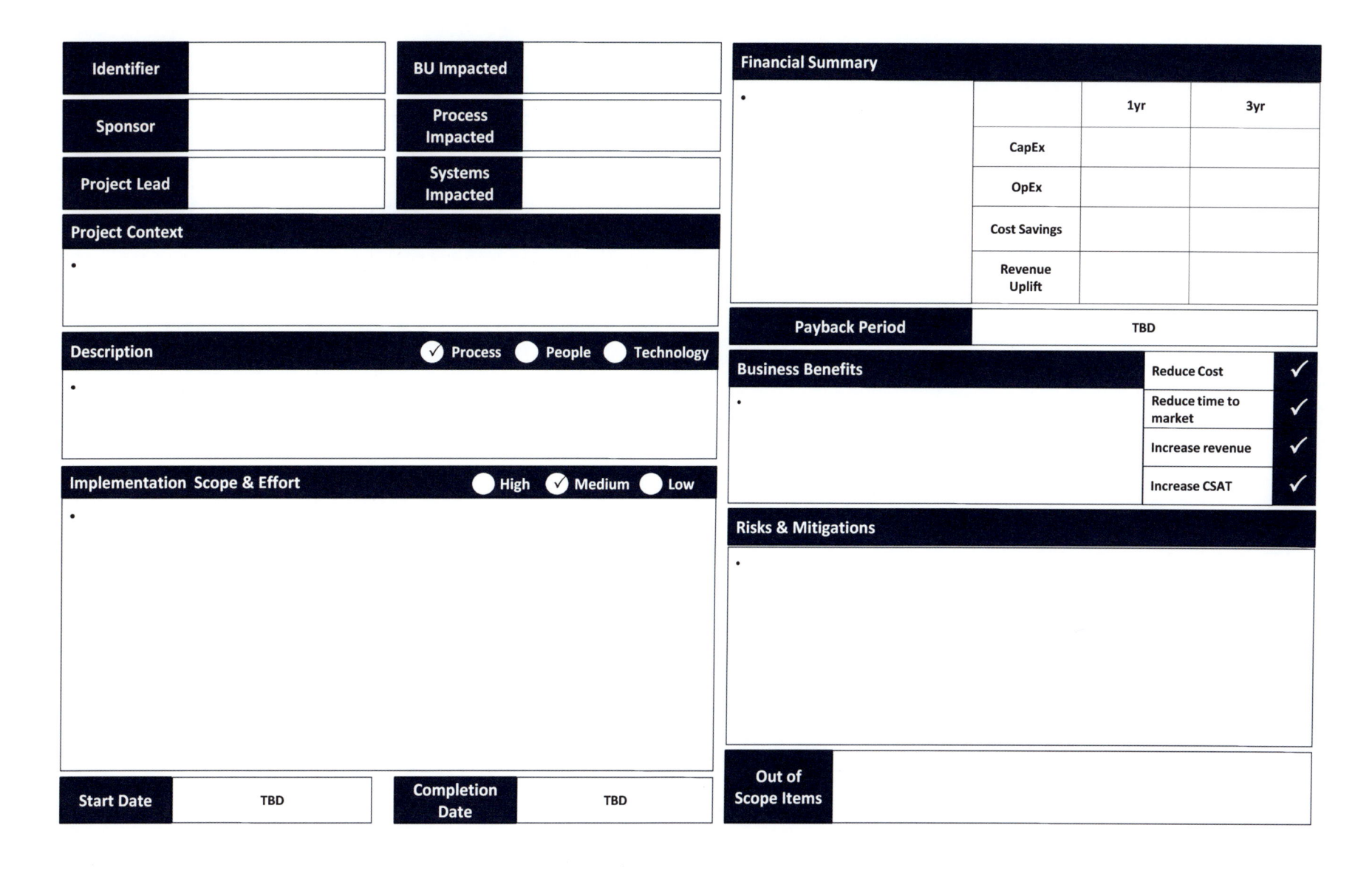

Identifier	
Sponsor	
Project Lead	

BU Impacted	
Process Impacted	
Systems Impacted	

Project Context

-

Description

(✓) Process ( ) People ( ) Technology

-

Implementation Scope & Effort

( ) High (✓) Medium ( ) Low

-

Start Date	TBD

Completion Date	TBD

Financial Summary

-

	1yr	3yr
CapEx		
OpEx		
Cost Savings		
Revenue Uplift		

Payback Period	TBD

Business Benefits

-

Reduce Cost	✓
Reduce time to market	✓
Increase revenue	✓
Increase CSAT	✓

Risks & Mitigations

-

Out of Scope Items	

Project Issues Register

A concise and proven template for capturing and presenting business project issues

Project Issues Register – Overview

What is it

The Project Issues Register is a proven, concise template for capturing the issues that are encountered during the delivery of a business initiative. The template allows the project leader and other team members to capture and report on the key issues impacting the delivery of a business initiative's objectives, activities and deliverables.

When to use it

The Project Issues Register Template is intended to be used during project delivery for capturing issues raised by team members and stakeholders. It also complements the Project Status Report during project communications, governance and reporting. Depending on the complexity of the project, a more sophisticated issues repository may be required in addition to this template. In this situation, the Project Issues Register Template is still very effective at communicating the key issues to an executive audience.

Why use it

It is essential during any project to effectively and efficiently capturing and report project issues to ensure timely and appropriate resolution. Oftentimes, project teams do not do this well, or do it in a way that makes it overly complex and cumbersome. The Project Issues Register template is proven at making this process simple, easy to use and effective at helping teams and projects focus on the most significant issues likely to impact the delivery of targeted outcomes.

Project Issues Register – Method

How you use it

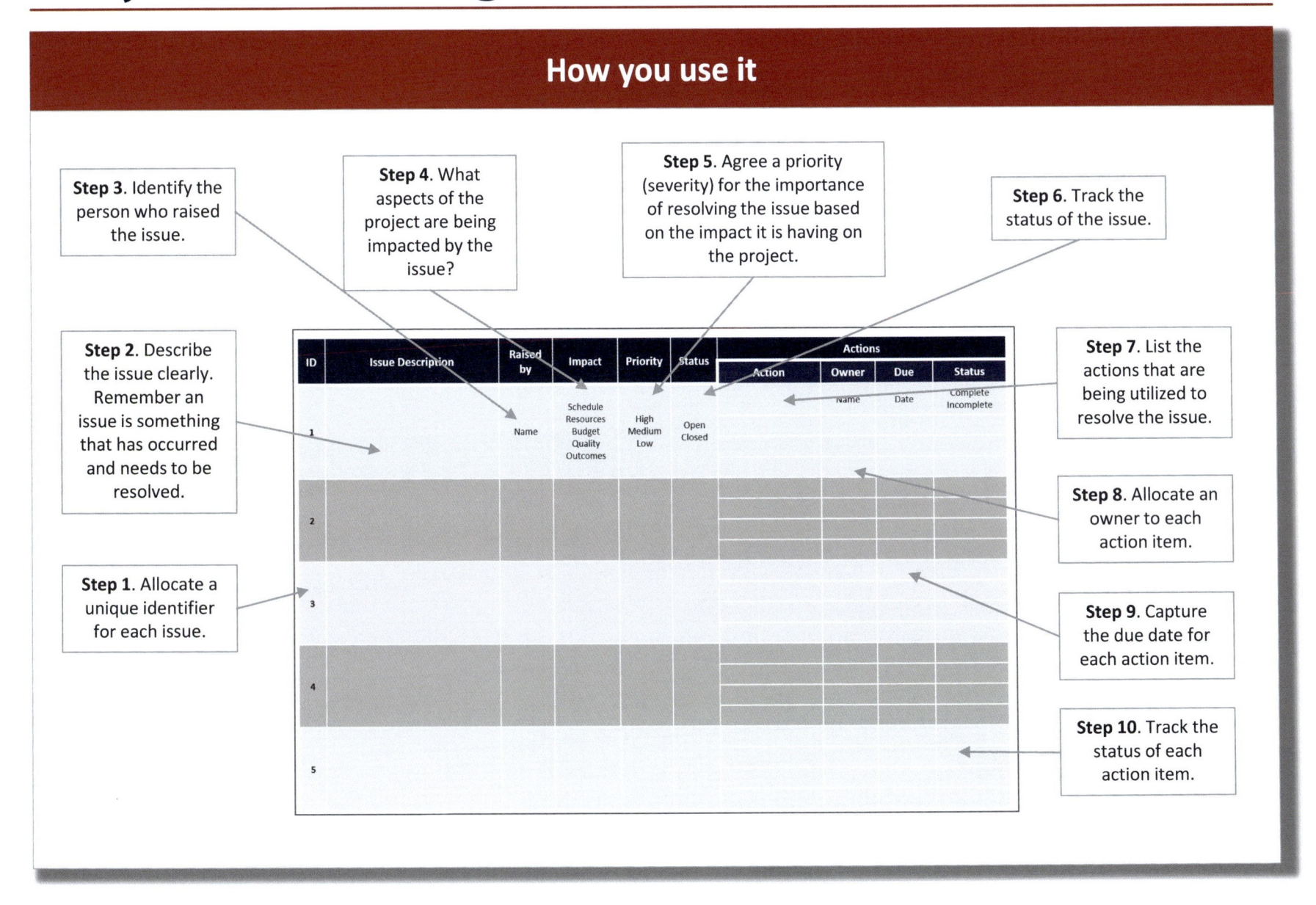

Step 3. Identify the person who raised the issue.

Step 4. What aspects of the project are being impacted by the issue?

Step 5. Agree a priority (severity) for the importance of resolving the issue based on the impact it is having on the project.

Step 6. Track the status of the issue.

Step 2. Describe the issue clearly. Remember an issue is something that has occurred and needs to be resolved.

Step 7. List the actions that are being utilized to resolve the issue.

Step 1. Allocate a unique identifier for each issue.

Step 8. Allocate an owner to each action item.

Step 9. Capture the due date for each action item.

Step 10. Track the status of each action item.

ID	Issue Description	Raised by	Impact	Priority	Status	Actions			
						Action	Owner	Due	Status
1		Name	Schedule Resources Budget Quality Outcomes	High Medium Low	Open Closed		Name	Date	Complete Incomplete
2									
3									
4									
5									

Project Issues Register – Template

ID	Issue Description	Raised by	Impact	Priority	Status	Actions			
						Action	Owner	Due	Status
1		Name	Schedule Resources Budget Quality Outcomes	High Medium Low	Open Closed		Name	Date	Complete Incomplete
2									
3									
4									
5									

Project Risk Register

A concise and proven template for capturing and presenting business project risks

Project Risk Register – Overview

What is it

The Project Risk Register is a proven, concise template for capturing the risks that may be experienced during the delivery of a business initiative. The template allows the project leader and other team members to capture and report on the key risks that have the potential to impact the delivery of a business initiative's objectives, activities and deliverables.

When to use it

The Project Risk Register Template is intended to be used during project delivery for capturing risks raised by team members and stakeholders. It also complements the Project Status Report during project communications, governance and reporting. Depending on the complexity of the project, a more sophisticated risk register may be required in addition to this template. In this situation, the Project Risk Register Template is still very effective at communicating the key risks to an executive audience.

Why use it

It is essential during any project to effectively and efficiently capturing and report project risks to ensure timely and appropriate mitigation. Oftentimes, project teams do not do this well, or do it in a way that makes it overly complex and cumbersome. The Project Risk Register template is proven at making this process simple, easy to use and effective at helping teams and projects focus on the most material risks that have the potential to impact the delivery of targeted outcomes.

Project Risk Register – Method

How you use it

Step 1. Allocate a unique identifier for each risk

Step 2. Describe the risk. Remember a risk is something that might happen, but has not yet happened.

Step 3. Identify the owner of the risk. Typically this is the person responsible for mitigating the risk

Step 4. If the risk did materialize, how severe would the impact be?

Step 5. How likely is the risk to occur?

Step 6. What aspect of the project would be impacted if the risk was to eventuate?

Step 7. Track the status of the risk.

Step 8. List the strategies / actions that will be employed to mitigate the risk

Step 9. Allocate an owner to each strategy / mitigation action

Step 10. Track the status of each mitigation strategy / action

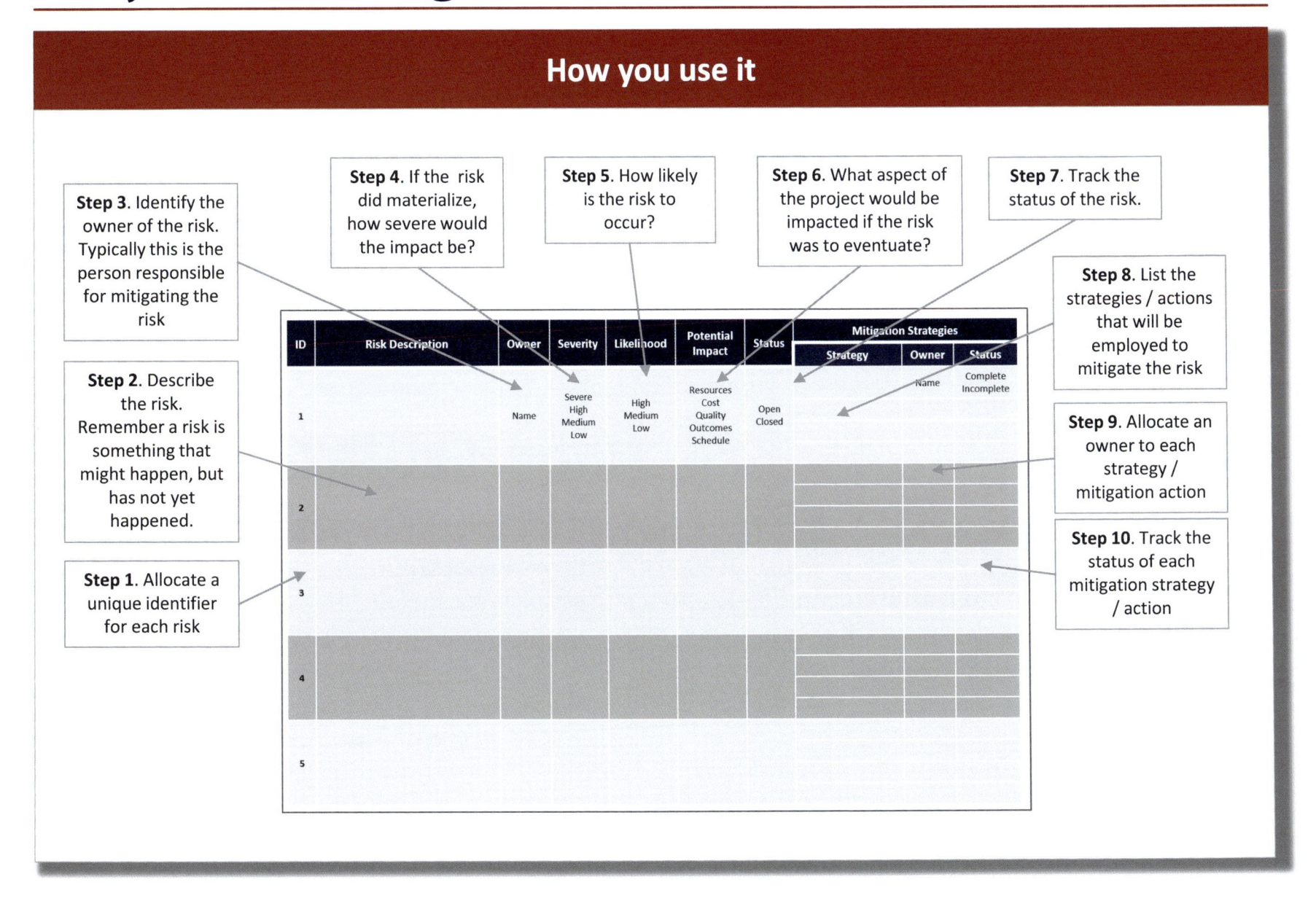

ID	Risk Description	Owner	Severity	Likelihood	Potential Impact	Status	Mitigation Strategies		
							Strategy	Owner	Status
1		Name	Severe / High / Medium / Low	High / Medium / Low	Resources / Cost / Quality / Outcomes / Schedule	Open / Closed		Name	Complete / Incomplete
2									
3									
4									
5									

Project Risk Register – Template

ID	Risk Description	Owner	Severity	Likelihood	Potential Impact	Status	Mitigation Strategies		
							Strategy	Owner	Status
1		Name	Severe High Medium Low	High Medium Low	Resources Cost Quality Outcomes Schedule	Open Closed		Name	Complete Incomplete
2									
3									
4									
5									

Project Status Report

A concise and proven format for providing executive project status updates to key stakeholders

Project Status Report – Overview

What is it

The Project Status Report Template is a concise and clear layout for reporting regular status updates to sponsors and other stakeholders for a business analysis, improvement or transformation initiative.

When to use it

Use the template on a regular basis (weekly is recommended) during a business analysis, improvement or transformation project to provide updates and progress reports to sponsors and stakeholders.

Why use it

In any business initiative it is imperative to provide regular and concise updates to stakeholders with information on scope, activities, deliverables, risks, issues and progress. This template is proven to be effective at providing these updates.

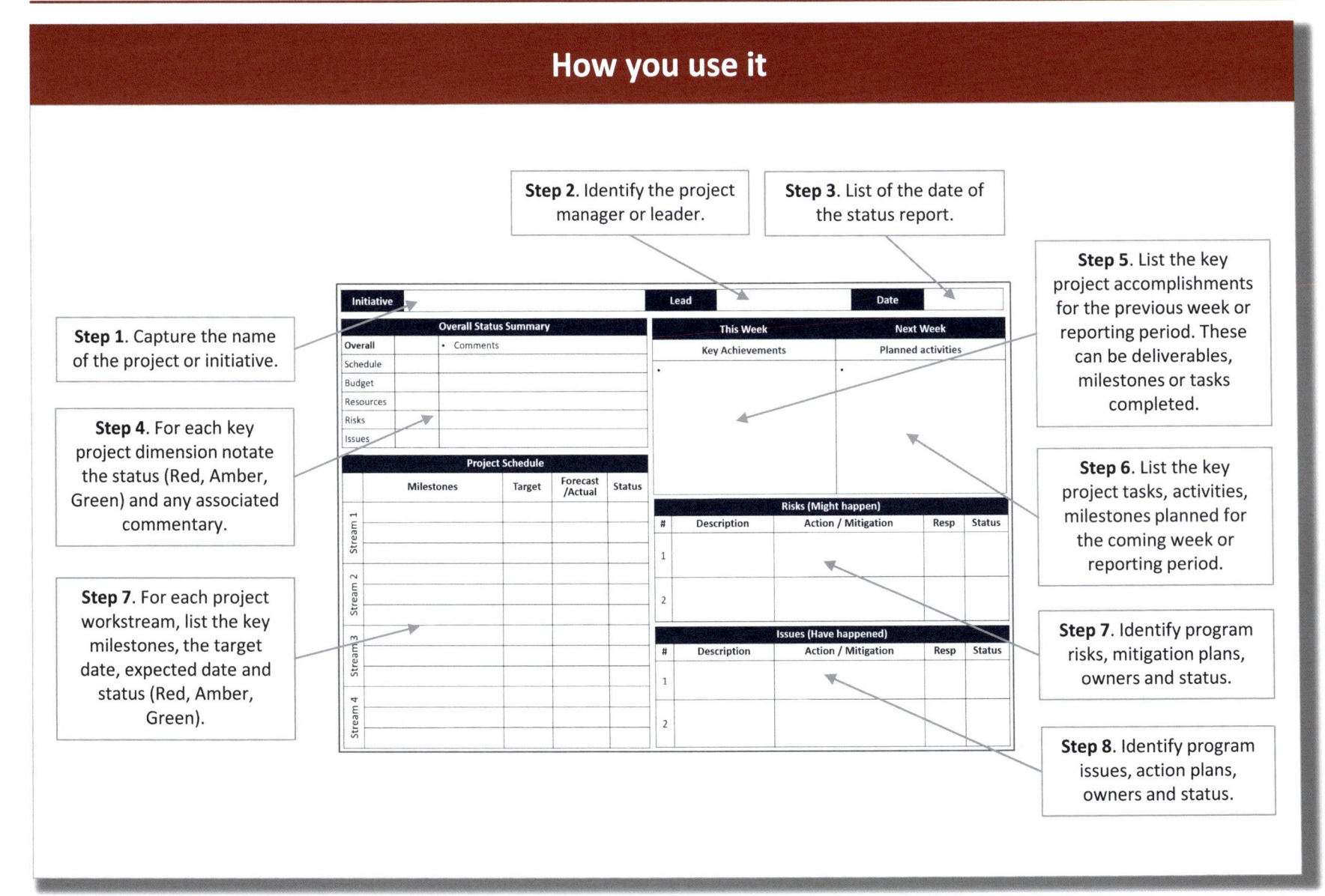

Project Status Report – Method

How you use it

Step 1. Capture the name of the project or initiative.

Step 2. Identify the project manager or leader.

Step 3. List of the date of the status report.

Step 4. For each key project dimension notate the status (Red, Amber, Green) and any associated commentary.

Step 5. List the key project accomplishments for the previous week or reporting period. These can be deliverables, milestones or tasks completed.

Step 6. List the key project tasks, activities, milestones planned for the coming week or reporting period.

Step 7. For each project workstream, list the key milestones, the target date, expected date and status (Red, Amber, Green).

Step 7. Identify program risks, mitigation plans, owners and status.

Step 8. Identify program issues, action plans, owners and status.

Project Status Report – Template

Initiative		Lead		Date	

Overall Status Summary

Overall		Comments
Schedule		
Budget		
Resources		
Risks		
Issues		

Project Schedule

	Milestones	Target	Forecast /Actual	Status
Stream 1				
Stream 2				
Stream 3				
Stream 4				

This Week / Next Week

This Week	Next Week
Key Achievements	Planned activities
•	•

Risks (Might happen)

#	Description	Action / Mitigation	Resp	Status
1				
2				

Issues (Have happened)

#	Description	Action / Mitigation	Resp	Status
1				
2				

Project Executive Update Template

A concise format for providing a business improvement project summary update to key senior stakeholders

Project Update Template – Overview

What is it

The Project Update Template is a simple, concise format template for communicating essential information to key stakeholders regarding progress, findings and benefits delivered as part of a business improvement initiative. It is complementary to the Project Status Update Template, however the Project Update Template is broader, provides additional context and focuses more on presenting findings, insights and benefits rather than reporting on the status of project delivery.

When to use it

The Project Update Template is best used when reporting to senior business executive stakeholders interested in the business outcomes being delivered on a project. The template should be used on a cadence appropriate for the initiative being delivered and at critical project milestones where there is important information (results, findings, benefits, insights) that need to be communicated.

Why use it

Clear, concise stakeholder communication is of critical success to any business improvement or transformation initiative. While it is important to have clear reporting as part of regular program governance mechanisms, it is also essential to report upwards and outwards on critical program benefits and insights over the course of the project. Being able to communicate to executives clearly without getting "bogged down" in project delivery details is a must-do for every project.

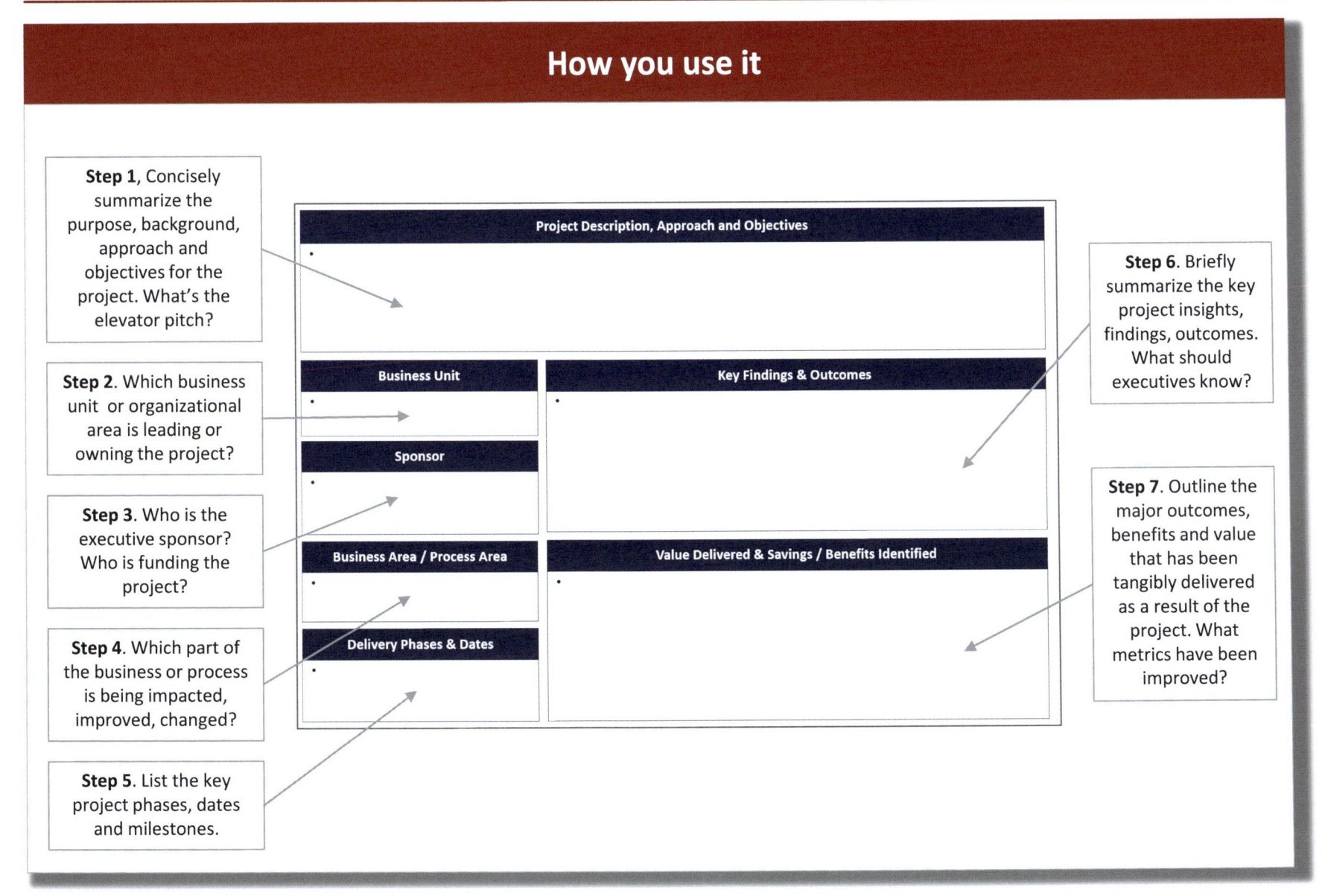

Project Update Template – Method

How you use it

Step 1. Concisely summarize the purpose, background, approach and objectives for the project. What's the elevator pitch?

Step 2. Which business unit or organizational area is leading or owning the project?

Step 3. Who is the executive sponsor? Who is funding the project?

Step 4. Which part of the business or process is being impacted, improved, changed?

Step 5. List the key project phases, dates and milestones.

Step 6. Briefly summarize the key project insights, findings, outcomes. What should executives know?

Step 7. Outline the major outcomes, benefits and value that has been tangibly delivered as a result of the project. What metrics have been improved?

Template Sections

- Project Description, Approach and Objectives
- Business Unit
- Sponsor
- Business Area / Process Area
- Delivery Phases & Dates
- Key Findings & Outcomes
- Value Delivered & Savings / Benefits Identified

Project Update Template – Template

Project Description, Approach and Objectives

-

Business Unit

-

Sponsor

-

Business Area / Process Area

-

Delivery Phases & Dates

-

Key Findings & Outcomes

-

Value Delivered & Savings / Benefits Identified

-

Resource Management Plan

A template for tracking business transformation project roles, resources, allocations and focus areas

Resource Management Plan – Overview

What is it

The Resource Management Plan is mechanism for tracking resources that are allocated to a business transformation program or other type of business improvement initiative. It is highly customizable and allows a project manager or team leader to maintain visibility and track resources that are allocated to a project over its duration. The resource management plan should be developed in conjunction with the project plan and kept current as the plan evolves and as resources are changed.

When to use it

The Resource Management Plan should be developed at the commencement of a project during the planning cycle. Once a detailed project plan has been developed, teams and roles will be identified to deliver specific work products, whereby individual resources can be identified and allocated to fill each of the necessary roles. The resource plan should be reviewed regularly and updated as resources roll-on and off and as the plan evolves over the duration of the program.

Why use it

The ability of a program to deliver on its intended outcomes is a direct result of having the right resources, with the right skills, allocated for the right time / duration and working on the right things. Having a focused mechanism for tracking roles and resources is critical – this template is simple, proven, customizable to help manage roles and resources on your project.

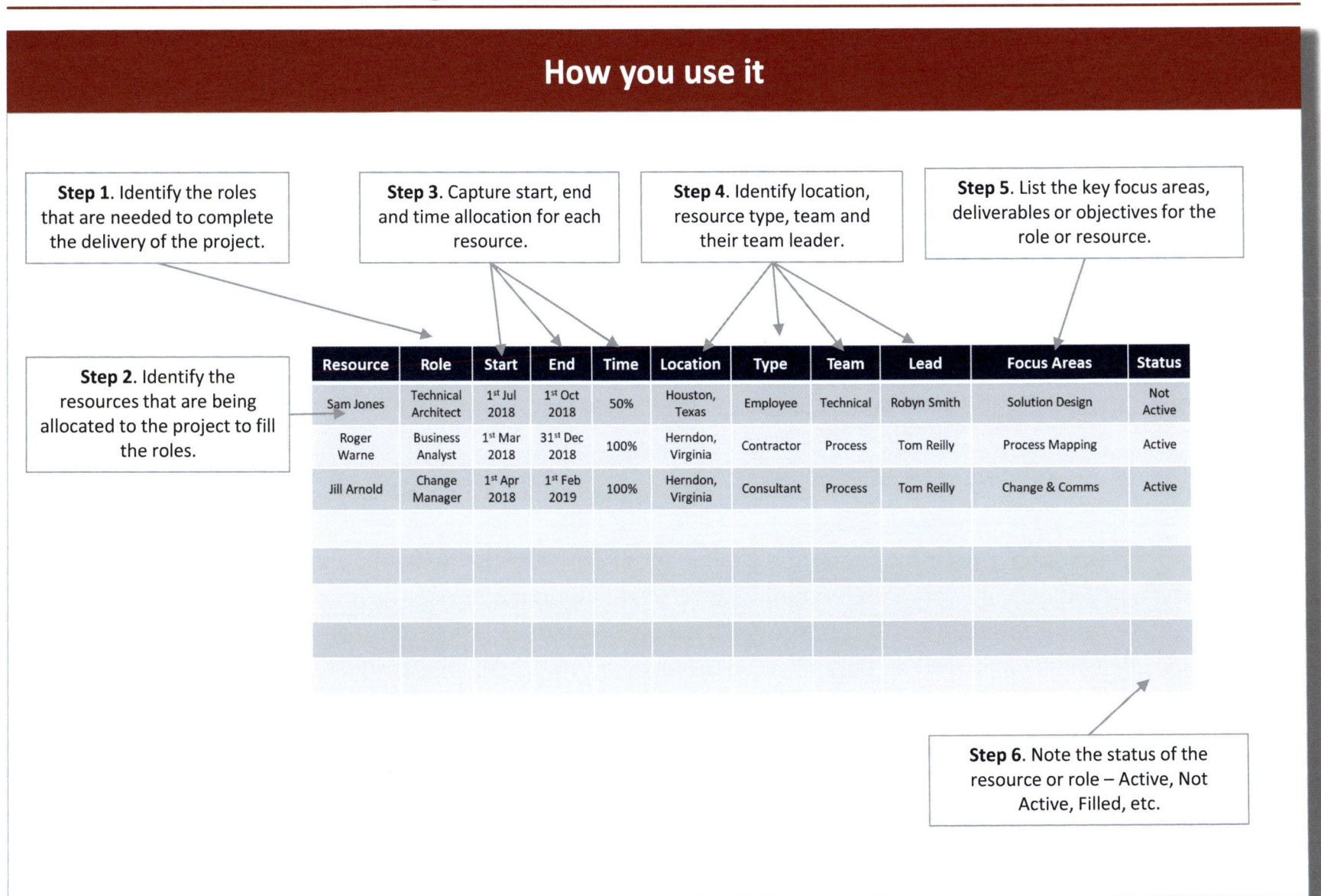

Resource Management Plan – Method

How you use it

Step 1. Identify the roles that are needed to complete the delivery of the project.

Step 2. Identify the resources that are being allocated to the project to fill the roles.

Step 3. Capture start, end and time allocation for each resource.

Step 4. Identify location, resource type, team and their team leader.

Step 5. List the key focus areas, deliverables or objectives for the role or resource.

Step 6. Note the status of the resource or role – Active, Not Active, Filled, etc.

Resource	Role	Start	End	Time	Location	Type	Team	Lead	Focus Areas	Status
Sam Jones	Technical Architect	1st Jul 2018	1st Oct 2018	50%	Houston, Texas	Employee	Technical	Robyn Smith	Solution Design	Not Active
Roger Warne	Business Analyst	1st Mar 2018	31st Dec 2018	100%	Herndon, Virginia	Contractor	Process	Tom Reilly	Process Mapping	Active
Jill Arnold	Change Manager	1st Apr 2018	1st Feb 2019	100%	Herndon, Virginia	Consultant	Process	Tom Reilly	Change & Comms	Active

Resource Management Plan – Template

Resource	Role	Start	End	Time	Location	Type	Team	Lead	Focus Areas	Status
Sam Jones	Technical Architect	1st Jul 2018	1st Oct 2018	50%	Houston, Texas	Employee	Technical	Robyn Smith	Solution Design	Not Active
Roger Warne	Business Analyst	1st Mar 2018	31st Dec 2018	100%	Herndon, Virginia	Contractor	Process	Tom Reilly	Process Mapping	Active
Jill Arnold	Change Manager	1st Apr 2018	1st Feb 2019	100%	Herndon, Virginia	Consultant	Process	Tom Reilly	Change & Comms	Active

Strategy Pyramid

A structured framework for development of business strategy linked to corporate vision and translated into transformation initiatives

Strategy Pyramid – Overview

What is it

The Strategy Pyramid is a framework to assist thinking through the development of a business strategy, linked with mission, vision and values and translated down to actions and objectives at the various levels and components of the business. The framework follows proven principles for business strategic planning while also being highly customizable to suit the specific application. The framework can be used for development of an overall business strategy or for a specific function within a business.

When to use it

The framework can be used as part of a strategic refresh cycle or as part of the development of a business transformation agenda – ensuring that the agenda is tightly coupled to the top line mission, vision and strategy. The framework can be used in its entirety – starting from the top and working to the bottom, or specific layers can be utilized and updated taking into consideration the other layers that have already been developed and are "fixed" inputs or pre-requisites.

Why use it

The Strategy Pyramid is a proven, structured approach for developing business strategies and transformation agendas – establishing a clear thread from "mission" down to "personal actions". It follows the principles of Hoshin Kanri - ensuring that the strategic goals of a business drive the progress and action at every level, thus eliminating the inefficiencies and misdirection that come from inconsistent strategies, goal misalignment and poor communication.

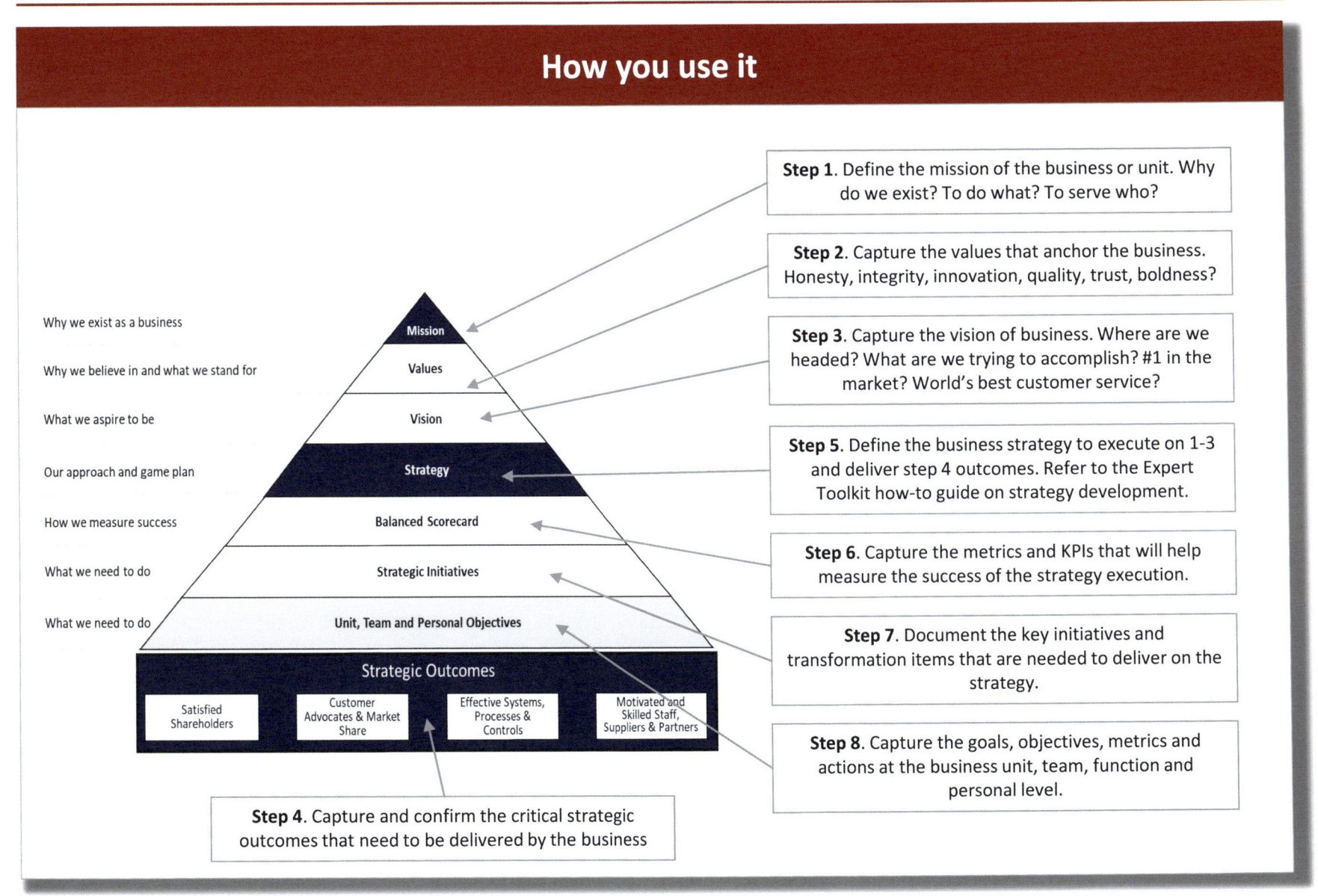

Strategy Pyramid – Method

How you use it

Pyramid levels (left to right labels):

- Why we exist as a business — **Mission**
- Why we believe in and what we stand for — **Values**
- What we aspire to be — **Vision**
- Our approach and game plan — **Strategy**
- How we measure success — **Balanced Scorecard**
- What we need to do — **Strategic Initiatives**
- What we need to do — **Unit, Team and Personal Objectives**

Strategic Outcomes:
- Satisfied Shareholders
- Customer Advocates & Market Share
- Effective Systems, Processes & Controls
- Motivated and Skilled Staff, Suppliers & Partners

Step 1. Define the mission of the business or unit. Why do we exist? To do what? To serve who?

Step 2. Capture the values that anchor the business. Honesty, integrity, innovation, quality, trust, boldness?

Step 3. Capture the vision of business. Where are we headed? What are we trying to accomplish? #1 in the market? World's best customer service?

Step 4. Capture and confirm the critical strategic outcomes that need to be delivered by the business

Step 5. Define the business strategy to execute on 1-3 and deliver step 4 outcomes. Refer to the Expert Toolkit how-to guide on strategy development.

Step 6. Capture the metrics and KPIs that will help measure the success of the strategy execution.

Step 7. Document the key initiatives and transformation items that are needed to deliver on the strategy.

Step 8. Capture the goals, objectives, metrics and actions at the business unit, team, function and personal level.

Strategy Pyramid – Framework

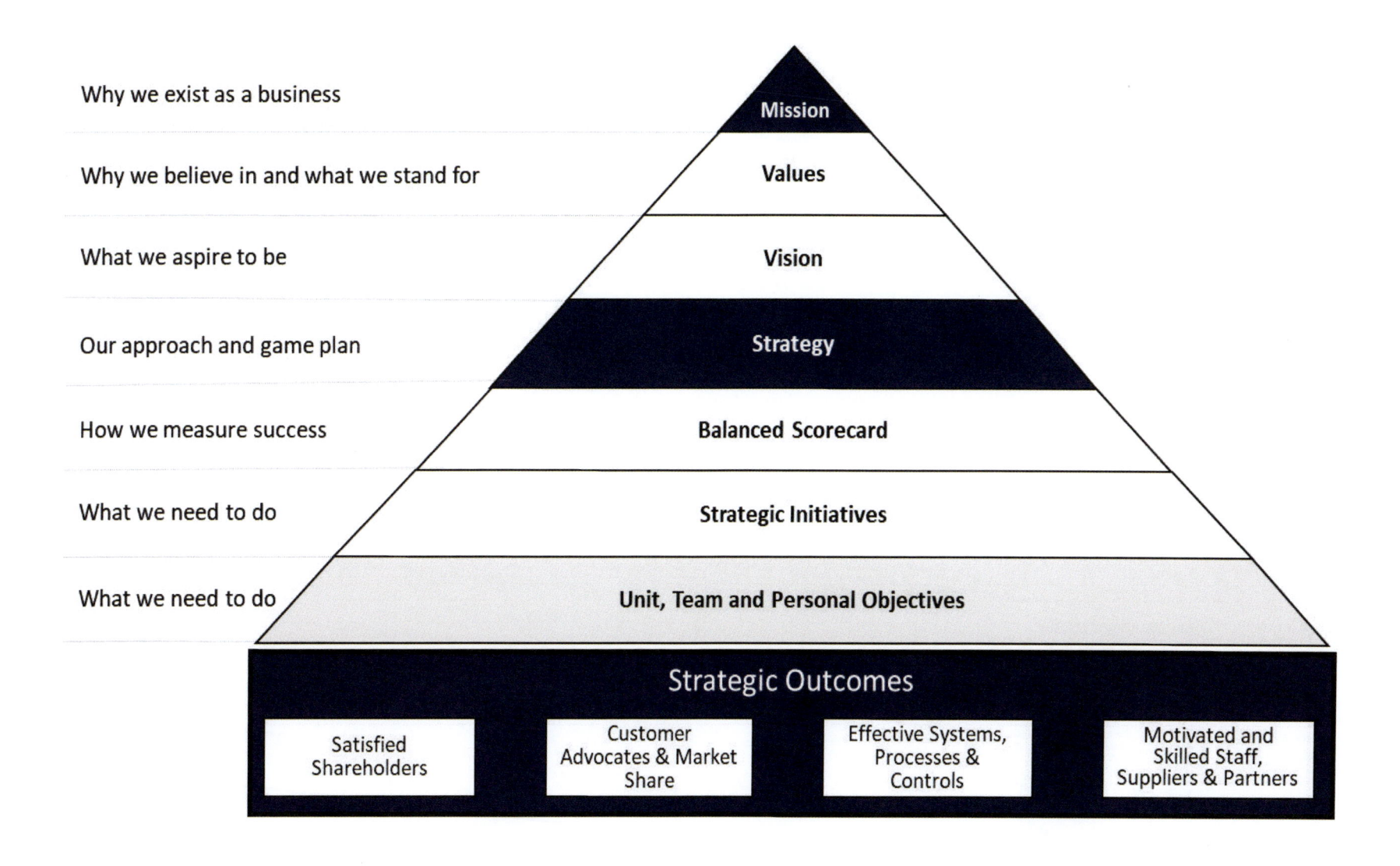

Description	Pyramid Level
Why we exist as a business	**Mission**
Why we believe in and what we stand for	**Values**
What we aspire to be	**Vision**
Our approach and game plan	**Strategy**
How we measure success	**Balanced Scorecard**
What we need to do	**Strategic Initiatives**
What we need to do	**Unit, Team and Personal Objectives**

Strategic Outcomes

- Satisfied Shareholders
- Customer Advocates & Market Share
- Effective Systems, Processes & Controls
- Motivated and Skilled Staff, Suppliers & Partners

Team Temperature Check Tool

A simple tool for gathering feedback and optimizing individual and team performance

Team Temperature Check Tool – Overview

What is it

The Team Temperature Check Tool is a simple mechanism for gathering feedback from project team members, workshop participants or other stakeholders involved in the delivery of an initiative or business event. The tool can be easily customized to suit the specific needs of the user and the feedback being sought from respondents. The tool allows critical information to be gathered quickly and for project adjustments to be made based on responses received.

When to use it

The Team Temperature Check Tool is ideally suited for use during a major business workshop or event that involves a wide variety of participants and stakeholders. It can also be used at various stages of a business project to gather team input anonymously and use this input to make modifications to items such as roles, approach, behaviors, scope, activities, deliverables or timeframes. The tool can be used in paper form or can be converted into a form of electronic survey.

Why use it

The Team Temperature Check Tool is very easy to administer but very powerful in terms of the team insights that can be gathered and utilized quickly. Team dynamics in a workshop or project are extremely critical and uncovering and addressing any team performance issues is paramount to operating as a high performing team aligned to the accomplishment of project objectives.

Team Temperature Check Tool – Method

How you use it

Step 1. Modify the questions / answer scales as necessary to suite your specific needs.

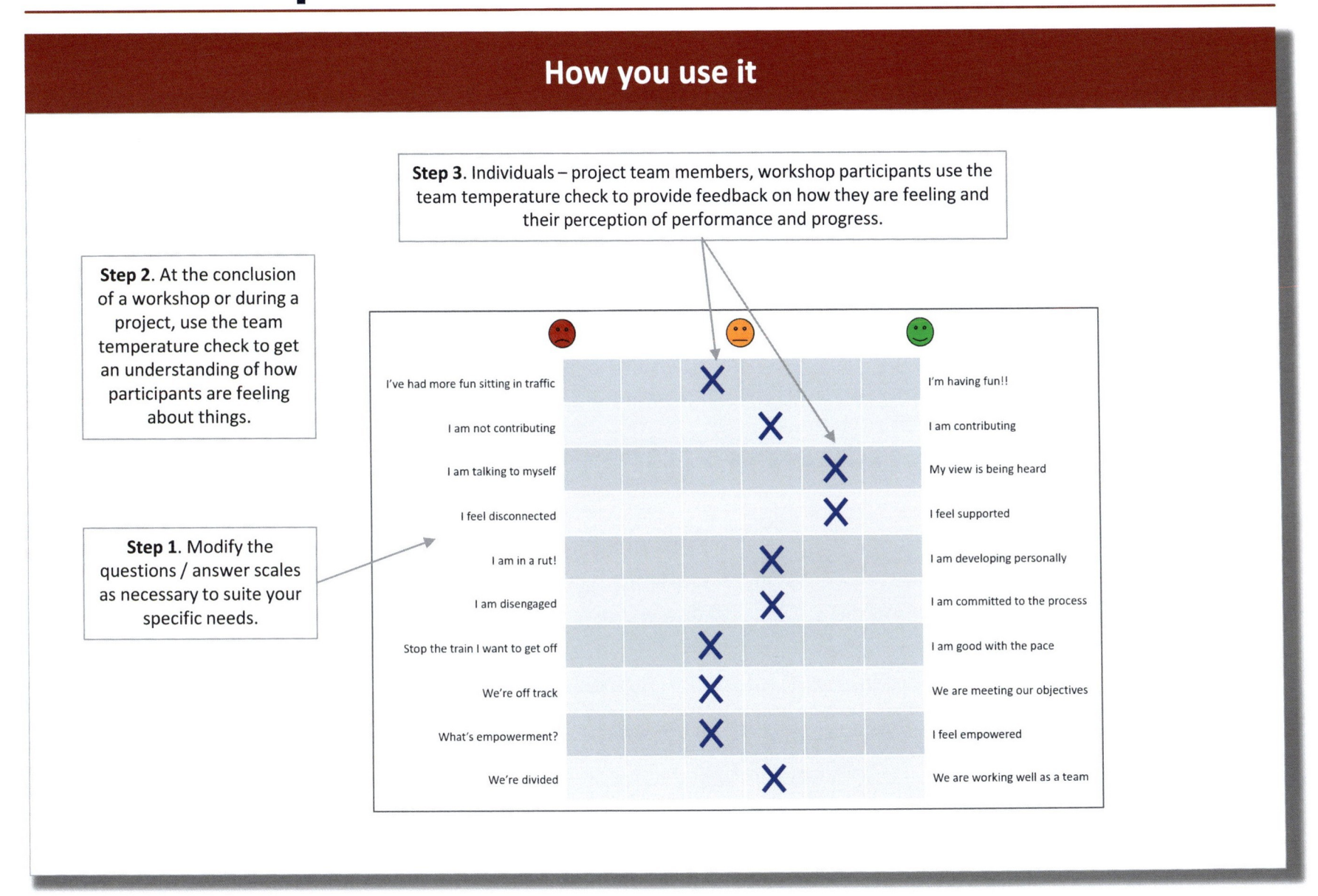

Step 2. At the conclusion of a workshop or during a project, use the team temperature check to get an understanding of how participants are feeling about things.

Step 3. Individuals – project team members, workshop participants use the team temperature check to provide feedback on how they are feeling and their perception of performance and progress.

Negative			Neutral			Positive
I've had more fun sitting in traffic			X			I'm having fun!!
I am not contributing				X		I am contributing
I am talking to myself					X	My view is being heard
I feel disconnected					X	I feel supported
I am in a rut!			X			I am developing personally
I am disengaged			X			I am committed to the process
Stop the train I want to get off		X				I am good with the pace
We're off track		X				We are meeting our objectives
What's empowerment?		X				I feel empowered
We're divided				X		We are working well as a team

Team Temperature Check Tool - Template

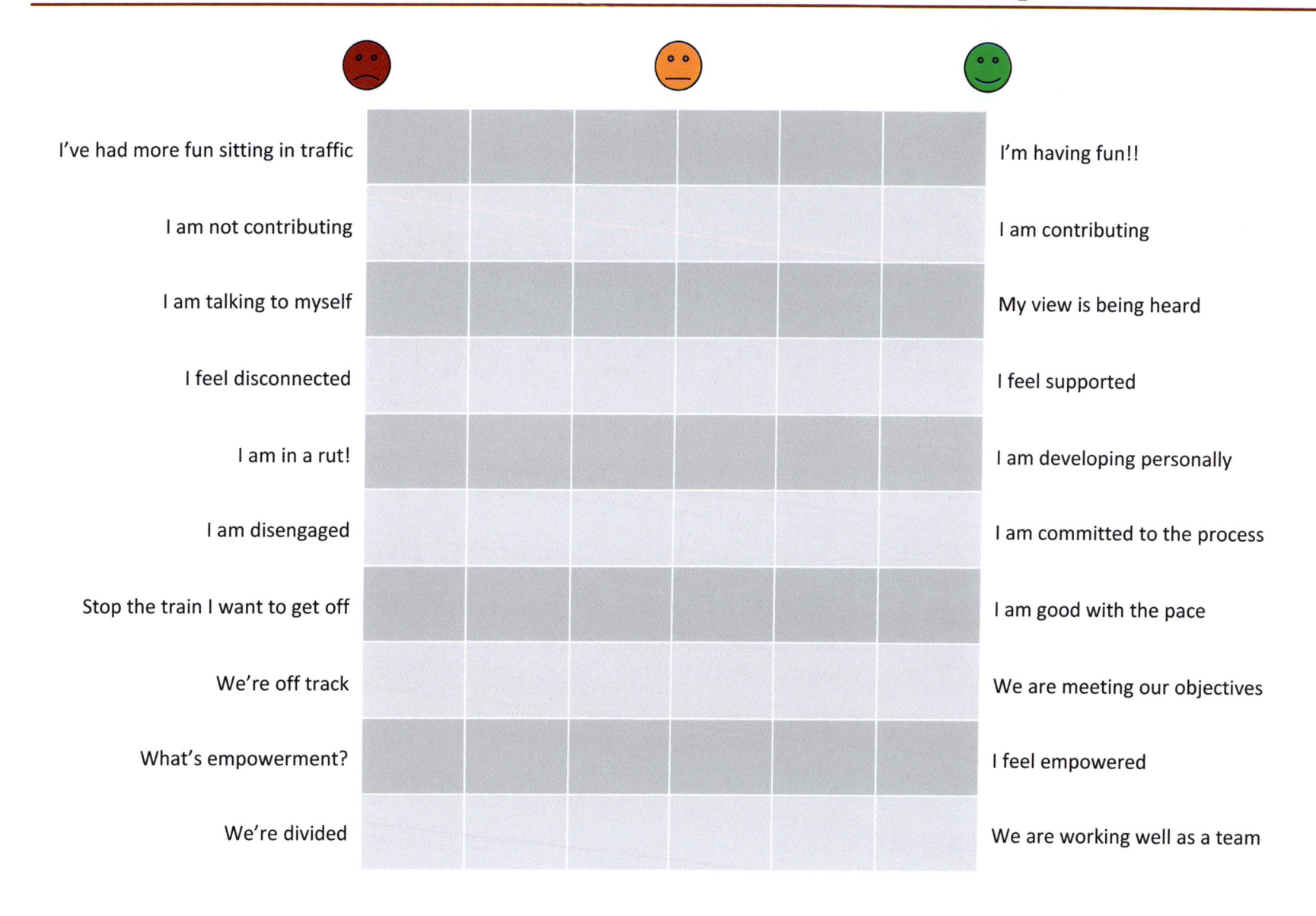

	☹		😐		🙂		
I've had more fun sitting in traffic							I'm having fun!!
I am not contributing							I am contributing
I am talking to myself							My view is being heard
I feel disconnected							I feel supported
I am in a rut!							I am developing personally
I am disengaged							I am committed to the process
Stop the train I want to get off							I am good with the pace
We're off track							We are meeting our objectives
What's empowerment?							I feel empowered
We're divided							We are working well as a team

Transformation Conclusion Survey

A focused staff questionnaire to assess the success of a business transformation program

Transformation Conclusion Survey – Overview

What is it

The Transformation Conclusion Survey is a questionnaire that can be utilized with staff, suppliers, partners and other stakeholders to assess their perspectives on the success of a business transformation after it has been delivered. The survey helps to formulate a broad view of the perspectives, attitudes and concerns of a wide variety of individuals who have been impacted by a transformation initiative. Once the survey has been delivered, the information gathered can be utilized to design follow-up actions or communications.

When to use it

The Transformation Conclusion Survey should be used after transformation program has been delivered, either in full or following a major change-initiating milestone. The survey should be used with the intent and the capability to address any key items of feedback received. It is also recommended that the survey be administered in a way that allows the data to be analyzed across cohorts in order that cohort-specific actions can be taken where necessary.

Why use it

For any Business Transformation Program to be successful and move through the awareness, acceptance, adoption cycle successfully, it is imperative that impacted stakeholders are understood, engaged and have their concerns promptly addressed. This survey is a simple, but proven mechanism for gauging the disposition of personnel after they have been involved or impacted by a business transformation program, providing critical data that allows for effective responses.

Transformation Conclusion Survey – Method

How you use it

Step 1. Choose the delivery mechanism for the survey – which can range from paper based, web survey to email voting.

Step 2. Identify the cohorts that need to be targeted for the survey. Consider staff groups, suppliers, partners, even customers.

Step 3. Identify individuals that sit within each of the identified cohorts and ensure that contact details are available and "permission to survey" exists.

Step 4. Modify the questions as necessary to suite the specific needs of your change program and the cohorts being engaged. What information is essential? Keep the survey to 5-10 questions (maximum).

Step 5. Issue the survey to the targeted cohorts using the preferred delivery mechanism.

Step 6. Individuals – project team members, users, people impacted by a transformation program – provide their responses to the survey questions.

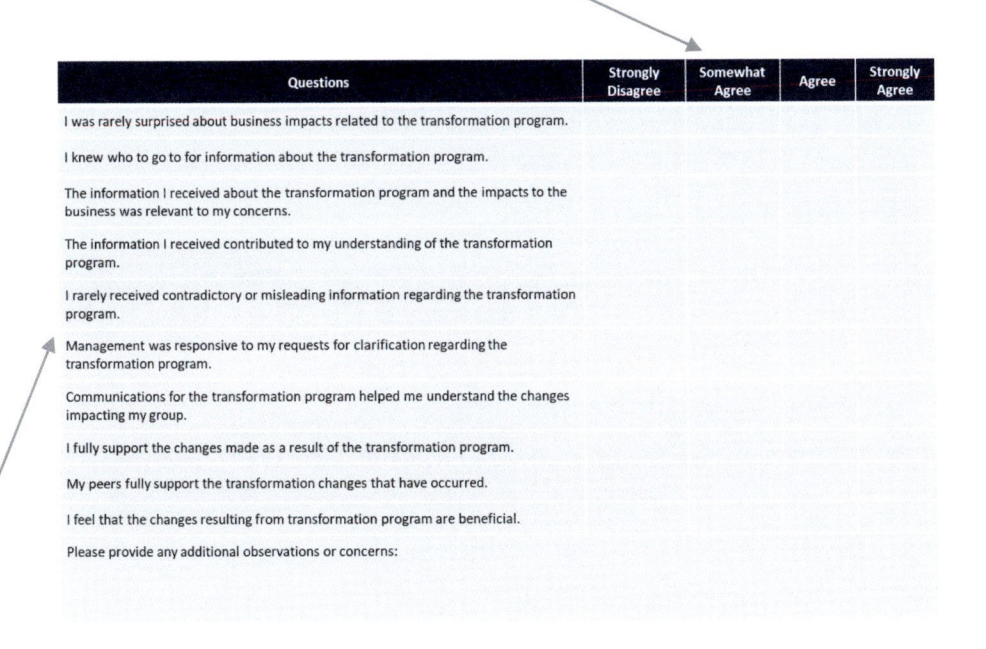

Questions	Strongly Disagree	Somewhat Agree	Agree	Strongly Agree
I was rarely surprised about business impacts related to the transformation program.				
I knew who to go to for information about the transformation program.				
The information I received about the transformation program and the impacts to the business was relevant to my concerns.				
The information I received contributed to my understanding of the transformation program.				
I rarely received contradictory or misleading information regarding the transformation program.				
Management was responsive to my requests for clarification regarding the transformation program.				
Communications for the transformation program helped me understand the changes impacting my group.				
I fully support the changes made as a result of the transformation program.				
My peers fully support the transformation changes that have occurred.				
I feel that the changes resulting from transformation program are beneficial.				
Please provide any additional observations or concerns:				

Step 7. Collate the survey responses and look for trends, patterns, anomalies and other insights. Develop action plans and targeted interventions where required to address items raised in the survey.

Transformation Conclusion Survey – Template

In relation to the transformation program just concluded, please answer the following questions by selecting one of the boxes indicated below. Strongly Disagree represents the most negative response, Strongly Agree the most positive.

Questions	Strongly Disagree	Somewhat Agree	Agree	Strongly Agree
I was rarely surprised about business impacts related to the transformation program.				
I knew who to reach out to for information about the transformation program.				
The information I received about the transformation program and the impacts to the business was relevant to my concerns.				
The information I received contributed to my understanding of the transformation program.				
I rarely received contradictory or misleading information regarding the transformation program.				
Management was responsive to my requests for clarification regarding the transformation program.				
Communications for the transformation program helped me understand the changes impacting my group.				
I fully support the business changes made as a result of the transformation program.				
My peers fully support the transformation changes that have occurred.				
I feel that the changes resulting from transformation program are beneficial to the business.				
Please provide any additional observations or concerns:				

Transformation Map Template

A proven template for clearly laying out the initiatives and sequencing of a business transformation program

Transformation Map Template – Overview

What is it

The Transformation Map Template is a visual method for laying out the key initiatives that are required to be delivered as part of a business transformation program. The typical format for a transformation map involves the current state being at the bottom left and the future state at the top right. The future state represents a new operating model, corporate vision or strategy and the initiatives outlined on the map represent the agreed "work packages" that need to be done in order to reach the desired future state.

When to use it

The Transformation Map Template should be used during transformation design and planning, after a future state vision has been identified, future state operating model defined, transformation solutions defined and prioritized. Confirmed transformation initiatives can then be plotted on the transformation map as a top down visualization to garner awareness, support and investment in the overarching transformation plan. Supporting each item on the transformation map should be detailed initiative charters – templates for these can be found on experttoolkit.com.

Why use it

A Transformation Map is a critical tool for gaining top-down agreement on the major buckets of work that need to be delivered and in what timeframe for a business transformation to deliver on its objectives. The two formats included in this Expert Toolkit Template are proven to work, easily customizable and will save you time when laying out your business transformation program.

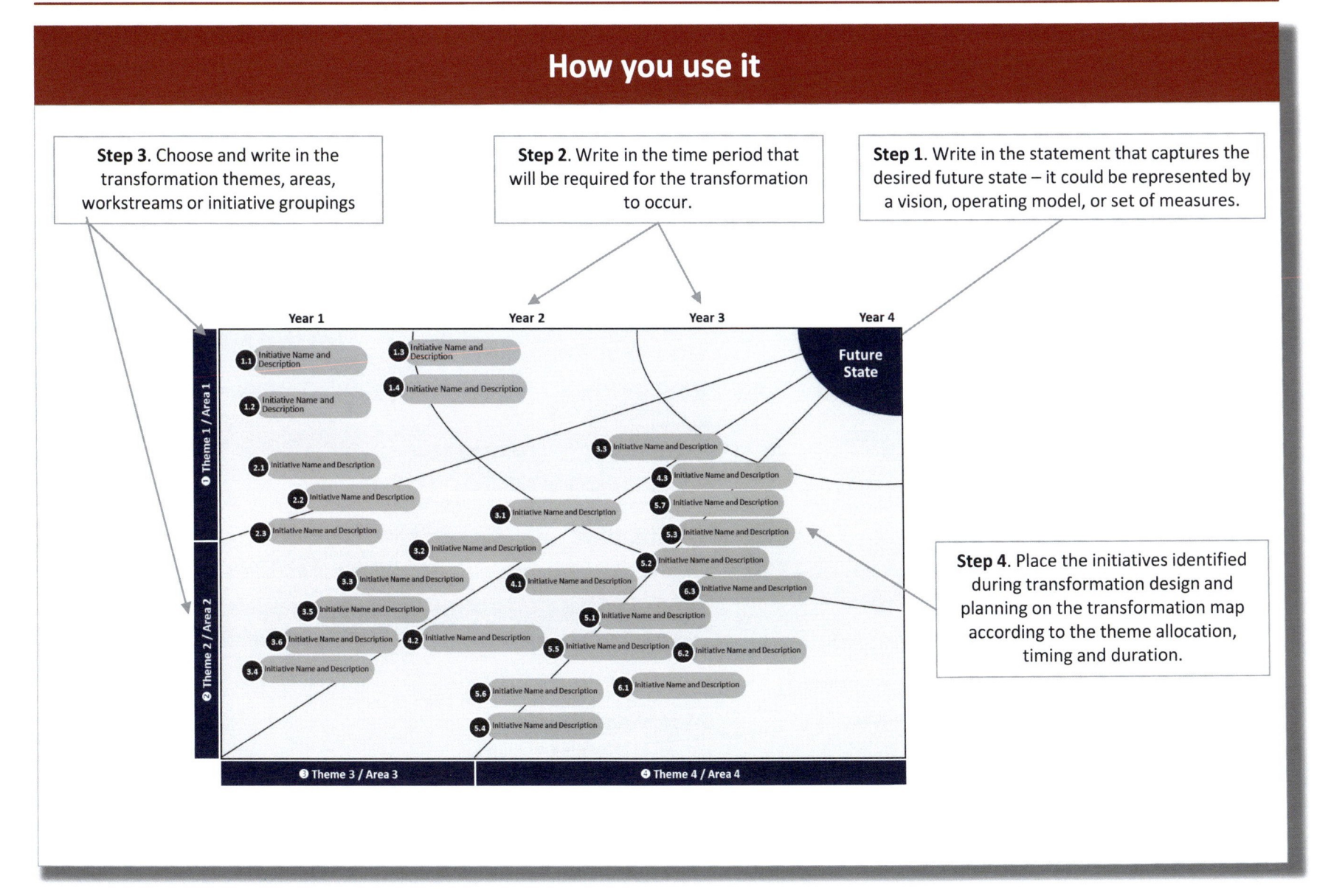

Transformation Map Template – Method

How you use it

Step 1. Write in the statement that captures the desired future state – it could be represented by a vision, operating model, or set of measures.

Step 2. Write in the time period that will be required for the transformation to occur.

Step 3. Choose and write in the transformation themes, areas, workstreams or initiative groupings

Step 4. Place the initiatives identified during transformation design and planning on the transformation map according to the theme allocation, timing and duration.

Transformation Map Template – Template (Option 1)

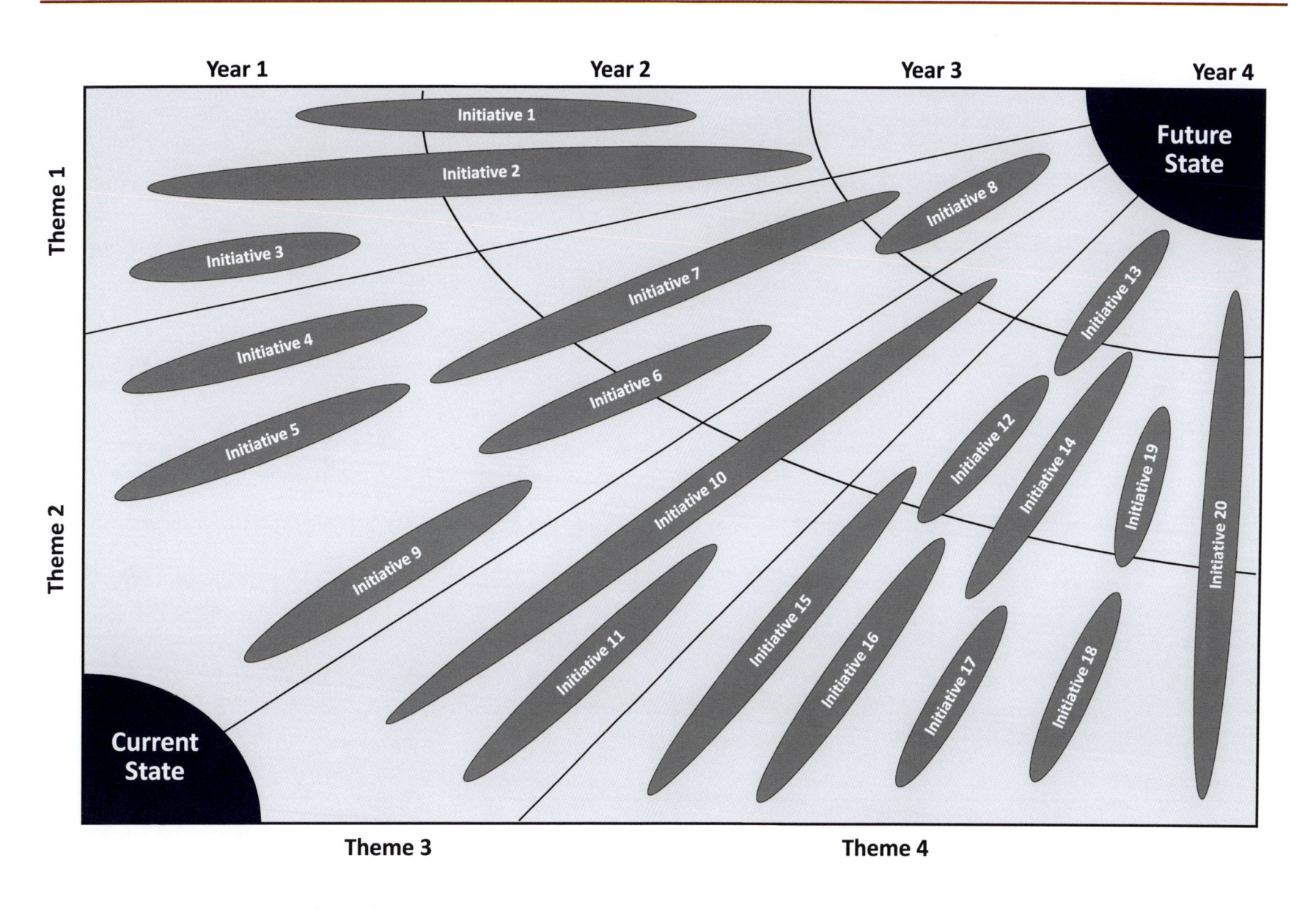

	Year 1	Year 2	Year 3	Year 4

Current State → **Future State**

Theme 1
- Initiative 1
- Initiative 2
- Initiative 3
- Initiative 4
- Initiative 5
- Initiative 7
- Initiative 8
- Initiative 13

Theme 2
- Initiative 6
- Initiative 9
- Initiative 10
- Initiative 12
- Initiative 14
- Initiative 19
- Initiative 20

Theme 3
- Initiative 11
- Initiative 15

Theme 4
- Initiative 16
- Initiative 17
- Initiative 18

Transformation Map Template – Template (Option 2)

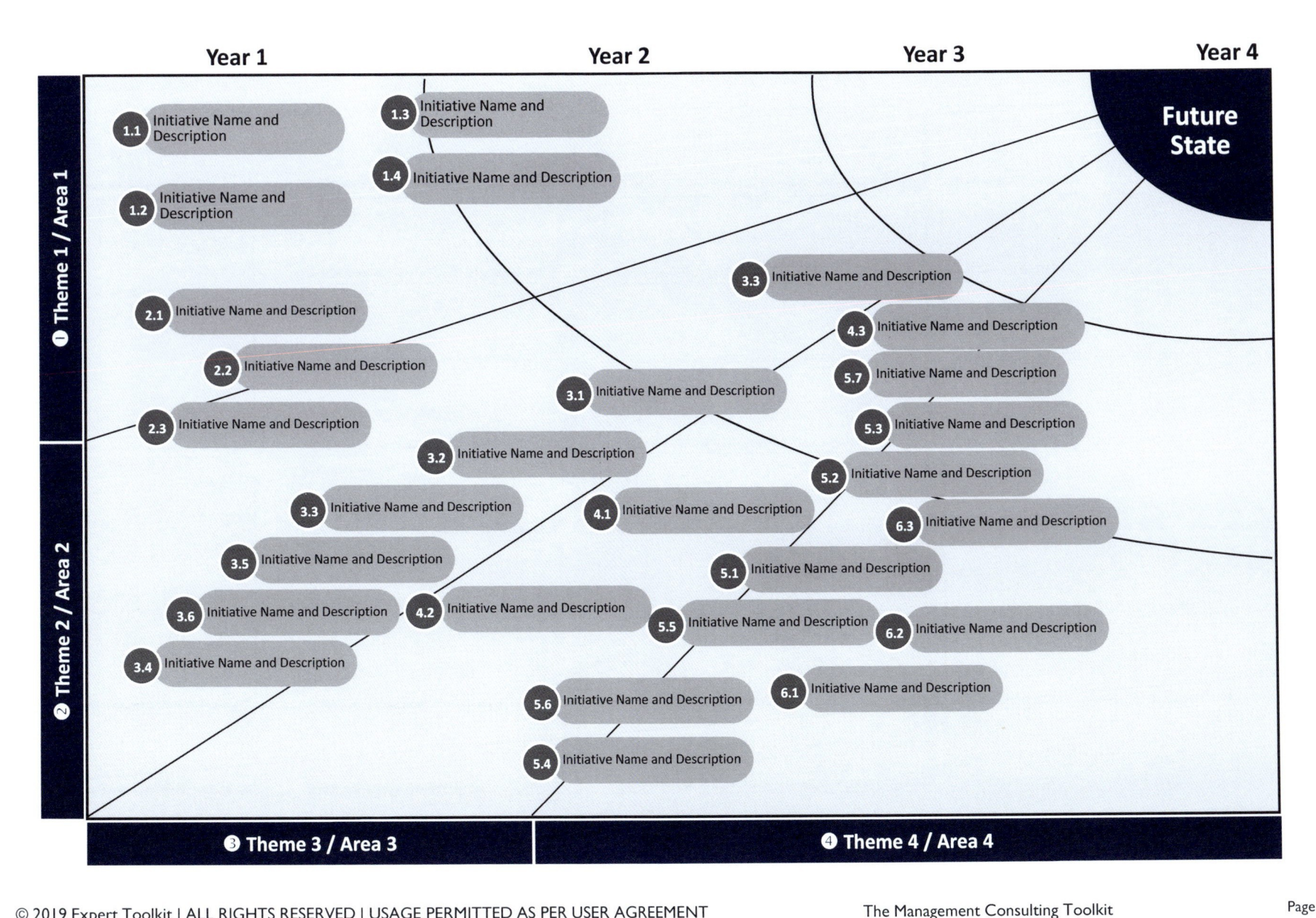

	Year 1	Year 2	Year 3	Year 4

① Theme 1 / Area 1
- 1.1 Initiative Name and Description
- 1.2 Initiative Name and Description
- 1.3 Initiative Name and Description
- 1.4 Initiative Name and Description
- 2.1 Initiative Name and Description
- 2.2 Initiative Name and Description
- 2.3 Initiative Name and Description
- 3.1 Initiative Name and Description
- 3.2 Initiative Name and Description
- 3.3 Initiative Name and Description
- 4.3 Initiative Name and Description
- 5.7 Initiative Name and Description
- 5.3 Initiative Name and Description
- 5.2 Initiative Name and Description

② Theme 2 / Area 2
- 3.3 Initiative Name and Description
- 3.5 Initiative Name and Description
- 3.6 Initiative Name and Description
- 3.4 Initiative Name and Description
- 4.1 Initiative Name and Description
- 4.2 Initiative Name and Description
- 5.1 Initiative Name and Description
- 5.5 Initiative Name and Description
- 5.6 Initiative Name and Description
- 5.4 Initiative Name and Description
- 6.3 Initiative Name and Description
- 6.2 Initiative Name and Description
- 6.1 Initiative Name and Description

③ Theme 3 / Area 3

④ Theme 4 / Area 4

Future State

Transformation Readiness Checklist

A proven checklist for assessing an organization's readiness to embark on a business transformation program

Transformation Readiness Checklist – Overview

What is it

The Transformation Readiness Checklist is a structured framework for assessing the readiness of a business transformation to be delivered successfully. The template enables a rapid, but broad health check to be performed on a transformation program with a focus on 6 dimensions that are proven to be essential for any major business initiative to succeed: Vision Clarity & Leadership; Communications and Commitment; Transformation Capability; Project Management; Culture; Stakeholders and Progress.

When to use it

The Transformation Readiness Checklist is most effective when used upon completion of transformation design and planning, after the design and communication of a clear end state (vision, operating model) and transformation plan. The initial read out from the readiness assessment should be used as the baseline and compared to subsequent assessments performed during the course of the program. The assessment should be performed with a group of transformation leadership and key stakeholders.

Why use it

For any major transformation to be successful, it's critical to understand how the organization and the program are positioned. This information can then be utilized to make adjustments prior to the commencement of the program and also for making course corrections during the life of the program. This checklist is simple, but concise and measures across attributes that are shown to strongly indicate whether an organization is "transformation ready" or not.

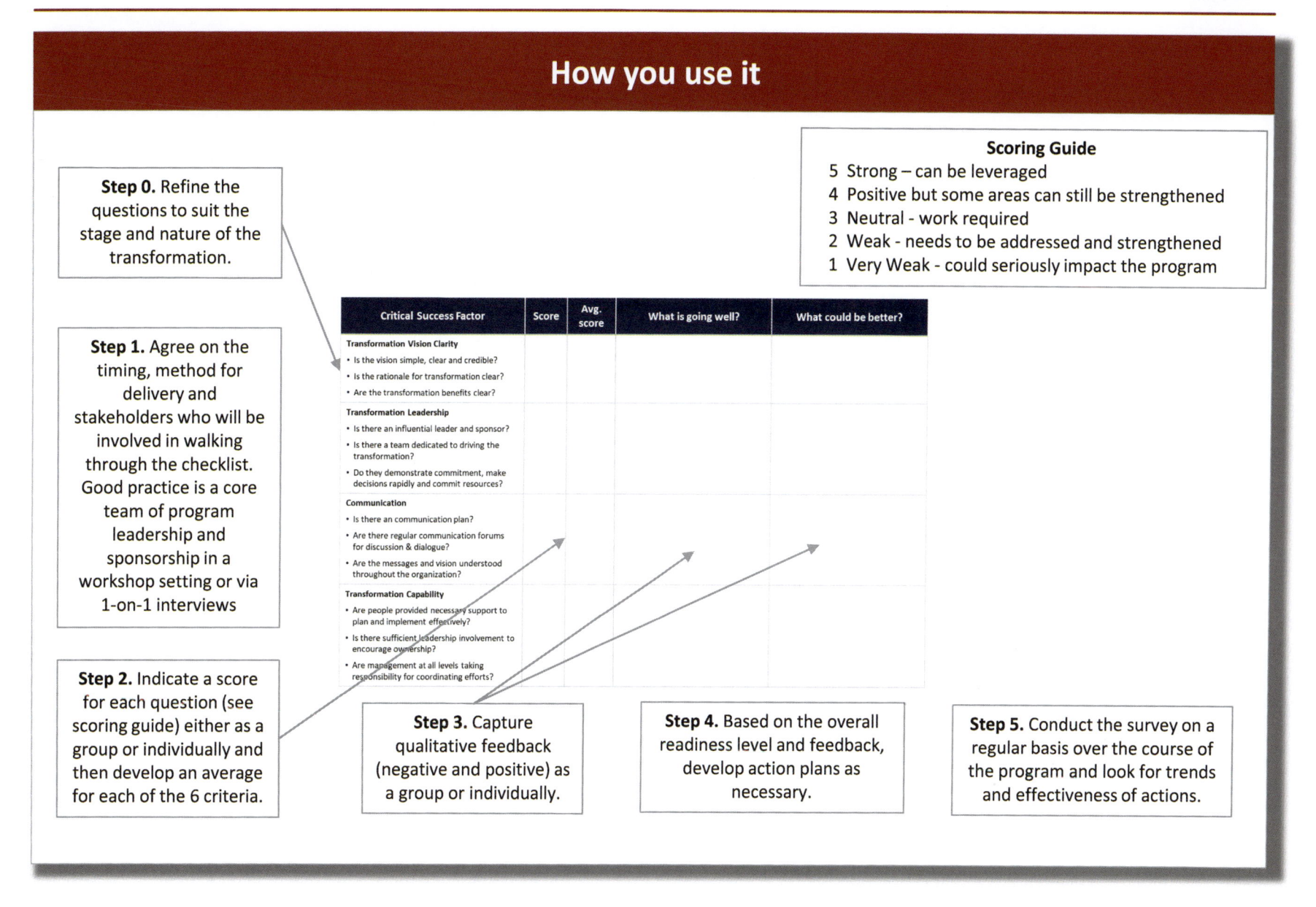

Transformation Readiness Checklist – Method

How you use it

Scoring Guide
5 Strong – can be leveraged
4 Positive but some areas can still be strengthened
3 Neutral - work required
2 Weak - needs to be addressed and strengthened
1 Very Weak - could seriously impact the program

Step 0. Refine the questions to suit the stage and nature of the transformation.

Step 1. Agree on the timing, method for delivery and stakeholders who will be involved in walking through the checklist. Good practice is a core team of program leadership and sponsorship in a workshop setting or via 1-on-1 interviews

Step 2. Indicate a score for each question (see scoring guide) either as a group or individually and then develop an average for each of the 6 criteria.

Critical Success Factor	Score	Avg. score	What is going well?	What could be better?
Transformation Vision Clarity • Is the vision simple, clear and credible? • Is the rationale for transformation clear? • Are the transformation benefits clear?				
Transformation Leadership • Is there an influential leader and sponsor? • Is there a team dedicated to driving the transformation? • Do they demonstrate commitment, make decisions rapidly and commit resources?				
Communication • Is there an communication plan? • Are there regular communication forums for discussion & dialogue? • Are the messages and vision understood throughout the organization?				
Transformation Capability • Are people provided necessary support to plan and implement effectively? • Is there sufficient leadership involvement to encourage ownership? • Are management at all levels taking responsibility for coordinating efforts?				

Step 3. Capture qualitative feedback (negative and positive) as a group or individually.

Step 4. Based on the overall readiness level and feedback, develop action plans as necessary.

Step 5. Conduct the survey on a regular basis over the course of the program and look for trends and effectiveness of actions.

Transformation Readiness Checklist – Template

Critical Success Factor	Score	Avg. score	What is going well?	What could be better?
Transformation Vision Clarity • Is the vision simple, clear and credible? • Is the rationale for transformation clear? • Are the transformation benefits clear?				
Transformation Leadership • Is there an influential leader and sponsor? • Is there a team dedicated to driving the transformation? • Do they demonstrate commitment, make decisions rapidly and commit resources?				
Communication • Is there an communication plan? • Are there regular communication forums for discussion & dialogue? • Are the messages and vision understood throughout the organization?				
Transformation Capability • Are people provided necessary support to plan and implement effectively? • Is there sufficient leadership involvement to encourage ownership? • Are management at all levels taking responsibility for coordinating efforts?				

Transformation Readiness Checklist – Template

Critical Success Factor	Score	Avg. score	What is going well?	What could be better?
Project Management • Are accountabilities clear? • Is there co-ordination and understanding between the various teams involved? • Are there processes for resolving issues and managing risks? • Are there processes and governance for monitoring and controlling the project?				
Stakeholder Commitment • Are key stakeholders bought into the plan? • Are sources of strength and resistance being anticipated? • Are plans in place to manage resistance?				
Culture • Is bad news being dealt with promptly? • Are those losing out being treated properly? • Are benefits being sold effectively? • Are managers leading by example? • Is commitment to transform rewarded?				
Progress • Is adequate forward progress being made? • Is senior management seen to be serious about driving transformation? • Are there early wins to mark progress? • Has performance management changed to be in line with new priorities ?				

Transformation Readiness Survey

A focused staff questionnaire to assess readiness and support for transformational business change

Transformation Readiness Survey – Overview

What is it

The Transformation Readiness Survey is a questionnaire that can be utilized with staff, suppliers, partners and other stakeholders to understand their preparedness for major business transformation. The survey helps to formulate a broad view of the perspectives, attitudes and concerns of a wide variety of individuals who will be impacted by a business transformation initiative. Once the survey has been delivered, the information gathered can be utilized to make any necessary program adjustments (e.g. communications).

When to use it

The Transformation Readiness Survey should be used after transformation planning and design have been completed and communicated across the organization but prior to transformation delivery and change commencing. Ideally, the survey should be used with sufficient time available to accommodate any key items of feedback received. It is also recommended that the survey be administered in a way that allows the data to be analyzed across cohorts in order that cohort-specific actions can be taken where necessary.

Why use it

For any Business Transformation Program to be successful and move through the awareness, acceptance, adoption cycle successfully, it is imperative that impacted stakeholders are understood, engaged and have their concerns promptly addressed. This survey is a simple, but proven mechanism for gauging the current disposition of personnel impacted by a business transformation program, gathering critical data that allows for effective responses to be designed and delivered to address any concerns and risks.

Transformation Readiness Survey – Method

How you use it

Step 1. Choose the delivery mechanism for the survey – which can range from paper based, web survey to email voting.

Step 2. Identify the cohorts that need to be targeted for the survey. Consider staff groups, suppliers, partners, even customers.

Step 3. Identify individuals that sit within each of the identified cohorts and ensure that contact details are available and "permission to survey" exists.

Step 4. Modify the questions as necessary to suite the specific needs of your change program and the cohorts being engaged. What information is essential? Keep the survey to 5-10 questions (maximum).

Step 5. Issue the survey to the targeted cohorts using the preferred delivery mechanism.

Step 6. Individuals – project team members, users, people impacted by a transformation program – provide their responses to the survey questions.

Questions	Strongly Disagree	Somewhat Agree	Agree	Strongly Agree
I have a clear understanding of the transformation program's strategy.				
I feel the transformation program is appropriately setup for success and risks are being adequately mitigated.				
I am clear about the *people* changes that are planned as a result of the transformation program.				
I am clear about the *process* changes that are planned as a result of the transformation program.				
I am clear about the *technology* changes that are planned as a result of the transformation program.				
I feel the transformation program is necessary.				
I am motivated to support the transformation program.				
My peers and colleagues are motivated to support the transformation program.				
I feel prepared for the changes that will be implemented by the transformation program.				
I feel that the changes are aligned with my groups' current culture/values.				
Please provide any additional observations or concerns:				

Step 7. Collate the survey responses and look for trends, patterns, anomalies and other insights. Develop action plans and targeted interventions where required to address items raised in the survey.

Transformation Readiness Survey – Template

In relation to the transformation program being undertaken, please answer the following questions by selecting one of the boxes indicated below. Strongly Disagree represents the most negative response, Strongly Agree the most positive.

Questions	Strongly Disagree	Somewhat Agree	Agree	Strongly Agree
I have a clear understanding of the transformation program's strategy.				
I feel the transformation program is appropriately setup for success and risks are being adequately mitigated.				
I am clear about the *people* changes that are planned as a result of the transformation program.				
I am clear about the *process* changes that are planned as a result of the transformation program.				
I am clear about the *technology* changes that are planned as a result of the transformation program.				
I feel the transformation program is necessary.				
I am motivated to support the transformation program.				
My peers and colleagues are motivated to support the transformation program.				
I feel prepared for the changes that will be implemented by the transformation program.				
I feel that the changes are aligned with my groups' current culture/values.				
Please provide any additional observations or concerns:				

Notes

Notes

Notes

Notes

Notes

Notes

Notes

Notes

Disclaimer

- Descriptions and other related information in this document are provided only to illustrate the methods covered. You are fully responsible for the use of these methods where you see appropriate. Expert Toolkit assumes no responsibility for any losses incurred by you or third parties arising from the use of these methods or information.

- Expert Toolkit has used reasonable care in preparing the information included in this document, but Expert Toolkit does not warrant that such information is error free. Expert Toolkit assumes no liability whatsoever for any damages incurred by you resulting from errors in or omissions from the information included herein.

- Expert Toolkit does not assume any liability for infringement of patents, copyrights, or other intellectual property rights of third parties by or arising from the use of Expert Toolkit information described in this document. No license, express, implied or otherwise, is granted hereby under any patents, copyrights or other intellectual property rights of Expert Toolkit or others.

- This document may not be reproduced or duplicated in any form, in whole or in part, without prior written consent of Expert Toolkit.

- The document contains statements that are general in nature and do not constitute recommendations to the reader as to the content's suitability, applicability or appropriateness.